Marx's Theory of Land, Rent and Cities

For Lavinia, Juliet, Georgia and Eleanor

Edinburgh Studies in Urban Political Economy

Series Editor: Franklin Obeng-Odoom

In a world characterised by cities, their disproportionate share of problems as well as prospects, and the limitations of mainstream urban economics as a compass, the *Edinburgh Studies in Urban Political Economy* series strives to publish books that seek to better understand, and to address, such challenges. The Global South is of particular interest, but it is by no means the only focus. As an alternative political economy series, it emphasises social sustainability of urban transformations, encourages the use of transdisciplinary political-economic approaches to urban economics, and welcomes books that are both heterodox and pluralist in their economics. Books in the series strive to both engage and to transcend mainstream urban economics, in methodologies, values, and visions, while placing their insights at the disposal of the wider fields of urban studies and political economy.

Titles in the *Edinburgh Studies in Urban Political Economy* series include:

Published:

Open Access *Coal and Energy in South Africa: Considering a Just Transition*
Lochner Marais, Philippe Burger, Maléne Campbell, Deirdre van Rooyen and Stuart Paul Denoon-Stevens

Open Access *Marx's Theory of Land, Rent and Cities*
Don Munro

Forthcoming:

Urban Inequality in a Nordic Welfare State
Mika Hyotylainen

Spatial Agency and Occupation: Foreign Domestic Helpers in Hong Kong
Evelyn Kwok

Marx's Theory of Land, Rent and Cities

Don Munro

EDINBURGH
University Press

Edinburgh University Press is one of the leading university presses in the UK. We publish academic books and journals in our selected subject areas across the humanities and social sciences, combining cutting-edge scholarship with high editorial and production values to produce academic works of lasting importance. For more information visit our website: edinburghuniversitypress.com

We are committed to making research available to a wide audience and are pleased to be publishing Platinum Open Access ebook editions of titles in this series.

Edinburgh University Press Ltd
The Tun – Holyrood Road, 12(2f) Jackson's Entry, Edinburgh EH8 8PJ

Typeset in 11 on 13pt Baskerville MT Pro
by Cheshire Typesetting Ltd, Cuddington, Cheshire, and
printed and bound in Great Britain.

A CIP record for this book is available from the British Library

ISBN 978 1 4744 9004 7 (hardback)
ISBN 978 1 4744 9006 1 (webready PDF)
ISBN 978 1 4744 9007 8 (epub)

Contents

List of Tables

Preface

There is something odd about the way most urban economic theory conceives of cities.

Political economy is generally understood as the study of how the economy shapes, and is shaped by, the legal, political and social institutions of a society. It studies the interactions between the economy, politics and society. *Urban* political economists therefore focus on the economic, political and social factors that affect urban development and urban life.

There are different schools of urban political economy. Some, influenced by microeconomics, describe how free markets and the economic law of supply and demand can explain issues as diverse as urban employment, housing, public transport, crime and local government finance. In contrast, Keynesian-influenced urban economists focus on the size and performance of urban economies. They measure the economic output of urban-based industries (such as manufacturing, construction, and wholesale and retail trade), household income and expenditure, and government spending. Eurostat, for example, publishes the 'Gross domestic product (GDP) at current market prices by metropolitan regions' for major cities throughout Europe, and the Bureau of Economic Analysis in the United States measures 'Gross Domestic Product by County'. In the third major school of urban economics, Marxist urban political economists often use labour, capital and the class struggle to explain cities holistically (showing why cities develop unevenly over time, or why particular patterns of suburbanisation develop as they do) and to explain specific urban issues (such as patterns in the built environment, the spatial distribution of unemployment and homelessness, and the causes of urban wealth and urban poverty).

These theories are making an important contribution to our knowledge of cities. This is more important now than ever before. Today, for the first time in human history, more than half of the world's population lives in cities. If current population trends continue unabated, more than two-thirds of the world's population (over 6 billion people) will live in cities by 2050.[1] Urban political economic research can provide valuable information for governments and communities wishing to build high-quality cities, where, for example, residents are prosperous and have good transport and communication infrastructure, a quality built and natural environment, inclusive and safe communities, affordable health, housing and education services, a vibrant cultural life, and good governance with community participation in decision making.

Urban political economy is also making an important contribution to our understanding of city life in the Global North and the Global South. For example, people living in cities in the Global North are continually affected by issues such as cyclical rises and falls in house prices, urban centralisation or urban sprawl, the cost of urban infrastructure (such as transport and communications), the influence of property developers and the real estate industry on local politics, and the capacity of local governments to deliver urban planning and social services. On the other hand, people living in cities in the Global South also face similar problems but without the resources that exist in cities in the Global North. In addition, many cities in the Global South are affected by the ongoing legacy of colonialisation, struggles to prevent the privatisation of customary land ('land grabbing'), overcrowding in favelas and shanty towns, and corruption.

In addition, cities in both the Global North and the Global South are directly contributing to, and being affected by, climate change and pollution. Urban population growth, land clearing to accommodate urban sprawl, and increased demand for natural resources and energy for city growth are putting unprecedented pressure on the world's climate and ecosystems. UN Habitat has estimated that cities, which cover less than 2 per cent of the Earth's surface, consume 78 per cent of the world's energy and produce more than 60 per cent of greenhouse gas emissions. Pollution is also mostly associated as a by-product of urban landscapes. The burning of fossil fuels is increasing carbon dioxide emissions, contributing to air pollution and global warming. In October 2018, the World Health Organization (WHO) calculated that 93 per cent of the world's children breathe toxic air every day.[2]

Less well appreciated is that urban political economic processes do not affect urban residents alone: they can and have caused national and global crises. The 2008 global financial crisis, for example, began with people in cities in the United States being encouraged by the finance, insurance and real estate industries to take out mortgages to buy their own home. When interest rates dropped, home refinancing surged from $460 billion in 2000 to $2.8 trillion in 2003, despite stagnant wages.[3] Subsequently, when interest rates rose, thousands defaulted on their mortgages, loan losses mounted and financial institutions (such as the 158-year-old Lehman Brothers investment bank) filed for bankruptcy. The US mortgage crisis spread to financial institutions around the world, triggered a collapse in cross-border trade, and caused 'the worst global recession in seven decades'.[4]

More recently, property development in cities in the Global South is threatening a global economic crisis. As this book goes to press, the Evergrande Group, the largest property developer by sales in China in 2020, is facing bankruptcy. Evergrande has more than 1,300 development and construction projects in 280 cities in China.[5] It is struggling to repay more than $300 billion in liabilities, including nearly $20 billion in offshore bonds that were deemed to be in default when Evergrande missed several repayments in December 2021.[6] The collapse of Evergrande would affect detrimentally hundreds of thousands of people who have paid their deposits and are waiting for their new homes to be built; hundreds of city councils whose income depends heavily on taxes on urban real estate activity; tens of thousands of construction workers who would be unemployed; and an unknown number of bond holders from around the world who may never recover the $20 billion in bonds they loaned to Evergrande.

Urban political economy, in other words, investigates the similarities and differences between cities around the world. It shows how the relationships between urban economies, governments and communities affect, for better or for worse, the lives of the majority of the world's people who live in metropolises. It also shows that these relations between the economic, political and social forces and institutions have flow-on effects – externalities – that directly contribute to global economic growth, instability and climate change.

However, despite the important role urban political economics is playing in the world, there is something odd, something missing, that is undermining its full potential to analyse and understand cities.

Careful readers will have noticed a discrepancy between the theories of urban political economy and the character of cities. Urban political economics investigates cities using concepts such as market forces, aggregate demand labour, capital and class struggle.

On the other hand, almost all the issues discussed above – including housing prices and homelessness; public transport; the distribution of employment, wealth and poverty; the built and natural environment; urban centralisation and urban sprawl; local government taxation; the influence of property developers and the real estate industry on local politics; land clearing; mortgages; urban property development; urban planning; colonialisation; land grabbing; air pollution and climate change – directly or indirectly concern land.

In other words, what is odd about much urban political economy scholarship is that many urban issues arise because of the ownership and use of land, but land is often missing from the theoretical toolkit of political economists.[7]

This was not always the case. When political economy developed in the eighteenth and nineteenth centuries, its early theoreticians such as Adam Smith, Thomas Malthus, David Ricardo and Karl Marx all recognised that economies relied on, and were structured by, three factors of production: land, labour and capital. Landownership, land use, land-working peasants and the landowning class were directly relevant to issues such as the sources of wealth and economic development; the decline of agricultural societies and the rise of manufacturing societies based in cities; and the causes of cycles of economic boom, bust and restructure. While these thinkers studied the economically dominant land use of the day, agricultural land, their insights can be applied to the economically dominant land use of today: urban land.

Unfortunately, the historically and geographically aware methodologies of political economy were 'forgotten'[8] with the rise of neoclassical microeconomics and Keynesian macroeconomics in the twentieth century. The study of how particular economies and societies developed in different places around the world were replaced by an aspatial and ahistorical economics, with generalised laws, mathematical models and econometrics that, it was assumed, apply to all societies, in all places, at all times. How production, consumption and markets are organised (in capitalist societies) would, by this logic, equally apply to indigenous, ancient city-state, feudal and communist societies. I disagree.

The title *Marx's Theory of Land, Rent and Cities* neatly summarises the scope and approach of this book. It concentrates on cities, and not the economies or governments that are organised at provincial, national or global scales, even though it will be shown that cities are influenced by, and influence, national and global economics. It diagnoses cities using Marx's theory of landed property, rent and the landed property class, phenomena that take different forms in particular social and historical contexts.

Karl Marx used his theory of the social relations of land, labour and capital to suggest a radical questioning of cities. He asked why cities are established in the first place, what functions they carry out for society, why each city is different from others, and how cities change over time. To understand life within cities, he argued, it is necessary to first understand the underlying mode of production whereby resources from nature (land) are transformed by socially organised work (labour) into the goods and services people need to live and societies need to reproduce themselves over time. Depending on the mode of production, cities play different functions in society and develop different industries, labour forces, distributions of wealth and poverty, built environments, ruling classes and forms of political governance.

The purpose of this book is to provide a comprehensive, coherent and clear understanding of Marx's view of the role of land and rent in the economy, with a particular focus on how land and rent shape cities and the lives of people living in cities. It documents and discusses Marx's extensive writings about land, from his earliest writings to his last, to show how landed property, rent and the landowning class directly influence particular modes of production and the cities that are built to support those modes of production. This includes a comparative analysis of landed property and rent as they exist in indigenous, ancient and Asiatic communities and in feudal, capitalist and communist societies.

This book has four characteristics that make it different from most other publications on land, rent and cities.

First, and for the first time, this book brings together all Marx's available writings in English on land, rent and the landed property class. Bringing together all Marx's comments on land and rent fills a major gap in the literature. This book shows Marx did not merely rely on the concepts of labour and capital to explain socio-economic change but continuously acknowledged the role of land, labour and capital. It provides a fuller understanding of Marx's critique of political economy by demonstrating the social relations between landed property, labour and capital, and therefore provides insights into the nature, behaviour and limits of labour and capital that arise from the social relations of landed property.

Collating all Marx's available writings in English about land also has pedagogical benefits: an understanding of land can provide students with an accessible entry point into the complexities of issues such as surplus value, contradictory social relations, classes and the state.

This book includes Marx's early writings such as those on land as nature (*The German Ideology*); the abolition of landed property and the application of rent for public purposes (*The Communist Manifesto*); the dangers of the landed property class (*The Eighteenth Brumaire of Louis Bonaparte*); the critiques of political economy he wrote in his forties and fifties which investigate landed property and rent in capitalist and non-capitalist economies (*Grundrisse*, the three volumes of *Capital*, and *Theories of Surplus Value*); and his later works on revolutionary strategy (*Critique of the Gotha Programme*) and the drafts of his letters to Vera Zasulich (which consider the possibility of Russia bypassing the capitalist stage of development and building a communist society on the basis of the common ownership of land that existed in peasant villages at that time).

Second, land is defined both broadly and narrowly. Broadly, land refers to nature: all the non-human-produced, natural resources (such as soil, grasslands, forests, minerals, rivers and oceans) which, when transformed by labour, are the inputs to build and maintain cities and meet the food, shelter and other needs of people living in cities. Land also has non-utilitarian values: it has recreational, mental health, aesthetic, cultural and spiritual values that are important for people around the world.

More narrowly, from an economic point of view, however, the physical, chemical, mineralogical, hydrological, social, spatial, cultural and ecological properties of land (nature) are of secondary importance. Land becomes economically significant when it is owned as property: landed property. It is the *property rights* of communities, organisations and individuals that gives those landowners the power to intervene in and influence economic production. The rights of landownership – to use, benefit from and dispose of land as the owner sees fit, irrespective of the impact on land non-owners or the community as a whole – that are the crucial explanatory factor in political economy.

Third, this book presents Marx's writings thematically. The advantage of this approach is that it discusses Marx's views on land, rent and the landed property class in the context of his writings on surplus value, social relations, labour, capital and so on. An alternative approach, to list chronologically all of Marx's published and unpublished writings on urban landed property, rent and the landed property class was not taken because of the risk of divorcing these topics from Marx's wider project and, by doing so, producing a misleading understanding of these phenomena.

Fourth, this book is explicit about its historical materialist methodology. As discussed above, Marx always wrote about the particular forms that economics and politics took in particular societies. For example, he showed how the two fundamental factors of production, land and labour, are organised and combined differently in indigenous, ancient and Asiatic communities, and feudal and communist societies. He also showed how the tools, machinery, materials, equipment, buildings and technologies that are used by labour in production – the instruments of labour that exist in all economies – were transformed by the capitalist mode of production to become capital – the third factor of production in classical political economics. In addition, Marx's methodology is materialist: it holds that societies develop and change historically as a result of changes in pre-existing material factors and social interactions (such as property, labour, infrastructure, rent, technologies, institutions, social conflict and so on).

There are several related consequences arising from this methodology. It recognises that people are social beings: we are born into a society with pre-existing language, customs, institutions and organisations, and we live and work within this social context and its limits. People have agency: people, individually and collectively, can think, act and change the society of which they are a part, albeit within the resources and other limits that exist in particular societies. Historical change is idiographic: individual societies change throughout history because of particular factors and circumstances existing in a particular place and time.

This approach differs from other social science methods which posit that social change is caused by non-material factors (such as gods, ideas, or the ambitions and actions of 'great' men and women). It also contrasts with the methodology of neoclassical economics based on methodological individualism (where economic phenomena arise from individuals making 'rational' decisions and always wanting to maximise their self-interest, utility, pleasure, profits and so on) and its use of nomothetic generalisation (such as the 'law of supply and demand' or 'perfectly competitive markets will always settle into equilibrium in the long run') to explain economic behaviours and change.

Finally, orthodox economic methodology typically aims to describe, explain, forecast or perfect the economies of existing societies. Marx's historical materialist method, on the other hand, aims to develop practical knowledge that can be used to diagnose existing societies in order to develop new, better societies. 'The philosophers' and, Marx could have added, the economists 'have only interpreted the world, in various ways; the point is to change it'.[9]

Notes

1. United Nations Habitat, *World Cities Report 2020 – The Value of Sustainable Urbanization*, Nairobi, Kenya, United Nations Habitat (Human Settlements Programme), 2020, https://unhabitat.org/sites/default/files/2020/10/wcr_2020_report.pdf

2. United Nations, 'Cities and Pollution', n.d., https://www.un.org/en/climatechange/climate-solutions/cities-pollution#:~:text=Cities%20are%20major%20contributors%20to,cent%20of%20the%20Earth's%20surface

3. Financial Crisis Inquiry Commission, *The Financial Crisis Inquiry Report: Final Report of the National Commission on the Causes of the Financial and Economic Crisis in the United States*, Washington, DC, Financial Crisis Inquiry Commission, 2011, p. 5, https://www.govinfo.gov/content/pkg/GPO-FCIC/pdf/GPO-FCIC.pdf

4. 'The Global Recovery 10 Years after the 2008 Financial Meltdown', ch. 2, *World Economic Outlook*, Oct. 2018, Washington, DC, International Monetary Fund, https://www.imf.org/en/Publications/WEO/Issues/2018/09/24/world-economic-outlook-october-2018

5. 'Group Profile', Evergrande, n.d., https://mobilesite.evergrande.com/en/about.aspx?tags=2

6. The Economic Times, 'With Evergrande Debt Relief Deal, China Signals Stability Trumps Austerity', *The Economic Times*, 14 Jan. 2022, https://economictimes.indiatimes.com/news/international/business/with-evergrande-debt-relief-deal-china-signals-stability-trumps-austerity/articleshow/88895109.cms

7. There are exceptions to this general statement. Henri Lefebvre, David Harvey, Ben Fine, Doreen Massey and Alejandrina Catalano, Matthew Edel, Frank Stilwell and Franklin Obeng-Odoom, among others, have specifically explored how land affects cities from a Marxist perspective. Their approaches, and others, are discussed throughout this book.

8. G. M. Hodgson, *How Economics Forgot History: The Problems of Historical Specificity in Social Science*, London, Routledge, 2001.

9. K. Marx, *Theses on Feuerbach*, Moscow, Progress Publishers, 1969, https://www.marxists.org/archive/marx/works/1845/theses/theses.htm

Acknowledgements

I am very grateful to the many people who have helped make this book possible. Franklin Obeng-Odoom, Associate Professor at the Helsinki Institute of Sustainability Science, initiated this book, provided valuable editorial feedback and steered it through the commissioning and publication process. Professor Frank Stilwell and Associate Professor Bill Dunn at the University of Sydney provided invaluable intellectual advice and assistance over many years. The very useful feedback from three anonymous referees helped focus the argument in this book. The Marx Engels Archive provided priceless twenty-four-hour access to Marx's writings. The Edinburgh University Press commisioning team, including Gillian Leslie, Jenny Daly, Ersev Ersoy and Sarah Foyle, and the editing team, including Joannah Duncan, Robert Tuesley Anderson and Amanda Speake, turned the manuscript into a publication. Juliet Munro provided practical, intellectual and emotional support without which this project would never have been completed. Of course, all errors are the responsibility of the author.

CHAPTER 1

Introduction

The property in the soil is the original source of all wealth, and has become the great problem upon the solution of which depends the future of the working class.[1]

The century of cities

In 2007, the world changed fundamentally. For the first time in the history of humanity, more people in the world were living in cities than in rural regions.

For millennia, civilisations had been based on agriculture. Most people lived in low-density farms, hamlets, villages and other forms of small settlements, or on kinship or indigenous lands.[2] On occasions, some small settlements would expand and become centres of population, industry, trade and government, but compared to the rest of the society these towns and cities were small. From the 1500s to 1700s, in Western Europe, for example, only 10 to 12 per cent of the population lived in urban regions, and only about 5 per cent of the world's population lived in cities.[3]

Some of these agriculture-based civilisations built great cities. The earliest known evidence of high numbers of people living a concentrated, built environment with a diverse economy and some form of governance, taxes and public buildings is Çatalhöyük, in modern-day Turkey. Here a settlement of some 10,000 people existed from approximately 7100 BCE to 5700 BCE.[4] Jericho, in today's Palestine, is one of the earliest known walled cities with its fortifications dating back to 6800 BCE. Argos, Greece, has been continuously inhabited since 5000 BCE. Luxor, the city known to ancient Egyptians as Waset and Greeks as Thebes, dates from 3200 BCE. In Asia, Luoyang, built around 1600 BCE, is one of the four great ancient capitals of China. Quito, Ecuador; Benin, the oldest city in Nigeria; Beijing, China, and Varanasi, India, have been continuously inhabited since around 1000 BCE. Nakbe, Guatemala, one of the earliest documented Maya civilisation cities, has large structures that date to around 750 BCE.

Beginning in the 1700s, however, with the emergence of capitalism in Western Europe, there was a major migration of people from rural regions to cities (Table 1.1). New cities developed in Western Europe and its colonies. The growth of urbanisation was uneven across the world, but in the two

Table 1.1 Growth of urbanisation (percentage of population living in urban areas)								
	1500	1600	1700	1800	1900	2000	2016	2050
Japan	2.9	4.4	5.0	5.0	11.9	78.7	91.5	94.7
USA	0.2	0.7	2.0	6.1	40.0	79.1	81.9	89.2
South Korea	0.2	0.6	1.7	4.7	13.8	79.6	81.6	86.4
Latin America				14.0	20.0	75.5	80.2	87.8
Western Europe	10.6	12.2	12.8	21.4	40.6	76.0	79.6	87.0
China	6.5	7.0	5.9	6.0	6.6	35.9	56.7	80.0
World	4.1	5.2	5.1	7.3	16.4	46.7	54.4	68.4
Sub-Saharan Africa				4.0	5.0	35.0	41.6	58.1
India	4.4	4.6	4.9	6.4	11.9	27.7	33.2	52.8

Sources:
1. Global Change Data Lab, 'Urbanization over the past 500 years, 1500 to 2016', Oxford, Global Change Data Lab, n.d., https://ourworldindata.org/grapher/urbanization-last-500-years
2. United Nations, Department of Economic and Social Affairs, *World Urbanization Prospects: The 2018 Revision*, New York, United Nations Department of Economic and Social Affairs, 2019, https://population.un.org/wup/Publications/Files/WUP2018-Report.pdf

centuries between 1820 to 2016, Western Europe and the United States were the first to become highly urbanised.

Urbanisation spread. Japan and countries in Latin America and the Caribbean began to urbanise rapidly in the 1920s, and by 2016 were among the most industrialised regions in the world. South Korea and China began to urbanise around 1950, but while South Korea urbanised continuously to become one of the most industrialised nations in the world by 2016, China's rate of urbanisation decreased during the 1965–75 period of Mao's Cultural Revolution before recommencing. Based on the current trajectory, China will join the group of most urbanised nations in the world by 2050 with around 80 per cent of its people living in cities.[5]

On the other hand, sub-Saharan African and South Asian countries have urbanised later and more slowly than most other nations. Even so, on current trajectories, African nations on average will have around 60 per cent of their population living in cities by 2050 and India will have around 50 per cent of its population living in cities by that time.[6]

There are not only more people living in cities in the world; there are also more cities. In 2000, the world had 371 cities with 1 million inhabitants or more. By 2018, there were 548 cities with at least 1 million people. By 2030, there will be a projected 706 cities with at least 1 million residents.[7]

Table 1.2 Megacities, 1970–2035

	GLOBAL SOUTH				GLOBAL NORTH
	Asia	Africa	Latin America	Middle East	Europe, North America, Japan
1970					**Japan:** Tokyo **USA:** New York
2000	**China:** Beijing, Shanghai **India:** Mumbai, Delhi, Kolkata **Bangladesh:** Dhaka **Pakistan:** Karachi **South Korea:** Seoul **Philippines:** Manila	**Egypt:** Cairo	**Mexico:** Mexico City **Brazil:** São Paulo, Rio de Janeiro **Argentina:** Buenos Aires		**Japan:** Tokyo, Osaka **USA:** New York, Los Angeles **France:** Paris **Russia:** Moscow
2020	**China:** Beijing, Shanghai, Chongqing, Tianjin, Guangzhou-Guangdong, Shenzhen **India:** Mumbai, Delhi, Kolkata, Bangalore, Chennai **Bangladesh:** Dhaka **Pakistan:** Karachi, Lahore **Indonesia:** Jakarta **Thailand:** Krung Thep Maha Nakhon (Bangkok) **Philippines:** Manila	**Egypt:** Cairo **Nigeria:** Lagos **The Congo:** Kinshasa	**Mexico:** Mexico City **Brazil:** São Paulo, Rio De Janeiro **Argentina:** Buenos Aires **Colombia:** Bogota **Peru:** Lima	**Turkey:** Istanbul	**Japan:** Tokyo, Osaka **USA:** New York, Los Angeles **France:** Paris **Russia:** Moscow
2035	**China:** Beijing, Shanghai, Chongqing, Tianjin, Guangzhou-Guangdong, Shenzhen, Chengdu, Nanjing-Jiangsu, Wuhan, Xi'an-Shaanxi **India:** Mumbai, Delhi, Kolkata, Bangalore, Chennai, Ahmadabad, Surat **Bangladesh:** Dhaka **Pakistan:** Karachi, Lahore **Indonesia:** Jakarta **Thailand:** Krung Thep Maha Nakhon (Bangkok) **Malaysia:** Kuala Lumper **South Korea:** Thanh Pho Ho Chi Minh **Philippines:** Manila	**Egypt:** Cairo **Nigeria:** Lagos **The Congo:** Kinshasa **Angola:** Luanda **Tanzania:** Dar es Salaam	**Mexico:** Mexico City **Brazil:** São Paulo, Rio de Janeiro **Argentina:** Buenos Aires **Colombia:** Bogota **Peru:** Lima	**Turkey:** Istanbul **Iran:** Tehran **Iraq:** Bagdad	**Japan:** Tokyo, Osaka **USA:** New York, Los Angeles **France:** Paris **Russia:** Moscow **UK:** London

Sources: United Nations, Department of Economic and Social Affairs, *World Urbanization Prospects: The 2018 Revision*, New York, United Nations Department of Economic and Social Affairs, 2019, https://population.un.org/wup/Publications/Files/WUP2018-Report.pdf

The most recent development in the growth of urbanisation is the emergence of megacities. Megacities are urban conglomerations with 10 million inhabitants or more. In 1970, there were only two megacities in the world: Tokyo and New York. In 2000, there were twenty megacities, 70 per cent of which were based in the Global South, primarily in Asia, Africa and Latin America. By 2020, there were thirty-three megacities which were home to around 13 per cent of the world's urban population. Of these thirty-three megacities, 82 per cent were located in the Global South. By 2035, however, it is expected there will be forty-seven megacities in the world of which 85 per cent will be located in the Global South.[8] In debates about whether the growth of megacities in Africa is associated with economic development or not, preliminary findings suggest that urbanisation is strongly correlated with economic development.[9]

After millennia of people living in small, scattered communities and settlements around the globe, and after a transition period of only a few hundred years, the world is suddenly urban, and is becoming increasingly so.

These trends, of course, are not inevitable: they can be reshaped temporarily or permanently by public policies, pandemics, climate change and war, and societies typically reduce their levels of fertility as they become wealthier. But the trend is clear: the twenty-first century is the world's first century of cities, and the world's largest cities are Asian, Latin American and African.

Cities and the world

Cities are much more than large concentrations of people in a built environment. Cities are also the powerhouses of the world's economy. Economically, the world's cities produce more than 80 per cent of global output despite taking up merely 2 per cent of the Earth's land area.[10] Cities are centres of employment, investment, housing, health and education services, entertainment, culture and many other opportunities that benefit billions of people around the globe. Cities can be places of hope and potential; places where, as summarised in the eleventh-century German saying, 'Stadtluft macht frei nach Jahr und Tag'.[11]

But not for everyone. There is also a dark side to urban economic power. While the world's cities produce more than 80 per cent of global output, they also consume almost 80 per cent of the world's energy and account for over half of world's carbon dioxide emissions.[12] One-quarter of the world's urban population lives in city slums, mostly in East, Central and South Asia and sub-Saharan Africa.[13] Low-income and lower-middle-income countries face the greatest burdens arising from rapid urbanisation,[14] and without effective action, the number of people living in urban slums in the world could double to 2 billion.[15]

These Global North and Global South urban problems are intricately linked through global economic interdependencies in finance, migration, trade, investment and industrialisation.[16] For centuries, urban labour in the South (including slavery) has been exploited to build the wealth of cities in the North. Financiers in cities in the North speculate on the financialisation of urban property in the South and cause the cost of urban land in the South to rise steeply. Cost-cutting industrialists in the North continue to relocate their labour-intensive factories, 'dirty' industries and industrial waste to cities in the South.

As major centres of economic production, urbanisation is directly causing air, water and other forms of pollution including the production of solid wastes (such as plastics). These often have devastating impacts on urban dwellers.[17] For example, nearly 90 per cent of the air pollution-related deaths in the world occur in cities and towns in low- and middle-income countries, with nearly two out of three occurring in the newly urbanising regions in South-East Asia and the Western Pacific.[18]

Cities are major contributors to climate change, and they are also major causalities of climate change. Of the 136 biggest coastal cities in the world, 100 million people (or 20 per cent of their population) and US$4.7 trillion in assets are exposed to coastal flooding. With the growth of urbanisation, around 90 per cent of future urban expansion in developing countries is occurring near hazard-prone areas.[19] Similarly, climate change is contributing to food insecurity, fresh water shortages and the destruction of ecosystems. Combined with rapid urban sprawl, which often results in the destruction of fertile, agricultural land, many urban regions are losing their capacity to meet their own food needs.[20]

Health-wise, cities are also super-spreaders of infectious disease both within their environs and between cities. In 2008, for example, a novel influenza A (H1N1) virus infected people living in Mexico City. It quickly spread to the United States and then the world, killing up to 575,400 people, mostly younger, working-age people.[21] A decade later, the highly infectious coronavirus disease (COVID-19), first identified in the city of Wuhan, China, in December 2019, spread to every city in the world within 12 months, and within two years had killed around 5.5 million people.[22] Urbanisation is likely to increase the occurrence around the world of other diseases such as cholera and dengue.[23] On the other hand, creating more sustainable, healthy cities would deliver large societal and economic dividends. For example, making the world's cities healthy would reduce the capital required for urban infrastructure by US$15 trillion over fifteen years.[24]

Despite some similarities between some cities, no city in the world is alike. Each city is unique, with different population sizes and rates of ageing,[25] liveability,[26] economic, social and cultural attractiveness,[27] 'global cities' status (or not),[28] architectural and urban design look, levels of personal safety, locations and allied institutional/political arrangements'[29] and each has its own system of 'organised complexity'.[30]

Marxist approaches to urban land

There is a long tradition of Marxist analysis of cities, including debates about how capital, labour and land shape urban development. The first modern Marxist scholar to analyse urbanisation and urban development in a systematic way was Henri Lefebvre (1901–91), a French Marxist philosopher and sociologist. Lefebvre believed that cities needed to be studied carefully because they were the sites for future anti-capitalist revolution. This was a radical proposal at the time given revolutionaries such as Lenin, Che Guevara and Mao had all argued revolutions begin with peasants in the countryside.

Lefebvre argued that capitalism was reshaping cities to its own ends.[31] All aspects of urban life, including where people live, work, socialise and recreate, is shaped by capital in its search to make profit. This is not a unilateral process. The production of urban space, or more accurately, the co-production of urban space, emerges from the struggles between the collective action of the people who live in cities and the forces wishing to privatise and commodify urban resources and space. By 'space', Lefebvre referred to both 'natural' space (the three-dimensional, physical location and layout of cities) and 'social' or 'lived' space (the perceptions, meanings and experiences people have in their urban environment).

A key concept introduced by Lefebvre in *The Right to the City* is that cities need to be organised to meet the interests of those who inhabit the cities.[32] Specifically, the 'right to the city' involves two principles. First, the right to participate in the *production* of urban space (that is, to participate in the construction of both the built environment and the experiences one has living within the city); and second, the right to *appropriate* urban space (that is, the right to access, occupy and use existing urban space and to produce new forms of urban space so it meets the needs of urban inhabitants).[33] In other words, the right to the city is much more than having a say in the election of governments that carry out urban planning for cities. The right to the city means that urban residents (and not capital or the state) should be the final decision makers over how urban space is produced and used. This is a radical proposal because it challenges the usually sacrosanct property rights of capitalist landowners (and other types of commercial property) to use their property as they wish, irrespective of the impacts on property non-owners; instead, the use-rights of urban inhabitants takes precedence over the private property rights of individual landowners and capitalists.

Manuel Castells, a sociologist, criticised Lefebvre, arguing in *The Urban Question: A Marxist Approach* that urbanisation occurred and was structured by the imperative to create a labour force that was needed by capital.[34] In other words, cities are structured by the state which provides or funds health and housing services, education and training institutions, public transport and other social infrastructure – all types of 'collective consumption' – that are essential for the creation of the productive labour force that capital needs but is unwilling to pay for. In these circumstances Castells argued, many of the affected when the state provided its services (especially those from the middle class) would establish urban social movements to pressure the government to provide more or better-quality public services.

Nearly forty years later, Andy Merrifield wrote *The New Urban Question* in response to Castells.[35] He noted that the period of government-led urban development, where the state provided urban services and infrastructure, began to decline in the 1980s. After the economic slump of 1974–82, and with the rise of Prime Minister Margaret Thatcher in the UK and President Ronald Reagan in the United States, new neoliberal public policies were developed with the goal of dismantling the state as a strategy to restore higher levels of private sector profitability.[36]

By the 1990s, long-standing public assets were being privatised, giving the private sector ownership of profit-making monopolies such as airports, water services, toll roads and so on. In addition, hard-won government regulations, price controls and trade barriers that protected the interests of national industries, labour, consumers, tenants and residents were deregulated so that capital could cut costs, globalise and take other measures to maximise profits. The 'neoliberal principle of letting capital decide where to place production' directly contributed to urban phenomena such as gentrification (when government-provided rental housing was privatised and often replaced with expensive new apartments sold to wealthier owners) and mega-project-led urban redevelopment (where very large-scale private investment projects moved into suburbs, displacing the existing low-income and disenfranchised communities living there, and building large residential and commercial towers and privately owned recreational places).[37] Today, because of these changes, Merrifield argues, there is a need for a new form of urban-based politics, where labour and urban movements need to combine to repossess assets into public control and to reintroduce commons areas into cities which are under community control (rather than capital or the state).

Doreen Massey is best known for showing how cities are structured by the spatial divisions of labour, including the spatial division of gender.[38] However, one of Massey's earliest studies (with Alejandrina Catalano) provided empirical data on how landownership in cities affects capital accumulation.[39] In *Capital and Land: Landownership by capital*, Massey and Catalano analysed landed property owned by the aristocracy and church, by industrial capital (for production), and by financial investors owning land for rental and capital returns (but not land held by the construction industry or the state). With these data, they explored the causes of the land and property boom that occurred in the UK in the 1970s. This research and analysis was 'a first step towards a modern analysis of land and rent'.[40]

In the analysis of urban development and change, David Harvey's *The Limits to Capital* (1982) was, and continues to be, one of the most significant contributions to Marxist political economy generally, and the political economy of cities in particular.[41] Harvey argued that one essential characteristic of capital is that it must move continuously in a cycle of investment, production and profit-making. This cycle of investment, production and the realisation of profit is summarised symbolically as $M — C \dots P \dots C' — M'$ and is discussed in detail in Chapter 4. Essentially, money (M) is invested into buying commodities (C) which are transformed by labour in production (P) into new, higher-value commodities (C') which are sold (for M'), generating a profit. Because of competition and other pressures, this profit must be reinvested into yet another cycle of production to produce another round of profit. Importantly, this movement of capital is a change of form (from money to commodities to new, higher-value commodities to money-plus-profit) which occurs in space. For example, money moves from investors to buy raw materials which are transported to a factory where they are transformed by labour into new, higher-value commodities which are transported to wholesale and retail outlets where they are sold to customers for a profit which is forwarded to the original investor.

However, for this cycle of investment, production and profit-making to occur, capital must invest in factories, machinery, warehouses, transport infrastructure and other fixed assets. Capital invested in property, plant and equipment and infrastructure is made immobile in two senses: capital is 'fixed' in a built environment at a specific, unchanging location; and capital is immobile in the sense that these assets cannot easily be liquidated into cash and be moved back into the cycle of capital accumulation.

One of Harvey's most important contributions to urban political economy is his insight that capital investment must involve land markets and that 'The land market shapes the allocation of land and thereby shapes the geographical structures of production, exchange and consumption …'[42] In capitalism, he suggests, when land is freely traded it is both a 'commodity' and 'a form of fictitious capital'.[43] Landowners are 'a faction of money capitalists who simply have chosen, for whatever reason, to hold a claim on rent rather than on some other form of future revenues' and land markets are 'a special branch of the circulation of interest-bearing capital'.[44] In other words, rent is the mechanism whereby one faction of capital coordinates land use in such a way that it maximises capital accumulation as a whole. As a result of the intervention of landowners, capital constructs a capital-coordinated built environment in cities which facilitates both the imperative of capital to move through space (from money to commodities to sale to profit) and the imperative of capital to be fixed in space (as fixed assets and infrastructure).

Unfortunately for capital, these two imperatives, to flow and to be fixed, are contradictory. If there is a mismatch, with too much investment in one process or underinvestment in the other, this will cause delays in the cycle of capital flows or expensive overcapitalisation. Either way, capital is devalued and there is a tendency for the rate of profit to fall.

As a result of this contradiction, capital is forced to find new ways to become ever more profitable. One way it overcomes this crisis is for capital to reconfigure the urban space. For example, if a part of the built environment is too costly or not productive enough, capitalists can demolish those buildings, or pressure governments to build new infrastructure, and thus establish a new, modern and cheaper (or more productive) built environment. Second, capital can reconfigure space by selling up and relocating to a different suburb or city where there is a more productive built environment. A third spatial solution to capitalist crises of falling productivity is to move its factories and other fixed assets to another country.

In summary, Harvey argues the built environment of cities is slowly but continually restructured by capital as companies repeatedly invest in property, plant, equipment and infrastructure to make a profit, until, under pressure from a falling rate of profit, capital disinvests or restructures and moves to another city or another country. When this occurs, some or all of the city's built environment, often constructed over centuries, falls into disuse and disrepair, real estate values fall, the city deindustrialises, and unemployment rises. On the other hand, the city with the new investment has a boom in construction, real estate prices and employment rise, and a new built environment is established in the city. Capital accumulation restructures and expands the built environment of one city as it simultaneously destroys the built environment of another.

Finally, Harvey notes, this tendency of capital to find spatial solutions to overcome the crises of profitability, spatial solutions that continually restructure the built environment of cities around the world, cannot go on indefinitely. At some point, there is a crisis of capital accumulation which cannot be solved by moving to a more productive location (or through the development of new, more productive technology, which is an option discussed by Harvey but beyond the scope of this book). At this point, there is a massive devaluation of capital through bankruptcies, falling property values, factory closures, the sale of stockpiles of commodities at below-value prices and so on. There is also widespread unemployment. In such economic recessions or depressions, the built environment of cities changes again, but this time due to the failure of capital accumulation.

Harvey's explanation of how capital creates, restructures and destroys the built environment of cities may make capitalism seem like a system, a self-perpetuating 'machine' with no human input or agency. There is no mention of people, classes or class struggle (e.g. between capital and the landed property class over the payment of rent). Harvey has been criticised for the limited involvement of human agency in his theories. For example, Steven Katz noted that Harvey considered workers have agency in shaping the built environment (when they defend their existing homes from the pressures of capital, or when they move to other cities, creating a demand for housing, schools, shops, public infrastructure and other elements of the built environment) but that, in the workplace, workers are dominated by the imperatives of capital and have no agency.[45]

This tendency of Harvey's analysis to see social relations, in this case, as social relations of domination (rather than contradictory relations of struggle) also occurs in his later writings such as *Rebel City* where he neglects working-class initiatives in Italy (such as the autonomous Marxist tradition of working-class self-organisation, the associated forms of territorial-community activism, and the Wages For and Against Housework campaigns) which aim to restructure urban space for the good of residents rather than for profit by capital or land speculators,[46] as well as in his writings on accumulation by dispossession where he recognises the agency of urban social movements but not class struggle.[47] On the other hand, Harvey is acutely aware of the necessity of class struggle.[48]

Matthew Edel focuses more specifically on how landownership and rent contribute to the spatially uneven accumulation of capital that occurs in cities, and on the accompanying social segregation that it causes in cities.[49] Worker struggle can influence the magnitude of rent, and therefore worker struggle can directly affect the form of the urban built environment.[50] Suburbanisation (in the United States) can be understood as a class-based negotiated settlement between capital and organised labour working closely with progressive governments.[51]

Frank Stilwell built on the work of Harvey and Castells to show how urban development can be influenced by the role of the state.[52] Given the capacity of capital to move from city to city and country to country, many states are under pressure to use their powers to attract and retain 'footloose' capital. States can do this by regulating land use directly (through urban planning, land use zoning, building regulations and so on), providing publicly funded infrastructure to locations in order to attract or retain investment, providing funding to capital (through tax concessions, grants and so on), and exempting selected industries or companies from their environmental, competition or labour obligations. State intervention can be carried out on an ad hoc basis, but governments can also develop regional and urban development plans to attract new ('emerging') industries to the region, facilitate the transition of existing, often inefficient and polluting industries to new, technologically advanced industries, and/or facilitate the relocation of industries or firms from one region to another.

Finally, in this brief introduction to Marxist approaches to cities, it must be noted that almost all the debates on urbanisation refer to capitalist cities in the Global North, with very few considering urbanisation in the Global South. Across the Global South, urbanisation processes vary considerably (e.g. between middle-income and low-income countries, and between the continents of Latin America, Asia and Africa), and there are also some commonalities such as a rapid increase in the number of megacities (urban agglomerations with a population of more than 10 million), ongoing strong urban–rural linkages, and growing intra-urban inequalities.[53]

Since the 2000s, Lefebvre's 'right to the city' has inspired the development of critical urban studies in the Global South.[54] Lefebvre's right to the city has been useful in clarifying principles such as the right of inhabitants to produce cities for their use (rather than in the interests of private property), the right of inhabitants to appropriate their own space, and the need to promote the collective, popular and autonomous production of urban space by its inhabitants (rather than having cities planned and developed by professionals, consultants and experts in the service of private capitalist interests and the capitalist state).[55]

However, Lefebvre's broad vision has been narrowed by 'The Right to the City' announcements made by the United Nations commencing in 2016. The UN's 'right' to the city fits well with its programme of human rights and its associated Millennium Development Goals (such as the right of all people to have access to clean drinking water, affordable energy and decent work).

As a result, at least in sub-Saharan Africa, Lefebvre's revolutionary critique of urbanisation has had to be radically reconceptualised. For example, Lefebvre's view that urban dwellers need to seize the power of the state to gain control over cities needs to be heavily revised given the weaknesses of states in the Global South. Here, centuries of European colonialism established states with weak controls over urban space, where the state provision of welfare rarely exists, where the state is dependent on foreign investment for development, and where state repression, especially by authoritarian states, can sometimes be very violent. Second, Lefebvre's notion that urban inhabitants will combine and work together to produce and appropriate urban space is weakened in cities in the Global South which are marked with strong racial, ethnic, gender or caste divides. Third, Lefebvre's assumption that the right to the city depends, in part, on the participation of the urban working class is undermined when a large proportion of labour force in sub-Saharan cities carries out activities referred to as informal, and which are subject to high levels of political clientelism (where there is the exchange of goods and services between patrons, brokers and clients in return for political support).[56]

A practical problem affecting analyses of urban development in the Global

Table 1.3 Land tenure around the world

Nations	Main types of land tenure	Percentage of the world population
India, and many cities in Africa	Mostly state-owned land, some private and some indigenous title	35
China, Cuba, Vietnam, Russia, some ex-Soviet Bloc nations, Venezuela, Ethiopia; also Singapore	Mostly state-owned land, some collective ownership of rural land	25
Saudi Arabia, Morocco, Oman, Jordan, Kuwait and Qatar, and Pakistan	Feudal title	20
USA, Germany and France	Mostly privately owned land, plus some state ownership	10
Latin America	Mixture of public and private title, around 20% of land in indigenous title	10
Papua New Guinea, Fiji, Solomon Islands	Mostly indigenous title	0.15

Sources:
1. L. Cotula, C. Toulmin and C. Hesse, *Land Tenure and Administration in Africa: Lessons of Experience and Emerging Issues*, London, International Institute for Environment and Development, 2004, http://www.hubrural.org/IMG/pdf/iied_lt_cotula.pdf
2. 'Customary land use is omnipresent in West African cities and coexists alongside formal and informal land uses, a situation known as legal pluralism': P. M. Picard and H. Selod, *Customary Land Conversion and the Formation of the African City*, Washington, DC, World Bank, 2020, https://openknowledge.worldbank.org/bitstream/handle/10986/33484/Customary-Land-Conversion-and-the-Formation-of-the-African-City.pdf?sequence=1&isAllowed=y
3. R. Monzon, 'Introducing Private-Property Rights to Cuba: How Cuba's New Constitution Paves the Way for Economic Growth', *Case Western Reserve Journal of International Law*, vol. 52, no. 1, 2020, https://scholarlycommons.law.case.edu/jil/vol52/iss1/28
4. Embassy of the Socialist Republic of Vietnam in the United States of America, *Land Regulations*, Washington, DC, Embassy of the Socialist Republic of Vietnam in the United States of America, n.d., http://vietnamembassy-usa.org/basic-page/land-regulations
5. A. Haila, *Urban Land Rent: Singapore as a Property State*, Hoboken, NJ, Wiley-Blackwell, 2015.
6. P. Giampaoli, and S. Aggarwal, *USAID Issue Brief: Land Tenure and Property Rights in Pakistan*, Washington, DC, United States Agency for International Development, 2010, https://www.land-links.org/wp-content/uploads/2016/09/USAID_Land_Tenure_Pakistan_Issue_Brief-2.pdf
7. Land Portal, *Collective Property in South America, Challenges and Perspectives*, Groningen, The Netherlands, Land Portal, 2017, https://landportal.org/debates/2017/collective-property-south-america-challenges-and-prospects
8. Pacific Data Hub, *National Minimum Development Indicators for Population*, Noumea, New Caledonia, The Pacific Community, 2020

North compared with the Global South is the different forms of land tenure that exist in the world. In the Global North, most land tenure consists of privately owned land with some state ownership of land. On the other hand, most people around the world live in societies where land is totally or predominantly held under state, collective, feudal or indigenous tenure – and not private ownership (Table 1.3). As a result, reports, such as the World Bank's study of cities in sub-Saharan Africa which concluded 'building the city depends on private rights over land and structures'[57] are inherently biased by their reliance on neoclassical economic assumptions and beliefs,[58] and too simplistic for nations that consider communal and other forms of land tenure to be legitimate forms of property. Indeed, the unsophisticated advocacy of the privatisation of urban land has, in many cases, created social and economic problems.[59]

The approach of this book

This book addresses a recognised gap in the literature[60] by documenting in his own words how Marx's theory of land, rent and the landed property class explains different forms of urban development.

It proposes that urban *land* is what makes the economies, built environment and governance of cities distinctive. Explanations of urban development based on capital, labour, class struggle and/or the state are therefore necessary but not sufficient until they include an understanding of the social relations of urban landed property.

This approach builds on, but differs from, previous Marxist analyses of urban development. The approach can be summarised in the five main themes that constitute the key arguments in this book.

The first theme is land as property. The power of land to shape urban economies derives from its existence as landed *property*. As property, land gives its owners a bundle of property rights (and interests in land) including the economic power to extract rent from others who want to use the land. This power of landownership – to own, benefit from and dispose of land as the owner sees fit, and to exclude others even though they may be affected by the land use – directly affects how urban economies grow, develop and fail.

The second theme is land and the mode of production. The power of landownership varies significantly depending on the particular mode of production of which it is a part. Cities have historically developed in different ways and with different functions depending, for example, on whether they were operating in indigenous, ancient, Asiatic, feudal, capitalist and communist societies. Understanding these differences in urban landownership provides insights into urban processes that are not possible if it is assumed land only exists in capitalist societies.

The third theme is land and rent. The most important economic power of landed property is the capacity of landowners to demand rent from others for the use of their land. Rent is not merely a payment of money as part of a lease contract, but in many modes of production it can take different forms such as the provision of services (such as free labour) and payment in kind (such as free goods). Irrespective of its form, rent is always a payment to the land owner for the use of the land.

The fourth theme is land and the state. The state exists in a contradictory relationship with landed property. On the one hand, states are political authorities which exercise control over territory (land) and the population that lives on that territory. A fundamental responsibility of every state is to have a monopoly of violence so it can secure, defend and maintain control over its territory from attacks by potential invaders outside the state's territory, and to enforce law and order over those people living within the borders of the territory. On the other hand, to achieve these goals (and others such as to provide economic and social infrastructure and services) states need resources. One way to acquire the necessary resources is for the state to transfer ownership of parts of its territory to individuals or groups in return for the payment of land taxes, real estate fees and other land-based charges. In other words, the successful existence of states relies both on having control over its own territory and relinquishing control of parcels of its land to others in return for the payment of resources.

The fifth theme is land and class. The existence of property laws, land institutions and real estate markets is always accompanied by a landed property class made up of property developers, land speculators, real estate lobbyists and others whose economic interests lie in profiting from land. The landed property class actively organises to protect its economic interests, strengthen its property rights, reduce environmental and other land use regulations, minimise land and building development codes, maximise government-funded provision of land-price enhancing urban infrastructure such as roads and utilities, and limit or abolish land taxes and charges. The landed property class typically organises to influence the state directly (through actions such as getting their members and supporters elected or appointed to law-making and law-implementing bodies including municipal councils) and indirectly (through methods such as lobbying, donations to political parties and the payment of bribes). Understanding urban land requires an understanding of the influence of the landed property class.

Chapter overview

The first six chapters focus in detail on Marx's writings about land and cities. He wrote hundreds of pages on land, landed property, rent, landlords, land workers (such as peasants, serfs and farm labourers), the state and nature. These writings are in his theoretical studies, notebooks, political statements, newspaper articles, notebooks and correspondence.[61] By documenting the range and depth of Marx's land writings, this book hopes to overcome past problems where 'debates over rent seem to flourish as never before, often with scant regard for Marx's theory'.[62] It documents what Marx actually wrote, primarily, and connects it to later interpretations only secondarily. It shows Marx had a comprehensive approach to land that complements and informs his better-known writings on labour and capital.

Chapter 2 introduces the reader to the core concepts needed to understand Marx's writings including land, rent, value and class. These seemingly simple concepts are, in fact, full of complex meanings and can easily be misunderstood without an awareness of Marx's theoretical roots in his critiques of Hegel's philosophy of dialectics, social change and human emancipation.

Chapter 3 considers Marx's approach to landed property in communities organised on the basis of three modes of production: indigenous communities, ancient (agricultural or slave) communities and Asiatic communities. Indigenous communities have rarely had cities, but ancient and Asiatic communities have very different forms of land use, rent and cities.

Chapter 4 examines Marx's approach to landed property in societies with three different modes of production: feudal, capitalist and communist societies. Again, each of these different societies has a different form of land use, rent and cities depending on whether the land is communally owned, privately owned or owned by the state.

Chapter 5 discusses in detail two major forms of rent in capitalist economies: differential rent and absolute rent. This chapter shows how the basis of rent is the surplus value produced by labour, which is captured by capital, and then extracted from capital by the landed property class. The chapter also shows the limits that exist on the magnitude of rent that can be appropriated by landowners.

Chapter 6 demonstrates the contradictory interdependence of land and the state; the political role of the landed property class; and the relations between the working class, capitalist class and the landed property class.

These chapters, considered together, produce some surprising conclusions. Land and labour are the two factors of production that are essential to political economies of communities and societies in all modes of production. It is only in capitalism that the private ownership of money, machinery, tools, materials, buildings and other forms of technology – capital – becomes the important third factor of production. Second, there cannot be a general theory of rent, because how rent is extracted from labour varies with each indigenous, ancient, Asiatic, feudal, capitalist or communist mode of production. Third, in spite of the widely discussed and acknowledged problematic relationship between much Marxist political economy and post-colonialisation,[63] Marx could also be seen as one of the world's first supporters of indigenous land rights, and an early environmentalist who recognised that the artificial division between humans and nature, especially in capitalism, would destroy nature and jeopardise the future of humanity.[64]

The last chapter identifies some practical implications arising from the first chapters. It identifies four land-based strategies that policymakers can use to promote inclusive urban economic, social and environmental change. These policy tools are land value taxes, land nationalisation, the strengthening of customary land rights, and community land title. These strategies provide alternatives to the policies promoted by some international and national organisations that assume urban development and economic growth will be fostered only by privatising land, establishing 'free' rather than fair real estate markets, and treating land as a commodity to be bought and sold for a profit.

This book will be of interest to three types of readers: first, advanced undergraduate students, postgraduate students and scholars, in the Global North and the Global South, who are researching in depth urban issues such as real estate, land use legislation and planning, land taxation, urban development, urban policy, the local state and urban inequality; second, those interested in critically evaluating Marx's political economic theories and methodology, especially those interested in reintegrating Marx's views of land into his critiques; and third, general readers who are interested in how cities in the Global North and Global South are changing and why, the world history of urban development, and Marx's approach to the environment.

Notes

1. K. Marx, 'The Nationalisation of the Land', *The International Herald*, no. 11, 15 June 1872, https://www.marxists.org/archive/marx/works/1872/04/nationalisation-land. htm
2. Global Change Data Lab, 'Urbanization over the Past 500 Years, 1500 to 2016', *Our World in Data*, Oxford, Global Change Data Lab, n.d., https://ourworldindata.org/gra pher/urbanization-last-500-years
3. Ibid.
4. United Nations Educational, Scientific and Cultural Organization, 'Neolithic Site of Çatalhöyük', *World Heritage List*, Paris, United Nations Educational, Scientific and Cultural Organization, n.d., https://whc.unesco.org/en/list/1405/
5. United Nations, Department of Economic and Social Affairs, *World Urbanization Prospects: The 2018 Revision*, New York, United Nations Department of Economic and Social Affairs, 2019, https://population.un.org/wup/Publications/Files/WUP2018-Report.pdf
6. Ibid.
7. United Nations, Department of Economic and Social Affairs, *The World's Cities in 2018 – Data Booklet*, New York, United Nations, Department of Economic and Social Affairs, 2018, https://www.un.org/en/events/citiesday/assets/pdf/the_worlds_cities_ in_2018_data_booklet.pdf

8. United Nations, Department of Economic and Social Affairs, *World Urbanization Prospects: The 2018 Revision*, New York, United Nations Department of Economic and Social Affairs, 2019, https://population.un.org/wup/Publications/Files/WUP2018-Report.pdf

9. F. Obeng-Odoom, '"Abnormal" Urbanization in Africa: A Dissenting View', *African Geographical Review*, vol. 29, no. 2, 2010, pp. 13–40.

10. United Nations, 'Cities and Pollution', *Climate Solutions*, New York, United Nations, n.d., https://www.un.org/en/climatechange/climate-solutions/cities-pollution.

11. 'City air makes you free after a year and a day.' This eleventh-century German saying describes a principle of law where serfs could flee feudal land and gain their freedom by living in cities.

12. United Nations, 'Cities and Pollution', *Climate Solutions*, New York, United Nations, n.d, https://www.un.org/en/climatechange/climate-solutions/cities-pollution

13 United Nations Habitat, *World Cities Report 2020 – The Value of Sustainable Urbanization*, Nairobi, United Nations Habitat (Human Settlements Programme), 2020, https://unhabitat.org/sites/default/files/2020/10/wcr_2020_report.pdf

14. United Nations, Department of Economic and Social Affairs, *World Urbanization Prospects: The 2018 Revision*, New York, United Nations Department of Economic and Social Affairs, 2019, https://population.un.org/wup/Publications/Files/WUP2018-Report.pdf.

15. United Nations Habitat, *The Challenge of Slums – Global Report on Human Settlements*, Nairobi, United Nations Habitat (Human Settlements Programme), 2003, https://unhabitat.org/sites/default/files/download-manager-files/The%20Challenge%20of%20Slums%20-%20Global%20Report%20on%20Human%20Settlements%202003.pdf

16. For example, T. Barnes, *Making Cars in the New India: Industry, Precarity and Informality*, Cambridge, Cambridge University Press, 2018 and *Informal Labour in Urban India: Three Cities, Three Journeys*, London, Routledge, 2015; F. Obeng-Odoom, *Oiling the Urban Economy: Land, Labour, Capital, and the State in Sekondi-Takoradi, Ghana*, London, Routledge, 2014, *Reconstructing Urban Economics: Towards a Political Economy of the Built Environment*, London, Zed Books, 2016, 'Transnational Corporations and Urban Development', *American Journal of Economics and Sociology*, vol. 77, no. 2, 2018, pp. 447–510, 'Valuing Unregistered Urban Land in Indonesia', *Evolutionary and Institutional Economics Review*, vol. 15, no. 2, 2018, pp. 315–340 and *Global Migration Beyond Limits: Ecology, Economics, and Political Economy*, Oxford, Oxford University Press, 2022; and L. Marais, p. Burger, M. Campbell, D. van Rooyen and S. Denoon-Stevens (eds), *Coal and Energy in Emalahleni, South Africa: Considering a Just Transition*, Edinburgh, Edinburgh University Press, 2022.

17. United Nations Habitat, *World Cities Report 2020 – The Value of Sustainable Urbanization*, Nairobi, United Nations Habitat (Human Settlements Programme), 2020, https://unhabitat.org/sites/default/files/2020/10/wcr_2020_report.pdf

18. World Health Organization, *WHO Releases Country Estimates on Air Pollution Exposure and Health Impact*, Geneva, World Health Organization, 2016, https://www.who.int/news/item/27-09-2016-who-releases-country-estimates-on-air-pollution-exposure-and-health-impact

19. World Bank, *Urban Development*, Washington, DC, World Bank, 2020, https://www.worldbank.org/en/topic/urbandevelopment/overview

20. Intergovernmental Panel on Climate Change, '1.2.1.2. Land Degradation', *Special Report on Climate Change and Land: An IPCC Special Report on Climate Change, Desertification, Land Degradation, Sustainable Land Management, Food Security, and Greenhouse Gas Fluxes in Terrestrial Systems*, Geneva, Intergovernmental Panel on Climate Change, 2019, https://www.ipcc.ch/srccl/chapter/chapter-1/

21. Centers for Disease Control and Prevention, *2009 H1N1 Pandemic (H1N1pdm09 virus)*, Washington, DC, Centers for Disease Control, 2019, https://www.cdc.gov/flu/pandemic-resources/2009-h1n1-pandemic.html

22. World Health Organization, *WHO Coronavirus (COVID-19) Dashboard*, Geneva, World Health Organization, https://covid19.who.int/

23. World Health Organization, 'Climate Change and Infectious Diseases', in *Climate Change and Human Health – Risks and Responses*, Geneva, World Health Organization, 2003, https://www.who.int/globalchange/publications/climchange.pdf

24. World Health Organization, *COP24 Special Report: Health & Climate Change*, Geneva, World Health Organization, 2018, https://apps.who.int/iris/handle/10665/276405

25. United Nations Department of Economic and Social Affairs, *World Urbanization Prospects* [online resources], New York, United Nations Department of Economic and Social Affairs, https://population.un.org/wup/

26. The Economist Intelligence Unit, *The Global Livability Index 2019*, London, The Economist Group, 2019, https://www.eiu.com/public/topical_report.aspx?campaignid=liveability2019

27. Resonance Consultancy, *The World's Best Cities 2021*, Vancouver, Resonance Consultancy, 2021, https://www.bestcities.org/

28. Kearney, *2020 Global Cities Index*, Chicago, IL, Kearney, 2020, https://www.kearney.com/global-cities/2020

29. A. J. Scott and M. Storper, 'The Nature of Cities: The Scope and Limits of Urban Theory', *International Journal of Urban and Regional Research*, 2014, https://luskin.ucla.edu/sites/default/files/ScottStorperpublibished.pdf

30. D. Pumain (ed.), *Theories and Models of Urbanisation: Geography, Economics and Computing Sciences*, Berlin, Springer, 2020.

31. H. Lefebvre, *The Production of Space*, Hoboken, NJ, Wiley-Blackwell, 1991, and *The Urban Revolution*, Minneapolis, MN, University of Minnesota Press, 2003.

32. H. Lefebvre, *The Right to the City* in *Writings on Cities*, ed. and trans. E. Kofman and E. Lebas, Hoboken, NJ, Wiley-Blackwell, 1995.

33. M. Purcell. 'Excavating Lefebvre: The Right to the City and Its Urban Politics of the Inhabitant', *GeoJournal*, vol. 58, 2002, pp. 99–108.

34. M. Castells, *The Urban Question: A Marxist Approach*, trans. A. Sheridan, London, Edward Arnold, 1977, original French version 1972.

35. A. Merrifield, *The New Urban Question*, London, Pluto Press, 2014.

36. J. O'Connor, 'Marxism and the Three Movements of Neoliberalism', *Critical Sociology*, vol. 36, no. 5, 2010, pp. 691–715.

37. A. Hankin, 'Megaprojects' Exclusionary Benefits: The Case of Local Government Policy Benefiting the Privileged Few', *Harvard Real Estate Review*, 17 May 2017, https://medium.com/harvard-real-estate-review/megaprojects-exclusionary-benefits-the-case-of-local-government-policy-benefiting-the-privileged-db4d1a8228bc

38. For example, D. Massey, *Spatial Divisions of Labor: Social Structures and the Geography of Production*, 2nd edn, Routledge: New York, 1995.

39. D. Massey and A. Catalano, *Capital and Land: Landownership by Capital in Great Britain*, London, Edward Arnold, 1978.

40. M. Edwards and D. Lovatt, 'Review: Capital and Land', *Capital and Class*, vol. 3, no. 3, 1979, pp. 144–6.

41. D. Harvey, *The Limits to Capital*, Oxford, Basil Blackwell, 1982.

42. Ibid., p. 331.

43. Ibid., p. 347.

44. Ibid., p. 345.

45. S. Katz, 'Towards a Sociological Definition of Rent: Notes of David Harvey's *The Limits to* Capital', *Antipode*, vol. 18, no. 1, 1986, pp. 64–78.

46. N. Gray, 'Whose Rebel City?', *Mute*, 18 Dec. 2012, https://www.metamute.org/edito rial/articles/whose-rebel-city

47. R. Das, 'David Harvey's Theory of Accumulation by Dispossession: A Marxist Critique', *World Review of Political Economy*, vol. 8, no. 4, Winter 2017, pp. 590–616.

48. D. Harvey, 'David Harvey on Class Struggle', video, LABOURNET TV, 2011, https://en.labournet.tv/video/6260/david-harvey-class-struggle

49. M. Edel, *Urban and Regional Economics: Marxist Perspectives*, Reading, Harwood Academic Publishers, 1992.

50. M. Edel, 'Urban Renewal and Land Use Conflicts', *Review of Radical Political Economics*, vol. 3, no. 3, 1971, pp. 76–89.

51. M. Edel, 'Rent Theory and Labor Strategy: Marx, George and the Urban Crisis', *Review of Radical Political Economics*, no. 4, 1977, pp. 1–15.

52. For example, F. Stilwell, *Understanding Cities and Regions: Spatial Political Economy*, Leichhardt, Pluto Press Australia, 1995.

53. W. Smit. 'Urbanisation in the Global South', *Global Public Health*, 26 Apr. 2021, https://doi.org/10.1093/acrefore/9780190632366.013.251

54. M. Morange and A. Spire, 'The Right to the City in the Global South: Perspectives from Africa', *Cybergeo: European Journal of Geography*, 20 May 2019, https://doi.org/10.4000/cybergeo.32217

55. Ibid.

56. Ibid.

57. S. V. Lall, J. V. Henderson and A. J. Venables, *Africa's Cities: Opening Doors to the World*, Washington, DC, World Bank, 2017, https://openknowledge.worldbank.org/handle/10986/25896

58. K. Elahi and F. Stilwell, 'Customary Land Tenure, Neoclassical Economics and Conceptual Bias', *Nuigini Agrisayens*, vol. 5, 2013, pp. 28–39.

59. F. Obeng-Odoom, 'Valuing Unregistered Urban Land in Indonesia', *Evolutionary and Institutional Economics Review, vol. 15*, no. 2, 2018, pp. 315–40.

60. C. Ward and M. B. Aalbers, 'The Shitty Rent Business: What's the Point of Land Rent Theory?', *Urban Studies*, vol. 53, no. 9 (2016), pp. 1760–83.

61. These are sourced primarily from the Marx/Engels Internet Archive at https://www.marxists.org/archive/marx/index.htm

62. B. Fine, 'Marx's Rent Theory Revisited? Landed Property, Nature and Value', *Economy and Society*, vol. 48, no. 3, 2019, pp. 450–61.

63. For example, V. Chibber, *Postcolonial Theory and the Spectre of Capital*, London, Verso, 2012; K. B. Anderson, *Marx at the Margins: On Nationalism, Ethnicity and Non-Western Societies*,

Chicago, IL, University of Chicago Press, 2016, and R. Warren (ed.), *The Debate on Postcolonial Theory and the Spectre of Capital*, London, Verso, 2017.

64. M. Le Page, 'Destruction of Nature Is as Big a Threat to Humanity as Climate Change', *New Scientist*, no. 3229, 11 May 2019.

CHAPTER 2

Foundational Concepts

Political economy proceeds from the fact of private property.[1]

Introduction

Before discussing Marx's specific comments on land, rent and cities, some preliminary remarks are needed to clarify the foundational concepts used in the following chapters.

This is necessary for two reasons. First, readers who are *not* familiar with political economic concepts (such as land, rent, capital, value, social relations, contradictions, class and the state) will find it useful to have an up-front explanation of these specialised terms.

Second, there is no single, universal, unchanging definition of economic categories (such as land, rent, state and cities) because the nature, scope and characteristics of these categories depends on the system of production of which they are a part. For example, in the analysis of the economy of any community or society 'nothing seems more natural than to begin with ground rent, with landed property, since this is bound up with the earth, the source of all production and of all being, and with the first form of production of all more or less settled societies – agriculture'.[2] This assumption is erroneous because, for example, who owns land, who uses it and for what purposes, and who can lease the land (if at all) is significantly different in an indigenous community (where the land is common property and used primarily for human sustenance) compared with land under a feudal mode of production (where the landownership is 'held' by a monarch who provides it to a feudal lord in return for fealty and military service).

In other words, to fully understand economic assets (such as land), economic practices (such as rent) and economic institutions (such as landed property) it is necessary to recognise their 'historical specificity'[3] and investigate them within their particular societal context.

Land

Economic conceptualisations of land are generally atheoretical and ahistorical. Historically political economists (such as the Physiocrats in France, and Adam Smith and David Ricardo in England) assumed land was agricultural land. Today, economists are more likely to include 'nature (minerals, water, fish in the oceans, the frequency spectrum, etc.)' and the 'physical sites or locations where production takes place'.[4]

Marx held land to have four important features. First, land is a part of the broader category of nature (e.g. 'an element of nature, say land').[5] By nature, Marx referred to the 'geological, hydrographical, climatic and so on'[6] characteristics of the 'sensuous external world', where the 'objects of nature' included 'plants, animals, stones, air, light, etc.'.[7] Throughout his writings, nature included soils, water, oceans, plants, pastures, animals, forests, ores and other physical, chemical and biotic factors within, on and above the Earth, and so on. Significantly, nature refers to those aspects of the material world that exist 'without human assistance, such as land, wind, water, metals in situ, and timber in virgin forests'[8] and which exist independently of people: 'The soil (and this, economically speaking, includes water) in the virgin state in which it supplies man with necessaries or the means of subsistence ready to hand, exists independently of him ...'[9]

Second, humanity has always existed in a relationship with nature. People directly live off nature. People consume the products of nature directly for 'food, heating, clothes, a dwelling, etc.' and use nature as materials, objects and 'natural' resources to produce the tools, technology, buildings and all other material aspects of the life of people. This relationship between people and nature is not voluntary or imagined: people 'must remain in continuous interchange' with nature if we are not to die.[10] This is why, in any civilisation, 'the first premise of all human history is, of course, the existence of living human individuals ... the first fact to be established is the physical organisation of these individuals and their consequent relation to the rest of nature.'[11]

More specifically, land and other components of nature have a use value for people, especially in the production by people of the goods and services they need to live. In the language of economists, land (nature) is a factor of production, the source of 'natural' resources for production.[12] Nature can produce edible foods, fish, trees and minerals and so on with no human intervention. However, people have to work individually and together if they are to separate the products of nature from their environment – to *gather* food, *catch* fish, *fell* timber or *extract* ores from the Earth – and to transform those 'subjects of labour' into the goods and services they need for their own sustenance (food, clothing, shelter and so on) and for the maintenance of the community into which they are born and live.[13]

Third, Marx was clear that land (nature) was not just important for utilitarian, economic reasons of production, but also has important *non*-economic values.

In one of his early writings, Marx noted that 'man's physical and spiritual life is linked to nature' because 'man is a part of nature'.[14] In the earliest communities, people developed a 'consciousness of nature, which first appears to men as a completely alien, all-powerful and unassailable force'.[15] This consciousness of nature, which was distinct from their consciousness of their community, distinguished people as separate from nature, and encouraged people to develop 'natural religions' based on the observation of the forces of nature.[16]

Marx's three understandings of land (nature), as the natural environment that exists independently of humans, as a source of natural resources for production, and as a source of non-economic qualities (such as indigenous identity, spirituality, mental health and aesthetics) have been developed in many different ways.[17] Classics include Karl Polanyi on the dangers of commodifying nature),[18] James O'Connor on how capitalism necessarily destroys nature in the endless accumulation of capital[19] and Paul Burkett on the role of the working class in environmental activism to save the planet and their lives.[20] In addition, these issues are addressed by the *Capitalism Nature Socialism* journal,[21] the *Monthly Review* journal[22] in the United States and the UK's Red-Green Study Group.[23]

The fourth feature of land that was crucial for all of Marx's analyses was that, in almost all economies throughout human history, land has been property. Recognising land as landed property, or real estate, draws attention to the societal rules that govern land: who has access to, use of and control over certain parts of nature; who is excluded from the use of the land (even though they may have a greater need for the natural resources); and the extent to which ownership of land should be subject to controls by society for the common good. This is discussed in detail next.

Land as property

For Marx, the most important economic characteristic of land was that it could be taken into *ownership* and be treated as *property*. He developed this understanding of the character of landed property when he studied law at the Universities of Bonn and Berlin. From his earliest writings to his last, Marx consistently discussed land as being nature that had been taken into private, state or collective ownership, giving landowners a powerful influence over the economy. For example, 'The property in the soil is the original source of all wealth, and has become the great problem upon the solution of which depends the future of the working class,'[24] or 'In general the relationship of large and small landed property is like that of big and small capital' or 'the monstrous power wielded by landed property, when united hand in hand with industrial capital, enables it to be used against labourers engaged in their wage struggle'.[25]

What are the characteristics of landed property that made it of such interest to Marx? And how does Marx's approach to landed property differ from the 'property rights school' of economics which, like Marx, recognised there is a relation between economics and the law, but which, unlike Marx, attempted to provide a foundation for microeconomic theory[26] and urban studies.[27]

Commonly understood, 'ownership' of an asset (such as a parcel of land) implies an individual owner has an absolute, undivided, exclusive control over that asset. This concept of individual private ownership as absolute power over a thing is expressed in the ancient Roman maxim: 'ius utendi fruendi et abutendi res sua quatenus juris ratio patitur' ['where the owner of a thing has three different rights over that thing – to use, take the fruits of, and dispose of freely – with all other people being excluded from enjoying these rights over that thing'][28]

In reality, landed property is very rarely a situation where an individual has unitary and total control over a parcel of land. Instead, landed property is more practically understood as 'divided property' where multiple bearers have different rights in the same parcel of land.

In the approximately eighty countries with a common law tradition, ownership of property is often described as consisting of a 'bundle' of rights, where multiple people hold different and often conflicting rights in the same asset. For example, the right of the landowner to *use* a parcel of land is limited by the rights of the local government authority over that land (say, to enforce zoning regulations on the type of house that can be built on the land). The right of the landowner to *take the fruits* of the land site (say, to lease the house for rent) is limited by the rights of the renter (say, to have ease of access to the site and certainty over the length of time the renter can hold and use the land and house). The right of the landowner to *dispose* of the land (say, to sell the land to another) is limited by the rights of others over the land (e.g. if a financial institution has a mortgage over the land, which makes it, the mortgagee, the legal owner of the land until the mortgage is repaid). Finally, the right of the landowner to *exclude* all others from the use, benefits or disposal of the land is limited under certain circumstances (such as when a government uses its powers of compulsory acquisition to acquire that land for public infrastructure such as schools, roads, hospitals and parks).

In the approximately 120 countries with a civil law tradition, there is a unitary or monopoly concept of ownership, which, in general, cannot be divided or shared between different parties (as in common law countries). Instead, the rights of ownership over landed property create 'divided property' through the right of usufruct. In these countries, and consistent with the ancient Roman concept of ownership (discussed above), a landowner has the rights to use, benefit from and dispose of the land. Under the right of usufruct, the landowner can 'divide' their ownership rights so that another person (or persons) can have a temporary right to use and benefit from the land (but not the right to dispose of, alter or damage the land). For example, a landowner may provide their land to others for their exclusive use and benefit (so they can use the land to build, farm, lease, mortgage, bequest and so on) until, after a period of time, the interests in the land revert back to the original owner.

The fifth feature of land that is crucial for Marx's analyses is that landed property rights establish interrelationships – or social relations of dependency, obligation and contradiction – between the different parties who hold various rights over the land. The idea of divided property, or multiple bearers of rights in the same parcel of land, is not a uniquely Western idea, but establishing 'the interrelationships of the various competing rights' originated in the Western system of land rights during the feudal period.[29] The rights, privileges and responsibilities between different landowners, land users and land non-owners establish social relations of power between them that are made explicit in the contracts, leases, mortgages, bequests and so on between those owners, users and non-owners. These social relations of power are enforced by the state and its institutions including the legislature, land planning and regulatory system and agencies, taxation authorities, land and environment courts, the judiciary and police.

The extent to which landowners can impose their rights over land, and the extent to which land non-owners can protect their interests in the land, change over time depending on the balance of power between landowners and land non-owners. Even though the 'rights' of property may appear to be universal, unchanging, pre-existing, ethically and legally rightful, they are socially constructed and enforced by the police and courts and other institutions of the state. It is '[o]nly through legal determinations, which the society attributes to the factual property', that private property receives 'the quality of rightful property'.[30] These 'rights' of property are embedded in legislation, legal principles, land use regulations, administrative procedures, customs and practices which are developed by people, interest groups and the state over centuries. Land rights change over time, often incrementally, depending on the conflicts, and the balance of power, between landowner interest groups and land non-owner interest groups.

Marx's understanding of land as the social relations of power between all those who have different rights over the use, benefits and disposal of a piece of land is distinctly different from the 'property rights school' of thinking developed by scholars such as Svetozar Pejovic[31] and Ronald Coase and promoted by the University of Chicago since the 1960s. Coase held that land can be thought of as a bundle of rights but added: 'We may speak of a person owning land and using it as a factor of production but what the land-owner in fact possesses is the right to carry out a circumscribed list of actions.'[32] His argument was that property rights are merely a 'list of actions', a catalogue or inventory of permitted uses held by an individual landowner. This school's assumption that individuals can be thought of as existing as solitary atoms and the rights of property held by different people establish no social relations with, dependencies on or responsibilities to others (its methodological individualism) blinded it to the fact that people live in social relationships with each other and are influenced, and limited by each other. People are 'living carriers' of the legal and economic relations that are needed for the operation and reproduction of the society of which they are a part.[33]

The significance of landed property as the social relations between the different groups who hold rights in landed property are explored fully in coming chapters. As will be shown in following chapters, property rights which establish social relations of power between two classes of people (landowners and land non-owners) are one of the most powerful institutions that shape all societies in the world. This understanding of land-as-property also helps us explore and critique many real-world dynamics in cities such as the power of landowners over tenants, conflicts between landowners and capital over rent, and the existence of a landed property class which lobbies, funds and in other ways influences governments to protect the rights of property developers and the urban real estate industry.

Dialectical social relations

A further refinement is needed to clarify Marx's approach to the social relations of landed property. This is that the social relations of land are *dialectical* social relations.

Dialectics was first written about by the ancient Greeks. For philosophers such as Socrates, Plato and Aristotle, dialectics described a method of philosophical argument where one person would enter into a (debating) relationship with another by putting a view (the thesis), while the second person in the relationship would propose the opposite view (the antithesis), and then the back-and-forth debate between the two would produce new knowledge or a deeper understanding of the issues (the synthesis). Hegel used this concept of a dialectical relationship to argue that the clash of ideas or consciousnesses will develop a more sophisticated understanding of the world and, indeed, contribute to a better world itself: 'Dialectics is what drives the development of both reason as well as of things in the world.'[34]

Marx critiqued Hegel's argument saying it was not the contradiction between people's ideas or consciousness that caused the world to develop but the contradiction between material factors and actors that caused societies to develop. The most important contradictory relationships in a society, relationships that both structured the society and caused it to change, are those between the different groups who produce the goods and services people and society need to reproduce themselves over time.

In the case of land in a capitalist economy, for example, landowners owning land and wanting to earn a rent, and capitalists owning technology and wanting to produce a profit, enter into an arrangement with each other where the landowner leases their land to the capitalist for a period of time (and collects rent) and the capitalist gains use of the land for a period of time (and pays rent). This is a dialectical social relationship: it is a *mutually dependent* relationship between two *opposed* interests that causes both interest groups to change how they operate and produce wider material changes in the industry and economy.[35]

A capitalist may be forced to become more efficient or to innovate so they can pay the rent, or diversify their operations and buy land rather than lease land so that 'a large part of landed property falls into the hands of the capitalists and those capitalists thus become simultaneously landowners'. The owners of capital may take legal and political action against landowners to try to reduce rental payments, undermine the political power of the landowning class, limit the 'rights' of landowners, defend their own political and economic power, and generally promote the capacity of capital to maximise profit. On the other hand, the landowner may be forced to reduce their rent, or diversify into new industries such that 'large landowners become at the same time industrialists'.[36] Landed property owners may also defend their rights over property; protect their existing assets and try to increase the size of their landholdings; combine into associations to protect their levels of rent; and directly and indirectly influence the state to seek support in their struggles against capital.[37]

However, in capitalism, what if the contradictions in the mutually dependent but dialectical relationship between land and capital cannot be resolved? Ultimately, while land can exercise a degree of power over capital, it is geographically fixed. On the other hand, for capital, if the contradictions within the relationship become unresolvable and the competition on capital to continually grow its profits is too great, capital can always relocate to another suburb, city or nation: 'Capital by its nature drives beyond every spatial barrier … [T]he annihilation of space by time – becomes an extraordinary necessity for it.'[38]

Land tenure

In property law, land tenure refers to the legal regime or regimes that exists in every society which determines who can hold (or own) land and use land, for how long and under what conditions. The system of land tenure specifies the rights and responsibilities of landowners and others who use the land, the role of the state or other relevant authority overseeing and enforcing the land tenure system, and procedures to prevent tenure disputes and prosecute corruption. Six common forms of land tenure in the world today are public, private, communal, collective, indigenous and customary tenure.[39]

Land tenure systems may be based on official laws and policies, informal or customary arrangements, or both. For example, feudal tenure is based on official arrangements: the ruler or Crown owns the land and allocates parcels of land to landlords (in return for the provision of fees or services), each of whom then subdivides their allocation and doles the smaller land parcels to tenants (in return for payment of money or services).

Customary tenure, the set of rules and norms that govern community ownership, allocation, use and transfer of land (and other natural resources), 'are often based on traditional, unwritten, and locally relevant rules about how to use and allocate land and resources [and] facilitate social cohesion'.[40] Typically, this system of land tenure takes into account the significance of the land for economic purposes (for food, fuel, fibre, shelter and so on) as well as non-economic purposes (such as social stability, cultural identity and environmental sustainability)[41] Customary duties to the land often include providing long-term custodianship of the land for future generations. Common land tenure systems often combine both official and unofficial arrangements, where ownership of land is held indivisibly by a community and where rights cannot be divided and allocated to individual members of the community and are often held in trust for current and future members.[42]

Land title is an administrative system for publicly registering that a parcel of landed property with defined boundaries was acquired and includes any conditions that apply to the ownership of the land (such as the existence of easements over the land or other limitations on the ownership rights of the landowner). Typically, the administrative infrastructure and funding needed to identify, document and store title over land, and enforce 'ownership' of those titles, is provided by the state, which also provides a degree of certainty and legitimacy for the landownership system.[43]

Stronger claims for the benefits of land title systems were made by Hernando de Soto in 2000 in his book *Mysteries of Capital*. He claimed in the section on 'Why Property Law Does Not Work Outside the West' that new and improved systems of land title are needed in Global South countries to reduce illegal land acquisitions, improve housing, strengthen the operations of housing markets, and improve the capacity of poor people to access finance (through mortgages and other real estate-based financial instruments), and more generally, improve the operation of capitalism in the Global South. He also argued that introducing systems that officially registered landed property would deliver an additional non-economic benefit: 'Widespread legal property will even help solve one of their [the government's and the elite's] loudest and most persistent complaints about the expanding urban poor – the need for more 'law and order.' ... The right to property also engenders respect for law.'[44]

De Soto's claimed benefits of land titling systems have been criticised as being empirically false and theoretically flawed;[45] ineffective without other improvements to judicial systems and bankruptcy codes, and a restructuring financial market regulations;[46] reductionist by inadequately addressing all the legal, economic and social notions that make up 'security of tenure';[47] and limited in that it does not take into account alternative methods of land valuation such as those in Indonesia where estimates of fair compensation for land occur irrespective of whether the land is registered or not.[48] Even so, the World Bank (2019) continues to fund the establishment of land title systems in countries in the Global South with the narrow purpose that landowners can 'use land titles to access credit to improve their land and dwellings – and expand businesses or open new ones, generating jobs, boosting productivity, and increasing incomes'.[49]

As will be shown in coming chapters, Marx always held that different land tenure systems could not be analysed as standalone systems, and they are always structured by the particular mode of production that supports the existence and reproduction of each society.

Rent

Rent is commonly thought of as a payment made by one party (such as a renter) to another (the lessor) for the temporary use of something (such as a dwelling). In economics, rent has several other meanings. For political economists such as David Ricardo, rent was 'the portion of the produce of the earth, which is paid to the landlord for the use of the original and indestructible powers of the soil'.[50] Ricardo stressed that rent is a distinct payment with its own 'economic laws' (which are unlike the economic laws that describe the payment of wages for labour or profit for the use of capital). He added that the quantity of rent is determined by the fertility, location or other advantages of particular plots of land such that the best land earns the highest rent, middle-quality land earns middle quantities of rent and the worst land site will earn no rent.

Neoclassical microeconomics changed the concept of rent to include factors other than land (natural resources), and introduced the idea that 'rent' was the 'excess earnings over the amount necessary to keep the factor in its present occupation'. There are modifications of this approach, such as von Thünen's idea that land rent is affected by geographical distance such that rent equals the yield of the land (market price of the commodities less production costs) less the cost of freight to take the produce to market.[51]

The key issues for Marx, however, were that rent arises solely from ownership of land (he often called it ground rent) and does not arise from the quality of the land (such as its fertility or location) or from its distance to the market; rent of land, he argued, 'is established as a result of the struggle between tenant and landlord'.[52] Rent, in other words, 'is a product of society and not of the soil'.[53]

Marx also made a clear distinction between *ground* rent and *building* rent: while *ground* rent always is the tribute paid to a landowner for their permission to utilise for a period the earth over which they have exclusive property rights, this differs from *building* rent which consists of returns on capital invested in land (such as investment in residential or commercial housing, industrial buildings and retail shopping centres). For example, a landowner who invests capital and builds a new warehouse on the land, and then leases the land (and its new warehouse) to a capitalist, will receive two payments in the 'rent': the actual ground rent for the lease of the land, plus a payment for the capital that was used to build the warehouse (plus interest and amortisation on the capital invested in building). The payment of the interest on the capital does not constitute ground rent, which, Marx insists, is always paid only for the use of the land.[54]

What, then, is the source of rent if not the fertility of soil? Marx shows rent always originates with, and is extracted from, the direct producers who work the land, be they slaves, serfs, peasants or farm labourers.[55] Chapters 3, 4 and 5 in particular will explore in detail how 'Rent results from the *social relations* in which the exploitation of the land takes place'.[56]

Land and value

Another key concept that is at the heart of Marx's explanation of land and rent is that of value, including the measurement of value.

In all societies, irrespective of their mode of production, people exchange goods and services with each other. With friends and family, for example, these exchanges may be based on a reciprocal sharing arrangement, or unilateral gift giving. However, economic exchanges (such as the exchange of labour for wages, or access to land for rent) are much more complex exchanges and, unlike exchanges with family and friends, typically involve transfers between strangers.

The classical political economists noted that, in the economy, people generally exchanged goods and services of equal value. The question then arose: what is the source of value, and how can it be measured? Adam Smith, David Ricardo, John Stuart Mill[57] and Thomas Malthus[58] developed the labour theory of value to explain how economic exchanges occurred. The labour theory of value theory holds that goods and services exchange on the basis of their value, that is, the amount of labour (measured as labour-time) that was necessary to produce the goods and services. The benefits of the labour theory of value include: it is measurable (in units of labour-hours spent producing a commodity); labour-time is a relatively stable measure of value in markets and can be used to analyse the GDP of nations;[59] and labour measures of value can explain why commodities exchange at a ratio fixed by the relative differences in the labour times used to make the commodities (e.g. 1,000 simple products, each made with five hours of labour, will be needed to exchange for one complex product, made with 5,000 hours of labour). The labour theory of value is clearly different from microeconomic theory, which stipulates economic exchanges occur in a market based on the subjective, non-measurable evaluations of psychological 'utility' or 'preferences' of the buyer and seller,[60] although it does have some relevance to Keynesian economics.[61]

Marx was critical of some aspects of the classical economists' labour theory of value. For example, he clarified that value needed to be measured by the labour-time which is *socially necessary* to produce goods and services.[62] By 'the labour time socially necessary for its production' Marx meant the average amount of labour, or the labour time 'required to produce an article under the normal conditions of production, and with the average degree of skill and intensity prevalent at the time'.[63]

Marx also saw a significant flaw in the political economists' theory of value. Given that the value of labour and capital could be measured (in units of the labour hours socially necessary for their production), what then was the value of land. Land, water, trees, minerals and all the other elements of nature are created and exist naturally: they are not a product of labour, and therefore, by definition, natural resources have no value. If land has no value, it therefore contributes no value to the production of commodities. On what basis then is land bought and sold; if it has no value, how is its price determined when it is exchanged in the market? Furthermore, why is rent (one form of value) paid for the use of land if it is a 'free gift of Nature' and adds no value to production:

> Natural elements entering as agents into production, and which cost nothing, no matter what role they play in production, do not enter as components of capital, but as a free gift of Nature to capital, that is, as a free gift of Nature's productive power to labour, which, however, appears as the productiveness of capital, as all other productivity under the capitalist mode of production.[64]

Marx's solution to this apparent dilemma for the labour theory of value is discussed in detail in Chapter 5.

Mode of production

Every 'social formation' (community or society), with its people, families, government and other institutions, and culture, must have a well-organised, continuously operating system for producing the material basis of that social formation. That is, every society must have the industries, workforce, technology, markets and other economic processes to produce enough goods and services for people to sustain themselves and for the social formation to reproduce itself over time. Specifically, the economy needs to produce the food, clothing, shelter and other necessities for people to live, as well as the physical infrastructure (such as communications and transport), social infrastructure (such as childcare and education), system of government, defence force and so on, that the society needs to maintain and perpetuate itself. In other words, in all communities and societies, 'The first historical act is thus the production of the means to satisfy these needs, the production of material life itself.'[65]

In general, the production of the material bases of communities and societies always rests on some common economic characteristics such as having access to natural resources (land), people to work (labour) to transform those natural resources into useful goods and services, tools and machinery, transport routes and other infrastructure, markets, some form of currency or finance, and so on. In practice, throughout history, communities and societies have developed many different ways to organise all these elements of production; that is, into different modes of production. Furthermore, depending on how production is organised, one sector of industry will always dominate and structure the others: 'There is in every social formation a particular branch of production which determines the position and importance of all the others, and the relations obtaining in this branch accordingly determine the relations of all other branches as well.'[66]

Marx identified six basic modes of production: the indigenous, ancient, Asiatic, feudal, capitalist and communist modes of production. Each mode of production divides all the people in the community or society in particular ways that make production possible. For example, the mode of production divides the population into producers and consumers, into different industries (such as agriculture, manufacturing, construction, transport and finance),[67] as well as into production and commerce,[68] and into those who carry out mental labour and physical labour, the private sector and the public sector, and so on. Each mode of production has its own form of landed property; its own ways of organising who in the society works (the labour force) and who controls the labour force; its own ways of producing the necessary goods and services needed for the sustenance of the population and the maintenance of the society itself; its own arrangements for who captures any surplus-to-requirements goods and services (wealth) that are produced by labour, and its own particular ruling class which rules the society in such a way that it perpetuates the mode of production and its associated hierarchy of rulers and the ruled.

It is important to clarify that these modes of production did *not* develop in a sequential, mechanical or linear way. Marx, especially in his writings on land (as will be shown in this book), made it clear that it is not the case that the indigenous mode of production existed at the dawn of humanity, the ancient and Asiatic modes appeared two millennia ago, the feudal mode of production existed only in the Middle Ages, capitalism emerged in England and the Netherlands in the sixteenth to seventeenth centuries, and that the communist mode of production will replace capitalism in the future. Instead, as will be shown, all of these modes of production continue to exist to some degree in the world today, in parallel and often in competition with each other.

When each mode of production establishes particular population-wide divisions of labour between land and labour, country and city, production and commerce, and so on, the mode of production also establishes *social relations* between these divided groups. The divided groups, which may have contradictory economic interests, are also dependent on each other. They must enter into social relations with each other so they can coordinate, collaborate, exchange and, when necessary, struggle against, the other so that they can achieve their interests. In other words: 'In order to produce, [people] enter into definite connections and relations to one another, and only within these social connections and relations does their influence upon nature operate – i.e., does production take place.'[69]

This society-wide division of the population into economic groups that make up the mode of production, and the concomitant social relations that are established between these groups so people can meet their own needs (and the needs of the society as a whole), also has a strong influence over the non-economic aspects of society. The interest groups with the most power and resources within the mode of production, often in the face of opposition by those with the least power and resources, struggle to control the way the society is governed, the nature and structure of the social institutions in the society (such as law and order, education, health, media and the family), and the cultural norms and values of the society. The relationship between the economic foundation of societies and the social, political and intellectual components of society is summarised in one of Marx's most famous, and debated,[70] statements:

> In the social production of their existence, men inevitably enter into definite relations, which are independent of their will, namely relations of production appropriate to a given stage in the development of their material forces of production. The totality of these relations of production constitutes the economic structure of society, the real foundation, on which arises a legal and political superstructure and to which correspond definite forms of social consciousness. The mode of production of material life conditions the general process of social, political and intellectual life. It is not the consciousness of men that determines their existence, but their social existence that determines their consciousness.[71]

This book will show that one of the major divisions of labour that occur in all modes of production is 'the separation of the towns from the country'.[72] Each mode of production establishes its own types of cities with particular economic and political functions that are needed to support and defend the particular mode of production. These cities are structured within the limits set by the particular mode of production and are continually shaped by the imperatives of landed property, different forms of rent and the actions of the landowning class. On occasions, struggles by classes within cities have also brought about revolutionary changes to the prevailing mode of production itself.

Human emancipation

Some newcomers to political economy (and economics more narrowly) find it disconcerting that Marx's political economics seems so intertwined with calls for revolution. In developing his critique of the dominant mode of production that existed in his time, capitalism, Marx was explicit that he wanted to disclose 'the special laws that regulate the origin, existence, development, death of a given social organism [capitalism] and its replacement by another and higher one'.[73]

Marx was impressed by capitalism as a system of production. For example, Marx and Engels noted in *The Communist Manifesto*: 'The bourgeoisie, during its

8

rule of scarce one hundred years, has created more massive and more colossal productive forces than have all preceding generations together.'[74] They added that capitalism had also 'created enormous cities [and] greatly increased the urban population as compared with the rural'. However, this mode of production also *necessarily* subjugates 'Nature's forces to man',[75] exploits the majority of people (workers), produces for profit rather than the needs of people, and systematically creates unemployment, poverty, homelessness, social inequalities and other social ills.

The core problem with the capitalist mode of production is that it controls the lives of billions of people without any democratic control. In many nations around the world, people have a degree of democratic control over their governments, but they have no control over the capitalist laws that operate in ways that are 'independent of their will'.[76] Capitalism is a 'social process that goes on behind the backs of the producers' which appears 'to be fixed by custom'.[77]

This is why Marx was not interested in describing, explaining or forecasting the behaviour of capitalist markets, industries or economies – as is the objective of orthodox economists – but wanted to emancipate people from the inhumane and undemocratically controlled regulation of their lives. He wanted to replace capitalism with a democratic, non-exploitative and non-destructive mode of production that produces enough goods and services to meet the needs of all people. Only when societies have a government *and* an economy that is under the democratic control of working people will there ever be true human emancipation.[78]

Notes

1. K. Marx, 'Estranged Labour', *Economic and Philosophic Manuscripts of 1844*, Moscow: Progress Publishers, 1959, https://www.marxists.org/archive/marx/works/1844/epm/1st.htm
2. K. Marx, *Grundrisse der Kritik der politischen Ökonomie* [1857–8], first published Moscow, Marx–Engels Institute, 1939; English translation available at https://www.marxists.org/archive/marx/works/1857/grundrisse/ch01.htm
3. G. M. Hodgson, *How Economics Forgot History: The Problems of Historical Specificity in Social Science*, London, Routledge, 2001.
4. J. Ryan-Collins, T. Lloyd and L. Macfarlane, *Rethinking the Economics of Land and Housing*, London, Zed Books, 2017, p. 38.
5. K. Marx, *Theories of Surplus Value*, https://www.marxists.org/archive/marx/works/1863/theories-surplus-value/ch09.htm#s3
6. K. Marx and F. Engels, *The German Ideology*, pt 1.A, Moscow, Progress Publishers, 1968, https://www.marxists.org/archive/marx/works/1845/german-ideology/ch01a.htm
7. Marx, 'Estranged Labour'.
8. K. Marx, *Capital*, vol. I, ch. 8, Moscow, Progress Publishers, 1887, https://www.marxists.org/archive/marx/works/1867-c1/ch08.htm
9. Ibid., vol. I, ch. 7, https://www.marxists.org/archive/marx/works/1867-c1/ch07.htm#1a
10. Ibid.

11. Marx and Engels, *The German Ideology*, pt 1.A.
12. As Marx and Engels noted in *The German Ideology*: 'The first premise of all human history is, of course, the existence of living human individuals. Thus, the first fact to be established is the physical organisation of these individuals and their consequent relation to the rest of nature.'
13. Ibid.
14. Marx, 'Estranged Labour'.
15. Marx and Engels, *The German Ideology*, pt 1.A.
16. 'Natural' religions assume God, soul and spirits are a part of nature, unlike those based on divine revelation.
17. T. Benton, 'What Karl Marx Has to Say about Today's Environmental Problems', *The Conversation* (Australian edn), 5 June 2018, https://theconversation.com/what-karl-marx-has-to-say-about-todays-environmental-problems-97479
18. K. Polanyi, *The Great Transformation: The Political and Economic Origins of Our Time*, Boston, MA, Beacon Press, 2018.
19. J. O'Connor, *Natural Causes: Essays in Ecological Marxism*, New York, Guilford Press, 1998.
20. P. Burkett, *Marx and Nature: A Red and Green Perspective*, Chicago, IL, Haymarket Books, 2014.
21. For example, J. O'Connor, 'Capitalism, Nature, Socialism: A Theoretical Introduction', *Capitalism Nature Socialism*, vol. 1, no. 1, 1988, pp. 11–38.
22. For example, J. Bellamy Foster, B. Clark and R. York, *The Ecological Rift: Capitalism's War on the Earth*, New York, New York University Press, 2010.
23. For example, Red-Green Study Group's *What on Earth is to be Done?*, Manchester, Red-Green Study Group, 1995, http://redgreenstudygroup.org.uk/what-on-earth-is-to-be-done/
24. K. Marx, 'The Nationalisation of the Land', *International Herald*, no. 11, 15 June 1872, https://www.marxists.org/archive/marx/*The* works/1872/04/nationalisation-land.htm
25. K. Marx, *Capital*, vol. III, Moscow, Progress Publishers, 1956, https://www.marxists.org/archive/marx/works/1894-c3/ch46.htm
26. For example, N. Furniss, 'The Political Implications of the Public Choice-Property Rights School', *The American Political Science Review*, vol. 72, no. 2, 1978, pp. 399–410.
27. For example, M. B. Havel, 'The Effect of Formal Property Rights Regime on Urban Development and Planning Methods in the Context of Post-Socialist Transformation: An Institutional Approach', in R. Levine-Schnur (ed.), *Measuring the Effectiveness of Real Estate Regulation*, New York, Springer, 2020.
28. E. Zendeli, 'The Notion and Legal Space of Exercising the Right to Ownership', *Journal of Civil and Legal Sciences*, vol. 2, 2013, p. 104.
29. H. J. Berman, *Law and Revolution: The Formation of the Western Legal Tradition*, Cambridge, MA, Harvard University Press, 1983, p. 312.
30. K. Marx, *Critique of Hegel's Philosophy of Right*, pt 5, Cambridge: Cambridge University Press, 1970, https://www.marxists.org/archive/marx/works/1843/critique-hpr/ch05.htm
31. S. Pejovich (ed.), *The Economics of Property Rights*, Cheltenham, Edward Elgar Publishing, 2001.
32. R. H. Coase, 'The Problem of Social Cost', *Journal of Law and Economics*, vol. 3, 1960, pp. 1–44.

33. K. Marx, *Grundrisse*, London, Penguin Books in association with *New Left Review*, 1973, ch. 10, https://www.marxists.org/archive/marx/works/1857/grundrisse/ch10.htm#p540

34. J. E. Maybee, 'Hegel's Dialectics', *The Stanford Encyclopedia of Philosophy*, Winter 2020 Edition, Edward N. Zalta (ed.), https://plato.stanford.edu/archives/win2020/entries/hegel-dialectics/

35. K. Marx, 'Antithesis of Capital and Labour', *Economic and Philosophic Manuscripts of 1844*, Moscow, Progress Publishers, 1959, https://www.marxists.org/archive/marx/works/1844/manuscripts/second.htm

36. K. Marx, 'Rent of Land', *Economic and Philosophic Manuscripts of 1844*, Moscow, Progress Publishers, 1959, https://www.marxists.org/archive/marx/works/1844/manuscripts/rent.htm

37. For example, The Centre for Public Integrity, 'Case Study: The Property and Construction Industry', *Industry Political Donations and Disclosable Payments*, Washington, DC, The Center for Public Integrity, 2021, https://publicintegrity.org.au/wp-content/uploads/2021/01/Donations-case-study-property-and-construction-industry-1.pdf

38. K. Marx, 'The Chapter on Capital', *Grundrisse*, ch. 10, London: Penguin Books in association with *New Left Review*, 1973, https://www.marxists.org/archive/marx/works/1857/grundrisse/ch10.htm

39. Food and Agriculture Organization, *Voluntary Guidelines on the Responsible Governance of Tenure of Land, Fisheries and Forests in the Context of National Food Security*, Rome, Food and Agriculture Organization, 2012, http://www.fao.org/3/i2801e/i2801e.pdf

40. United States Agency for International Development, 'What Is Land Tenure?', *LandLinks*, Washington, DC, United States Agency for International Development, n.d., https://www.land-links.org/what-is-land-tenure/

41. Food and Agriculture Organization, *Voluntary Guidelines on the Responsible Governance of Tenure of Land, Fisheries and Forests in the Context of National Food Security*, Rome, Food and Agriculture Organization, 2012, http://www.fao.org/3/i2801e/i2801e.pdf

42. For a recent discussion of the nature and economic potential of the commons, see F. Obeng-Odoom, *The Commons in an Age of Uncertainty: Decolonizing Nature, Economy, and Society*, Toronto, University of Toronto Press, 2020.

43. An alternative land registration system is the deed registration system which documents that there was a transfer of property from one person or party to another, but without necessarily recording the ownership rights of, and limits on, the landowner.

44. H. de Soto, *The Mystery of Capital: Why Capitalism Triumphs in the West and Fails Everywhere Else*, London, Transworld Digital, 2010.

45. A. Gilbert, 'On the *Mystery of Capital* and the Myths of Hernando de Soto: What Difference Does Legal Title Make?', *International Development Planning Review* (formerly *Third World Planning Review*), vol. 24, no. 1, 2002, pp. 1–19; and D. Bromley, 'Formalising Property Relations in the Developing World: The Wrong Prescription for the Wrong Malady', *Land Use Policy*, vol. 26, 2008, pp. 20–7.

46. J. Clift, 'Hearing the Dogs Bark', *Finance and Development Magazine*, Washington, DC, International Monetary Fund, Dec. 2003, pp. 8–11.

47. F. Obeng-Odoom and F. Stilwell, 'Security of Tenure in International Development Discourse', *International Development Planning Review*, vol. 35, no. 4, 2013, pp. 315–33.

48. F. Obeng-Odoom, 'Valuing Unregistered Urban Land in Indonesia', *Evolutionary and Institutional Economics Review*, vol. 15, 2018, pp. 315–40.

49. W. Zakout, 'Stand with Us to Help Make Land Rights a Reality for Millions of Women around the World', *Sustainable Cities Blog*, Washington, DC, World Bank, 9 May 2019, https://blogs.worldbank.org/sustainablecities/make-land-rights-a-reality-millions-women-around-world

50. D. Ricardo, 'On Rent', *On the Principles of Political Economy and Taxation*, London, John Murray, 1817, https://www.marxists.org/reference/subject/economics/ricardo/tax/ch02.htm

51. C. Clark, 'Von Thunen's Isolated State', *Oxford Economic Papers*, vol. 19, no. 3, 1967, pp. 370–7.

52. Marx, 'Rent of Land'.

53. K. Marx, *The Poverty of Philosophy*, ch. 2.4, Moscow, Progress Publishers, 1955, https://www.marxists.org/archive/marx/works/1847/poverty-philosophy/ch02d.htm

54. Marx, *Capital*, vol. III, ch. 37, https://www.marxists.org/archive/marx/works/1894-c3/ch37.htm

55. Ibid., vol. III, ch. 47, https://www.marxists.org/archive/marx/works/1894-c3/ch47.htm

56. Marx, *The Poverty of Philosophy*, ch. 2.4, https://www.marxists.org/archive/marx/works/1847/poverty-philosophy/ch02d.htm

57. W. J. Barber, *A History of Economic Thought*, London, Penguin Books, 1991.

58. G. de Vivo, 'Malthus's Theory of the Constant Value of Labour', *Contributions to Political Economy*, vol. 31, no. 1, 2012, pp. 103–20.

59. A. M. Shaikh and A. Tonak, *Measuring the Wealth of Nations: The Political Economy of National Accounts*, Cambridge, Cambridge University Press, 1996.

60. P. C. Dooley, *The Labour Theory of Value*, 1st edn, London, Routledge, 2005.

61. B. Dunn, *Keynes and Marx*, Manchester, Manchester University Press, 2021.

62. Marx, *Capital*, vol. I, ch. 6, https://www.marxists.org/archive/marx/works/1867-c1/ch06.htm

63. Ibid., vol. 1, ch. 1, https://www.marxists.org/archive/marx/works/1867-c1/ch01.htm

64. Ibid., vol. III, ch. 44, https://www.marxists.org/archive/marx/works/1894-c3/ch44.htm

65. Marx and Engels, *The German Ideology*. In contrast, economic theorists begin their analyses of societies by assuming the prior existence of markets or isolated, rational, profit-maximising individuals (microeconomics) or measures of a nation's gross domestic product (macroeconomics), while political scientists typically begin their analyses of societies by assuming the prior existence of power, politicians, governments and/or a state.

66. K. Marx, Preface to *A Contribution to the Critique of Political Economy*, Moscow, Progress Publishers, 1977, https://www.marxists.org/archive/marx/works/1859/critique-pol-economy/preface.htm

67. Marx, *Capital*, vol. I. ch. 14, https://www.marxists.org/archive/marx/works/1867-c1/ch14.htm

68. Marx and Engels, *The German Ideology*, pt 1.C, https://www.marxists.org/archive/marx/works/1845/german-ideology/ch01c.htm

69. K. Marx, 'Nature and Growth of Capital', *Wage Labour and Capital*, Marxists Internet Archive, 1993, https://www.marxists.org/archive/marx/works/1847/wage-labour/ch05.htm

70. R. Beamish, 'Base and Superstructure', in G. Ritzer (ed.), *Blackwell Encyclopedia of Sociology*, Hoboken, NJ, John Wiley & Sons, 2017, pp. 224–6.
71. Marx, Preface to *A Contribution to the Critique of Political Economy*, https://www.marxists.org/archive/marx/works/1859/critique-pol-economy/preface.htm
72. Marx, *The Poverty of Philosophy*, ch. 2, https://www.marxists.org/archive/marx/works/1847/poverty-philosophy/ch02b.htm
73. Marx, *Capital*, vol. I, Afterword to the Second German Edition, https://www.marxists.org/archive/marx/works/1867-c1/p3.htm
74. K. Marx and F. Engels, *The Manifesto of the Communist Party*, https://www.marxists.org/archive/marx/works/1848/communist-manifesto/ch01.htm
75. Ibid.
76. Marx, Preface to *A Contribution to the Critique of Political Economy*.
77. Marx, *Capital*, vol. I, ch. 1, https://www.marxists.org/archive/marx/works/1867-c1/ch01.htm
78. International Workingman's Association, 'Resolution of the London Conference on Working Class Political Action, as adopted by the London Conference of the International, September, 1871', https://www.marxists.org/archive/marx/works/1871/09/politics-re solution.htm

CHAPTER 3

Indigenous, Ancient and Asiatic Land

The history of classical antiquity is the history of cities, but of cities founded on landed property and on agriculture; Asiatic history is a kind of indifferent unity of town and countryside (the really large cities must be regarded here merely as royal camps, as works of artifice erected over the economic construction proper) ...[1]

Introduction

Throughout human history, different civilisations have developed on the basis of their own particular modes of production.[2] This chapter discusses three of them: the indigenous, ancient and Asiatic modes of production.[3] Each mode of production establishes its own form of landed property, rent and cities.

Despite their differences, these three modes of production are considered together because they are all the material foundations of communities (*Gemeinschaft*), social totalities based on family, extended kin, neighbours and clans, and common ancestors: that is, communities where members share 'blood, language, customs'.[4]

Analysing these modes of production and their associated communities provides insights into many contemporary issues including struggles over indigenous land rights, societies based on nationalised land, the activities of the landed property class, the nature of the state, and how social contradictions cause social and economic change.

Marx discussed these communities at length in *The German Ideology*, *Grundrisse* and volume III of *Capital*, and made passing reference to them in many of his other writings identified throughout the chapter. Despite their abundance of insights for economists, sociologists, political scientists and others, Marx's writings on indigenous, ancient and Asiatic civilisations have been given relatively little sustained attention except by scholar-activists such as Georg Lukacs and Karl Korsch.[5]

Indigenous mode of production

The first mode of production discussed by Marx was the mode of production that is common to *Stamm* communities around the world.

Stamm is often translated into English as 'tribes', 'clans' or 'gens' (e.g. 'the tribal mode of production'), but in the twenty-first century *Stamm* is more accurately understood as referring to indigenous communities made up of Aboriginal, First Peoples and First Nations peoples. These communities have three common characteristics. First, these communities are based on a shared kinship, ancestry or heritage. Second, they are collective owners of the land upon which they live and produce. Third, they are a social unity where all members organise together to work on their common land for the good of the community and its members. That is, in the indigenous mode of production, there is no division between the members of the community, the proprietors of the land, and the workers of the land: there is a unity between community, property and labour.

The indigenous mode of production is one of the 'pre-capitalist economic formations'.[6] It takes various forms around the world depending on the productivity of the land and the type of internal organisation of labour used by the community to gain their sustenance from the land. The indigenous mode of production includes nomadic production (such as hunting and gathering, or pastoralism); the use of land management techniques (such as the use of fire) to strengthen the productivity of the land in a sustainable way and without damaging nature; and, in communities with a highly organised common workforce, agriculture.[7] The indigenous mode of production based on community-organised agriculture, such as is or was found in 'Mexico, and especially Peru, among the Ancient Celts, and some tribes of India',[8] was able to established complex, long-lasting civilisations centred on cities with palaces, temples, marketplaces and other buildings.

This pre-capitalist mode of production continues to be of importance to millions of people in the world today. Pastoralism, for example, contributes up to 80 per cent to the agricultural gross domestic product (GDP) of many African countries and makes up two-thirds of Mongolia's GDP.[9] As well as a producing meat, milk, hides and leather goods for use and for sale domestically, pastoralism is also a source of internationally traded goods such as cashmere fibre (from China) and leather and leather goods (from Ethiopia).[10]

Land is crucial to the indigenous mode of production: 'The earth is the great laboratory, the arsenal which provides both the means and the materials of labour, and also the location, the *basis* of the community.'[11] The land is the collective property of all the members of the community: 'they regard themselves as its *communal proprietors* ... Only in so far as the individual is a member – in the literal and figurative sense – of such a community, does he regard himself as an owner or possessor.'[12] Typically, use of the land is overseen by the heads of the kinship groups, elders or other customary authorities. Access to, use of and transfer of land are regulated in accordance with the indigenous community's customary traditions. The norms of customary tenure derive from and are sustained by the community itself. Indigenous members use the land for production directly (through hunting, gathering, fishing and pastoralism) and indirectly (by using the land for agriculture, mining, logging and associated productive purposes which transform the 'fruits' of the soil, rivers and oceans into food, shelter, clothing, fuel, technology, and other goods and services).

Indigenous communities which are established on the indigenous mode of production have two main characteristics. First, members of the community collectively own, and communally work, the land to produce the goods and services they need to sustain their individual lives and their community. Second, the identity of community members is integrally linked with their beliefs about their land. In this sense, then, there is no separation between people and nature: '*Property* therefore means *belonging to a clan* (community) (having subjective-objective existence in it); and … [is] a presupposition belonging to his individuality, as modes of his presence.'[13]

In 2017, the High Commission for Human Rights described the features of indigenous communities in similar terms to Marx: '… land is not merely an economic asset for indigenous peoples. It is [the] defining element for their identity, culture and their relationship to their ancestors and future generations. There is a need for recognition of indigenous land tenure systems …'[14]

The mode of existence of early indigenous communities was migratory because they lived through hunting and gathering, and nomadic pastoralism, a situation that suggests 'humankind is not settlement-prone by nature'.[15] When these early, nomadic families and groups of families found fertile, well-resourced land then the community would take possession of that land and settle: that is, 'the clan community, the natural community, appears not as a result of, but as a presupposition for the communal appropriation (temporary) and utilisation of the land'.[16] Indigenous community members held the land jointly and severally, and all are responsible for maintaining the use and health of the land as proprietors in common. They are hereditary owners of the land who also work the land, and they are workers on the land who also own the land. In other words, there is no societal division between those who own the land and those who work the land: the indigenous possessors of the land also hold, occupy, live on, work on, use, are stewards of, care for and identify with the land.

In the same way that ownership of the means of production – land – is collective, so too is indigenous production. Indigenous community members work together to produce the food, fuel, clothing and shelter they need for their own sustenance and for others in the community and for the reproduction of the community. Production includes community members applying their labour to the land directly (through activities such as hunting, gathering, fishing, plant cultivation, animal husbandry and mining) and indirectly (through domestic-level manufacturing such as hut construction, food preparation, production of utensils and other household items, fabric weaving, leatherworking, jewellery-making for personal adornment, production of pharmaceuticals and natural remedies, fashioning of tools and the making of weapons). As well as production of the material requirements of the individual members of the community and the community as a whole, members also work together in a coordinated way for non-economic reasons including governing the community, defending the territory, raising and educating children, maintaining cultural practices and so on.

Marx makes a further clarification about the nature of work in indigenous communities that is essential for understanding work in all communities and societies. People labour in communities for two different purposes: they provide *necessary labour* to produce the goods and services needed to sustain themselves and their family; and they provide *surplus labour* to produce the goods and services to sustain their communities. In indigenous communities, community members work for a period of time to produce goods and services that are *necessary* to sustain themselves and their families (this is *necessary labour*). They also work for a longer-than-necessary period of labour time to produce *surplus* goods and services required for the reproduction of the community (this is *surplus labour*). As will be shown in Chapters 4 and 5, these forms of surplus labour which produce surplus products is a nascent form of the profit and rent that exists in capitalist societies.

Marx also asks whether the social relation that indigenous people have with their land is a social relation of *production* or a relation of *consumption*. It could be argued that First Nations people have a mode of consumption rather than a mode of production, especially if it is assumed people merely have to consume the resources provided by the land (nature) in order to live. Instead, he argues that 'Even where the only task is to *find* and to *discover*, this soon requires exertion, labour – as in hunting, fishing, herding – and production (i.e. development) of certain capacities on the part of the subject.'[17] That is, even when food is provided by nature, indigenous community members need to apply their labour (physical effort over a period of time) in a coordinated way to collect, pick or capture the natural resources and to transform that raw material (using tools, machines, implements, utensils and other technologies) and prepare, cook, store, carry and in other ways convert nature into useable goods. In other words, what may appear as a social relation of *consumption* between people and nature is not possible without the prior establishment of a social relation of *production* between people and nature.

Marx also asked whether it was possible for privately owned property to exist in indigenous communities, and whether it was possible for individual community members to own and use communal property (such as land, tools, herd animals and so on) for their own private benefit rather than for the community as a whole. To answer this question, he noted the existence of *communal private property*. In indigenous communities, individuals can apply their own personal labour to communal property (such as land) to produce food, clothing, housing and other necessities that they need for their own personal benefit (or for the benefit of their immediate kin). The indigenous community has collective ownership of the land and all its features but does not own the personal labour of each member. That is, the land is communal property, but each worker is the owner of their own labour. Therefore, by working on the communal property (such as the community's land and waters) individual indigenous members may produce goods and services which they own privately: 'the labourer is the private owner of his own means of labour set in himself: the peasant of the land which he cultivates, the artisan of the tool which he handles.'[18] However, the individuals in community also have obligations to their community, and must work on the land to produce goods and services for the benefit of the community itself. For example, an individual may work on some indigenous land for their own private benefit (such as to gather food to eat or to make tools), and they are also obliged to provide a proportion of their labour (or their produce) to support the community (such as to defend the community from attack, or help raise and teach the community's children).

A number of questions about the nature of communal private property arise. One crucial question is: who decides where, and for how long, a person can work on indigenous land for their own private benefit and how much surplus work needs to be carried out for the perpetuation of the community? Similarly, if a member works on community land and produces an amount of produce they need for their own substance and a surplus-to-their-requirements amount of produce, how much can they keep for themselves and how much should be returned to the community? Finally, there is the question of the inheritance of communal private property: if a community member produces tools and materials for their own personal use, can they bequeath their tools, materials and surplus produce to their children and grandchildren, or must it all be returned to the community?

The answer to all these questions about communal private property (how much work must be provided for the benefit of the community, who owns any surplus-to-personal-requirements produce, and whether private property can be passed on to others) is decided by the community, of whom the relevant indigenous worker is a member. That is, all members of the community, or the customarily selected elders of the community, make decisions over the use, ownership and inheritance arrangements for privately made products that were created from the community-owned land.

The crucial point is that the decision about what to do with the economic surplus produced by personal labour of the community member working on indigenous land, and the tools produced by personal labour of the community member working on indigenous land, is decided socially – or *politically* – by the members of the indigenous community. As will be discussed in Chapter 4, this use of collective decision making over the economy, and any surplus-to-personal-requirements products, is radically different from the capitalist mode of production where the economic surplus produced by workers is automatically appropriated by the capitalist.

As a result of indigenous communities having no society-wide division of property in land, and no societal division of labour between owners and workers, so too these communities do not have classes. In indigenous communities where all own the land, there is a unity between 'the worker' and 'the conditions of production'. Unlike other modes of production where there is privatised ownership of land, in indigenous communities there is no class of landowners and land non-owners. Similarly, there is no division of the community into property-less workers and land- and tool-owning proprietors because the individual workers, the direct producers, also own the means of production.

This is not to say all members of this community are social equals. There are divisions of labour in these communities based on *non-economic* factors such as childbearing (a division between those who can and cannot bear children) and status (e.g. a division between the high-status elders who are the recognised custodians of cultural knowledge, law and practices and the majority of community members who are not elders). Other social divisions include those between kin and non-kin; community members and those who are in the indigenous community but not of the community (e.g. slaves, prisoners of war, visitors and so on); clan-based subgroups; and patriarchal or matriarchal divisions.

All these community divisions establish subgroups with interests that arise from their roles, status or occupations.[19] Conflicts of interest can arise between the different subgroups that may cause the parties to interact differently or may cause the broader changes in the practices or customs of the community. Important as these conflicts of interest can be, they are not deep-rooted, systemic contradictions that undermine or force changes to the indigenous community's mode of production, the material basis necessary for the perpetuation of the community and its people. There may also be other sources of community instability (such as inter-indigenous war, droughts and so on) but the underlying material basis for the production of the society itself is stable.

However, there is a significant economic repercussion arising from the stability of the indigenous mode of production. As will be seen in other modes of production, contradictory economic interests and conflicts between property owners and property non-owners create internal pressures within the economy to develop new tools, work practices and technology which improve efficiency, effectiveness or productivity of the economy. Indigenous communities do not have private property and class conflicts that drive change within the mode of production, and, as a result, technological development evolves very slowly. Instead of internal economic contradictions driving economic (and societal) change, change in these communities results from internal social causes (such as population change) and external causes (such as barter, colonialisation and war).

Marx's historical analysis of the indigenous mode of production and the communities that are based on it recognised that people are active social beings, born into and raised in communities, learning language and communicating with others, and working together to produce the material means of life and to reproduce their communities over time. He mentioned at one point, but did not expand on, that these 'early communal societies' had many of the characteristics of 'primitive communism'.[20]

His historical approach was radically different from the approach other political economists were taking at the time, and that many economists assume today. Influential philosophers of Marx's time included Thomas Hobbes, who argued in *Leviathan* (1651) that societies are made up of solitary individuals who have a 'natural' liberty and equality and a licence to undertake whatever actions are necessary to preserve themselves; and John Locke, who proposed in *Second Treatise of Government* (1689) that all societies are constituted by independent individuals who have a divinely granted liberty.[21] Marx was scathing of these ahistorical theories that assumed somewhere, somehow, the world had once been peopled by solitary, independent, free individuals: 'The solitary and isolated hunter or fisherman, who serves Adam Smith and Ricardo as a starting point [for their political economic theories], is one of the unimaginative fantasies of eighteenth-century romances à la Robinson Crusoe ...'[22]

As will be seen in following sections, these characteristics of the indigenous mode of production, with its communally held land and communally organised labour, are radically different from other modes of production that separate humans from nature, convert land into individually held property and establish a form of governance that exists independently of its communal members.

Ancient mode of production

Ancient communities (sometimes called attic, antique or antiquity communities) were the second form of community Marx identified.

With the release in 1981 of the classic *The Class Struggle in the Ancient Greek World* by G. E. M. de Ste. Croix, almost all analyses of ancient communities and the ancient mode of production have focused on one factor of production: labour. Ste. Croix argued that ancient Greece and Rome were established on a 'slave mode of production' and that these communities had a three-class social structure: a slave-owning, landowning ruling class; the majority of workers who were small producers (peasants, craftspeople and traders) producing for their own sustenance and contributing very little to the surplus (wealth) of the society; and the slaves who created the unpaid surpluses that were appropriated as wealth by the ruling class. Since then, there have been numerous debates over the relations between slavery in antiquity and class struggle,[23] democracy[24] and cities,[25] among many other issues.

Marx, on the other hand, always wrote about the significance of both factors of production – land and labour – when he wrote about the ancient mode of production. This section therefore aims to rebalance the traditional debates about labour in the ancient mode of production by focusing instead on the significance of ancient landed property (in particular, the development of a new form of landed property, public land) and its implications for the development of a new form of societal organisation: cities.

The prime examples of the ancient mode of production that Marx investigated were from ancient Greece, ancient Rome and ancient India, communities that existed from around the seventh century BCE to around the fourth century CE. However, he also noted this mode of operation existed in other continents and, in at least in the case of India, this mode of production continued to exist during his lifetime in the 1800s.

Ancient communities developed when many indigenous groups (discussed above) began to supplement their hunter-gatherer mode of production with agriculture, the domestication of livestock and other industries based on small, scattered farms and small villages. As these families, farms and villages became wealthier, they banded together to protect themselves from attack by outsiders, to develop shared infrastructure (such as roads and marketplaces), to establish warehouses that could store a common reserve of grain against bad harvests, and to develop specialised skills.

These ancient communities at first continued to maintain many characteristics reflecting their origins in indigenous communities – in particular, the common ownership of land and the requirement that only community members could make use of community land. As the main industry in the ancient mode of production was agriculture, at first most community members were self-managing peasants who held a parcel of (community-owned) agricultural land, applied their own labour to the land using their own tools, and produced the materials they needed for their own sustenance and the sustenance of their family. As well as working the land directly, families carried out small-scale domestic production to manufacture homecrafts (such as food, fuel and clothing) for their own sustenance and to barter with others. Marx argued that this ancient mode of production was 'the basis for the development of personal independence' but one that was still limited in many different ways.[26]

As part of the development of ancient communities, a new fortified urban centre was needed, often with military barracks, armouries, manufacturing workshops, grain storage, markets and related public purposes, as well as housing for those who lived in the new urban centre. As a result, the once unitary, commonly owned agricultural land that was the only form of property in the community was divided into two: land needed for an urban settlement which would carry out public purposes (*ager publicus*), and the surrounding agricultural hinterland that continued to be communal land used for private purposes.

This division of community-owned land into two types of uses – public land used by non-peasants for public purposes, and private land used by peasants for private and communal purposes – established a radically different form of landed property compared with the earlier indigenous form of landownership. The public-use landed property and the private-use landed property were physically and legally separate from each other, both had their own economic interests and priorities, and both were also mutually dependent on each other[27]

This division introduced a contradictory social relation between the holders of public land and the holders of private land. For example, the private peasant landholders (whose communal role is to produce the material goods and services needed for their own sustenance and the reproduction of the community as a whole) depended on the public city authorities (whose communal role is to defend the peasant landowners and, consequently, to tax all community members to resource its communal role). On the other hand, the public landholders found their capacity to defend, regulate and support the agricultural members of the community depended on the capacity of the peasant class to perform as the direct producers of the material resources needed by the city to carry out its functions.

This bifurcation of community land into the public land of the city and the privately held and worked land of the agricultural territory established a new social relation, a contradictory dynamic that drove social, economic, political and cultural change throughout the ancient world. The new cities concentrated the people and resources needed to protect and support the whole community. In addition, the city and its inhabitants developed new functions, architecture, technology and skills to strengthen its second role: the administration of the city and the governance of the community as a whole.

These new cities developed four new types of centralised services. First, the city built new public infrastructure (such as fortifications, military bases, centres for public warehouses and marketplaces for commerce and trade). Second, the city established new administrative arrangements to plan, manage and govern the urban population and its urban activities. Third, to pay for all this activity, cities institutionalised new forms of taxation and tax enforcement services so that peasants and urban dwellers alike provided the city with taxes, duties, levies other forms of obligatory payments. Fourth, the city developed a new form of governance so that the community members, most of whom lived and worked in the dispersed rural hinterland, could control and guide the city.

Cities became increasingly powerful. The leadership of the ancient community responsible for the community's governance, military, justice, economic, religious and other institutions was now based in the ancient city. Cities had the power to tax the community, impose controls over the population in times of war, and demand the provision of (surplus) goods and services from the direct producers and their families. Cities also had the armies under their control, providing city leaders with the military resources they needed to enforce their demands, if necessary.

Cities became richer. Large, wealthy and better-situated cities became transport hubs for trade with distant markets. Cities were educational, recreational and religious centres which attracted locals and foreigners, increasing the city's population and increasing the demand for agricultural products from the surrounding territory. A virtuous circle of growth occurred where cities grew demographically, politically, economically and culturally, creating local demand within the city for the produce of the surrounding agricultural territory as well as demands from other cities which could now be reached through the invention of new and larger forms of transport, warehouses and trade. Unless there were disruptions from war, disease, famine or other causes, the wealth of cities grew and peasants in the surrounding hinterland prospered as they produced for the expanding urban population and for trade beyond the city.

However, the expansion of cities also created divisions within ancient communities. Industrially, the community's traditional small-scale, domestic-level industry (where wives and daughters typically worked at home to produce spun, woven and related craft products) was undermined by the new urban artisans and their larger, more efficient urban-scale industries (such as pottery, leather goods, fabrics, utensils, and tools and technology). In addition, cities developed new urban-oriented industries, occupations and specialisations (including master artisans) which produced more and better-quality products as a result of the urban economies of scale and specialisation. Traditional barter or exchange of goods continued between local community members, but there was an expansion in urban production for trade with strangers living in other cities and further beyond. As inter-city trade expanded, cities built new, large-scale warehouse storage and larger forms of sea and land transport upon which the peasants in rural hinterland were increasingly dependent.

Structural changes also occurred in the governance of ancient communities. Historically, agricultural workers in the hinterland participated directly in the governance of their community, or at least, through their direct contact with the elders or other leaders of the community. With the development of the larger ancient communities based in cities came a new form of community governance with a new political institution: the state.

The city-state was a conglomeration of legal, taxing, regulatory and administrative institutions and workforce, supported by a military force, and overseen by a leadership group. The city-state was responsible for carrying out three, often contradictory objectives: to govern for the good of the city, for the good for the rural hinterland, and for the stability and protection of the community as a whole. As well as having these contradictory objectives, the state tended to be ruled by one of two contradictory interest groups. Leadership of the state fell into the hands of those wealthy enough and with enough time to manage the state. In practice, this meant the state was governed by the traditional ruling families from the peasantry (the patricians who could afford to leave their rural holdings to others to manage while they moved to live in the city) and members of the urban elites based in the city (such as master artisans from industry, bankers from finance, and the military). As a result of these conflicts, the state often changed its governance arrangements. Marx noted, for example, that governance in ancient communities such as Athens or Sparta took various institutional forms (such as a council, a citizen assembly, an oligarchy, a republic or a single despot such as an tyrant) depending on the balance of power between the conflicted vested interests.

However, despite their different rural and urban interests, the ruling parties would typically unite on issues affecting the stability and protection of the community as a whole, and the perpetuation of the state itself. The city inhabitants and the rural peasants may resist state taxation, regulation and the enforcement of decisions of the ruling class, but, when necessary, the ruling class would unite and impose the state's military forces to subdue any resistance.[28]

As the city-state expanded, and state power was consolidated, the state required ever more resources. Recall that, traditionally, peasants held their own plots of land on which they provided necessary labour to produce necessary goods to sustain themselves, and had a *customary* obligation to provide surplus labour to produce surplus goods for the benefit of the community as a whole. Increasingly, however, the city-state *compelled* the peasants (and urban workers) to provide surplus labour or surplus produce to the state, with the threat of the state imposing penalties or confiscating the peasants' land. The city-state, as an armed polity, could demand the continuous provision of unpaid, obligatory labour or surplus produce to the state. The state would use a proportion of the surplus for direct community-supporting purposes, but could also use the surplus for grand buildings, public circuses and other displays of wealth and power.

The development of the city-state in ancient communities also led to another far-reaching change in the course of human history, one which contributed to the destruction of the original indigenous and communal forms of land possession, and which spurred the development of new forms of industry and growth. This momentous change was the invention of currency in the seventh and sixth centuries BCE by cities in ancient Lydia (in today's Turkey), ancient Greece and ancient China. The British Museum has provided a summary of the origins of currency which is worth quoting in full:

> In small societies, there isn't really a great need for money, because you can generally trust your friends and neighbours to return any labour, food or goods in kind. The need for money, as we understand it, grows when you are dealing with strangers you may never see again and can't necessarily trust – that is, when you're trading in a cosmopolitan city … the answer was for the state to mint coins of pure gold and pure silver, of consistent weights that would have absolutely reliable value. It was the currency that you could trust in completely … The Lydians hit on the idea of the state, or the king, issuing standard weights and standard purity.

The stamps on them are the guarantee of the weight and the purity ... the gold standard starts here.[29]

Although Marx would generally agree with the comments of the British Museum about the emergence of money as a way to facilitate exchange between merchants in a pre-capitalist community, he would also want to put this view into perspective. The nature of money in an economy varies significantly depending on the dominant mode of production. That is, the properties, functions and forms of money in a community with an ancient mode of production (such as in Lydia) are very different from how money participates in other modes of production. In capitalism, for example, the connection between currency and the value of that coinage that existed in Lydia is lost: the national capitalist state may issue currency within its borders but it is not able to set the value of that currency.[30] Similarly, the authorisation of currency by the state, as in Lydia, does not necessarily occur in capitalism: in the case of international flows of capitalist credit, debt and money, 'there is no supranational state choosing units of account or having the power to tax at the international level'.[31]

Marx also argued that, along with the benefits of a state-guaranteed currency in ancient communities, came usury, where money was lent at high rates of interest to people: 'In Ancient Rome, beginning with the last years of the Republic, when manufacturing stood far below its average level of development in the Ancient world, merchant's capital, money-dealing capital, and usurer's capital developed to their highest point within the Ancient form.'[32] Usury promoted the function of money as a means of payment for commercial transactions instead of the traditional use of gift-giving (credit extended on a personal basis with an interpersonal balance maintained over the long term) or barter (where the buyer and seller exchanged their goods and services directly without the use of a medium of exchange). Usury introduced to commerce the capacity to separate in time the two different actions of purchasing and payment. Money developed as a means of payment where payment was based not on the exchange of goods or services of equivalent value, but on the repayment of money plus interest. Over time, usury also concentrated money wealth in the hands of a few lenders who could operate in the economy and make profit without altering the mode of production itself. Here, in ancient societies, a primitive form of financial dealing and new proto-banks developed that would, under very different circumstances, become a key feature of the capitalist mode of production.

A case study of the ancient mode of production in India
In volume I of *Capital*, Marx gave a detailed example of the operation of the ancient mode of production as it had occurred in Indian communities for centuries, and which continued to exist in some communities in his day. This case

study is of particular interest because, unlike the mode of production in ancient Greece, it is not dependent on slavery.

All members of the community have common ownership ('possession in common') of their land. The communal land, ranging from 100 acres to several thousand acres, was capable of producing all the material resources needed for the maintenance and reproduction of the community. Typically, the land consisted of a large agricultural region with a small amount of land where a small village was located.

The majority of the community members live and work on the land. These direct producers work on the land directly (such as by tilling the fields for agriculture) or indirectly (such as by spinning and weaving agricultural products to produce handicrafts, an early form of domestic manufacture). Of the goods and services produced by the direct producers, most (but not all) of those products were divided between themselves for their direct consumption.

However, a small proportion of the agricultural and handicrafts products (made by the direct producers) that is surplus to the sustenance needs of the direct producers is provided (as 'rent in kind') to the relatively few community members who live and work in the village. In the village, these dozen or so individuals (depending on the size and productivity of the communal land) lead and regulate the community and also provide infrastructure that is needed for the good of the community. They are effectively a nascent state governing the community as a whole. These community members who make up the community's State include:

> the 'chief inhabitant,' who is judge, police, and tax-gatherer in one; the bookkeeper, who keeps the accounts of the tillage and registers everything relating thereto; another official, who prosecutes criminals, protects strangers travelling through and escorts them to the next village; the boundary man, who guards the boundaries against neighbouring communities; the water-overseer, who distributes the water from the common tanks for irrigation; the Brahmin, who conducts the religious services; the schoolmaster, who on the sand teaches the children reading and writing; the calendar-Brahmin, or astrologer, who makes known the lucky or unlucky days for seed-time and harvest, and for every other kind of agricultural work; a smith and a carpenter, who make and repair all the agricultural implements; the potter, who makes all the pottery of the village; the barber, the washerman, who washes clothes, the silversmith, here and there the poet, who in some communities replaces the silversmith, in others the schoolmaster.[33]

This model of a community which is built on an ancient mode of production is resilient. If the population increases to the point that the direct producers can no longer produce enough from the land to sustain the community, the community splits into two. The new community is founded, with the same division of labour (between the direct producers and the state), on unoccupied land. Once again, all community members are proprietors of the community's land, and the direct producers work the land to produce the goods and services needed for their own sustenance plus an additional, surplus that is appropriated (as rent) by the members of the state.

Ancient land and rent

Marx makes almost no reference to the existence of rent paid for the use of land in the ancient mode of production. This is understandable given two aspects of the ancient mode of production.

First, most users of agricultural land were peasants who were members of the community, owners of their own means of production (their communal plot of land, their tools, and other equipment and resources) and direct producers of their own means of sustenance. As noted above, 'ownership of means of production by the producer himself was at the same time the basis for political status, the independence of the citizen'.[34] In this situation, rent did not exist because the direct producer who worked the land was also the proprietor of their own plot of (communal) land.

Second, in many cases where there was a concentration of landholdings (with one landholder taking control of many adjacent, smaller plots of land), the direct producers on these large agricultural farms were slaves. There was no category of rent paid for the use of land because all the produce of slaves working on the land was automatically owned by the slave-owning landowner. In ancient Rome, for example:

> The rich had got possession of the greater part of the undivided land. ... [They] bought, therefore, some of the pieces of land lying near theirs, and belonging to the poor, with the acquiescence of their owners, and took some by force, so that they now were cultivating widely extended domains, instead of isolated fields. Then they employed slaves in agriculture and cattle-breeding, because freemen would have been taken from labour for military service. The possession of slaves brought them great gain ... Thus the powerful men drew all wealth to themselves, and all the land swarmed with slaves.[35]

The case study of an Indian community (discussed above) was one occasion when Marx mentioned rent arising in a community based on an ancient mode of production. He did not discuss the rent in any detail except to clarify it was not rent paid as money but was 'rent in kind'.[36] Rent in kind consists of goods produced on the land by the labour of the direct producer that are surplus to the sustenance needs of the direct producer and which are paid to the landowner for the use of their land. In this case, the payment of rent in kind is not paid to the landowner (who is the direct producer) but to the nascent state. In this case, where the direct producer is confronted by the state, the payment of the surplus product could also be considered as a tax; this is a situation where 'rent and taxes coincide, or rather, there exists no tax which differs from this form of ground-rent'.[37] We will return to this distinction fully in the section on the Asiatic mode of production (below).

Ancient cities and change

Over time, the ancient mode of production was transformed from internal changes (such as the development of new technologies, the growth or decline of the size of the population and workforce, the development of expertise by urban artisans, and struggles between the slave-owning, landowning class, the peasant/citizen class and the class of chattel slaves) and from external changes (such as inter-urban trade, migration, territorial expansion and war).

These changes stimulated major changes in the culture, values and world-view of those living in the city-states. The traditional land-based peasants with values based on ethnic homogeneity, family, social stability and reliance on kinship members continued to be important in the agricultural hinterland. However, in the cities, wealth and power was increasingly centred on the lead-ers of the state and the new urban-based military, manufacturing, commer-cial, merchant and finance industries. Cities were increasingly multicultural and cosmopolitan as they attracted foreign merchants, scholars, pilgrims and others from outside the community's traditional kinship groups. With this influx of new people into the cities came new ideas, fashions, ways of working and religions. Furthermore, culturally, the widespread use of slavery was the very antithesis of the free, self-sufficient peasant who was an equal member with all others in their traditional community. These social and cultural tensions between the countryside and the city, in turn, contributed to further changes in these communities.

It is important to reiterate that ancient modes of production, unlike capitalism (discussed in the next chapter), were never driven by pressure to accrue wealth or profit. Marx argues that the objective of ancient communities, and the way the mode of production was organised, was to create good citizens. The mode of production where agricultural peasants worked on land to produce the prod-ucts they needed for consumption, for the sustenance of people, and where their surplus labour was used to produce surplus products which were used to resource the broader community (including the city-state), was designed to develop the character of the populace in general and the education, resourcefulness and leadership qualities of the city-state elites, in particular. That is, the ancient mode of production was not organised primarily to produce wealth. While the growth of wealth was an end in itself among some commercial professions (such as merchants and traders), ancient communities as a whole were structured by their mode of production for a civic purpose: 'Wealth does not appear as the aim of production, although Cato may well investigate which manner of cultivating a field brings the greatest rewards, and Brutus may even lend out his money at the best rates of interest. The question is always which mode of property creates the best citizens …'[38] This is why, Marx concludes, the 'childish world of antiquity' is in some ways a loftier community than capitalist societies.[39] Although not perfect by any means, the ancient community aspired to treat its community members as ends-in-themselves (not means to an end), and production was organised for the benefit of community members and the maintenance of the community. This is not to deny there were many serious inequities in the ancient communities: most economic and political benefits, for example, accrued only to male members of the community, many of these communities prospered from slavery, and the quality of the lives of many peasants living outside the cities were severely affected by technology change, trade, war and so on. However, despite these inequalities in ancient communities, Marx adds, capitalism by comparison is 'vulgar' because it sacrifices 'the human end-in-itself to an entirely external end' that is profit.[40]

Asiatic mode of production

The Asiatic mode of production is similar in some ways to the community-based indigenous and ancient modes of production.[41] The most significant differences are that in the Asiatic mode of production landed property is owned by a unitary ruler who personifies the community (an emperor or other absolute monarch), the land is possessed and used privately by the direct producers (local peasants and villagers) and there is a 'unity of agriculture and industry'.[42] Although Marx did not discuss the origins of the Asiatic mode of production, he made numerous references to its continued operation during his lifetime in India[43] and China, including noting that, in the case of the paper industry, 'India and China [have] two distinct antique Asiatic forms of the same industry'.[44]

Asiatic communities are communal in three ways. First, and as with indigenous and ancient communities, the community is organised on the basis of family and clan relations where members are related by blood, shared property and a common language and community ownership of the land. The community members can often trace their lineage, or in other ways show some sort of historical kinship connection with, the emperor (or other absolute ruler of the community) who represents and embodies the community and, in some empires, rules with the blessing of the gods under a 'Mandate of Heaven'.

Second, the community members, mostly agricultural peasants, typically work on small plots of communal land to produce their own food, fuel, clothing and shelter; own their own tools and equipment; produce additional goods in the domestic-scale industry that is undertaken by their family; and live together in the local village. The direct producers, the peasants, manage their own work practices on the land and, on occasions, work collectively with others in the fields or in the village. Villages complement the local peasant-based industry by providing the local community with specialised tradespeople and craftspeople, merchants and traders, local justice offices, religious and cultural institutions.

As a result, villages are the main basis for the organisation of life for most people in Asiatic communities. The agricultural production in rural regions surrounding villages, combined with small-scale industry, manufacturing and trade undertaken within villages, created local Asiatic communities that were generally self-sufficient, stable and long lasting: 'The simplicity of the organisation for production in these self-sufficing communities that constantly reproduce themselves in the same form, and when accidentally destroyed, spring up again on the spot and with the same name – this simplicity supplies the key to the secret of the unchangeableness of Asiatic societies ...'[45]

The third way that Asiatic communities are communal is that a unitary ruler (who personifies the community) owns all the land while the many small, village-based communities who live under the despot have use rights over the commune's land. In other words, 'the comprehensive unity standing above all these little communities appears as the higher proprietor or as the sole proprietor; the real communities hence only as hereditary possessors.'[46] As a result, there are only two forms of land title in the Asiatic mode of production: all the land in the empire or nation is the property of the monarch, emperor, despot or other unitary ruler (who embodies the community), while peasants villagers scattered across the territory have private use rights over their individual plots of land. That is, in Asiatic communities, land is communal property that is held in private possession.[47]

This Asiatic organisation of landed property is distinctly different from the indigenous and ancient forms of landed property in three ways. In terms of ownership and use of the community land, in indigenous communities all landownership and all land use rights are vested in the community members. In ancient communities, all landownership rights are vested in the community but there is a separation of land use rights into privately used land (for peasants) and publicly used land (for the city-state). In Asiatic communities, all landownership rights are vested in the Asiatic ruler (who personifies the Asiatic community) and there is a separation of land use rights into privately used land (for local peasants and villagers) and publicly used land (for the state).

In terms of who ultimately makes decisions over the use and the control of land, and the degree to which community members participate in the decision making, in indigenous communities the final decision typically lies with the elders but there is a degree of direct, participative democracy in the decision making through the day-to-day contact between the elders and the other community members. In ancient communities, the final decision over the control and use of land lies with the political aristocracy controlling the city-state, but there is a degree of direct, participative democracy in the decision making (as occurred in some city-states such as Athens and Sparta where peasants were also citizens).[48]

In Asiatic communities, the final decision over the control and use of land lies with the emperor (or other head of the state) who has absolute power over the empire and who makes decisions with no democratic input from the members of the community, the peasants and villagers who are geographically and institutionally far removed from the state.[49] Unlike community rule in indigenous and ancient communities, Asiatic peasants, villagers and the emperor are all members of the Asiatic community, but peasants and villagers are not members of the Asiatic state (including its associated state bureaucracy) and, in fact, are generally excluded from, and independent of, the rule of their community.[50]

One structural obligation within the Asiatic mode of production was that the emperor and his associated imperial state were responsible for the construction of irrigation systems and other large infrastructure projects around the empire. In China, for example, irrigation systems were essential for rice production by local peasants and villagers. However, the large financial outlay required for such infrastructure could not be afforded by individual villages but could be funded and organised by the power of the imperial state. The planning, construction and operation of infrastructure by the imperial state directly benefited peasants and villagers, but also brought added benefits for the state: building large infrastructure projects increased the legitimacy of the Asiatic mode of production, helped maintain economic and political stability across the empire, and publicly demonstrated the wealth, power and beneficence of the emperor to local village communities.

The Asiatic state used several different models to organise and fund the large-scale infrastructure. One model was for the state to fund the project directly and coordinate the logistics, sometimes over years, to organise local villagers and peasants to provide the labour power needed to build infrastructure that, when completed, benefitted those peasants and villagers. A second model used by the state was to fund and construct infrastructure, and then lease it to the peasants and the villagers, thus creating an ongoing revenue stream for the state.

Although the Asiatic mode of production with its unitary state could perpetuate a relatively stable and organised community, it was very easy for state control to become oppressive. The sole emperor had absolute control over all political power, the state's bureaucracy (including control over land, justice, taxation, economic and military institutions) and the religious institutions that deemed the ruler to be a sacred ruler and sometimes even a semi-god. Given this political, economic and military might, it was relatively easy for the emperor or the bureaucracy to intervene in the lives of villages and their local agricultural surroundings when it suited them.

Asiatic property and rent

In the Asiatic mode of production, the direct producers are the peasants and the villagers associated with the peasants. Together, they would apply their necessary labour to the land (nature) to produce the goods and services they needed for the sustenance of the local community and for the reproduction of the village.

In addition, the direct producers would work, providing their surplus labour, to produce surplus products for two main purposes. Surplus labour and produce were needed to build and maintain communal infrastructure (such as roads) and communal services (such as schools and health services) needed for the operation and growth of their local village. The provision of this surplus would, in general, be easily monitored by the village, be acknowledged by other villagers and bring direct benefits to the direct producers who lived in the villages or the surrounding countryside.

On the other hand, peasant and villager direct producers were typically compelled to provide surplus labour, surplus products and/or surplus money to the geographically and institutionally distant Asiatic ruler. As 'the *all-embracing unity*'[51] the ruler could appropriate the required surplus in many ways. As the unified and unitary expression of the community, the ruler could capture the surplus in the form of rent (for the use of the land), as taxes (for political, infrastructure and civic purposes), and as tributes and donations (for religious purposes). The appropriation of the surplus could be compelled through the use of both soft and hard power. For example, the ruler could compel the direct producers to provide the required amount of surplus through the use of political and legal pressure (which the emperor controlled as their sovereign), through the use of economic power (which the emperor controlled as their landlord), and through the use of religious obligation and duty (which the emperor controlled as their semi-divine leader). When necessary, the ruler could also enforce the provision of rent, taxation and tribute through their control of the armed forces.[52]

The logistics involved in producing and delivering the surplus to the ruler could occur in several different ways in the Asiatic community. Peasants and villagers, individually or collectively, could organise themselves to produce the surplus required by the local village (e.g. to stockpile grain as collective insurance against economic problems such as droughts or other natural disasters) and to produce the surplus required by the imperial ruler. Alternatively, the ruler (personally, or through their entourage, military officers, tax collectors and so on) could directly intervene in, oversee and direct how and when the peasants and villagers produced the required surplus. A variant, combining some of the elements of both these logistical approaches, was for the imperial ruler to delegate responsibility to the heads of villages or to heads of village families to organise the production and delivery of the required surplus to the state.

The main social (economic) contradiction in the Asiatic mode of production therefore is not between the peasants and the villagers, who are all direct producers who also live communally in their self-supporting village community. Instead, the main contradiction in the Asiatic mode of production is between the direct producers (the peasants and villagers in the local village community) and the state that demands the provision of surplus labour, surplus product or surplus money. This contradictory social relation between mutually dependent parties with mutually opposed interests arises because the villagers depend on the state to provide military protection, infrastructure and political stability, while the state depends on the villagers to provide surplus resources and subservience to the imperial ruler. In practice, local villages were subjected by imperial officials to strict regulatory and taxation controls to the point that villagers considered the state (and their officious bureaucratic representatives) to be the chief burden suffocating the life of local, village communities.[53]

The Asiatic mode of production also relied on the existence of two types of cities. One type of city was the imperial city: large fortified cities that were the home of the ruler and also centres of government and the bureaucracy, military bases, trade centres, and centres of science, learning, religion and art. One of the most famous imperial cities built under the Asiatic mode of production that is still in existence today is the Imperial City, part of the city of Beijing, which was built during the Ming and Qing dynasties and which has the Forbidden City at its centre.

The second type of city that was developed to support the Asiatic mode of production were provincial cities. Provincial cities were often built at locations which were favourable for trade, tax collection and territorial defence purposes, and, if necessary, where the cities could provide surveillance and military control over the villages within their hinterland. Marx says of these provincial cities that 'In Asiatic societies, where the monarch appears as the exclusive proprietor of the agricultural surplus product, whole cities arise, which are at bottom nothing more than wandering encampments …'[54]

The Asiatic mode of production is politically, economically and socially very stable. Marx concluded 'the Asiatic form necessarily hangs on most tenaciously and for the longest time … due to its presupposition that the individual does not become independent *vis-à-vis* the commune; that there is a self-sustaining circle of production, unity of agriculture and manufactures, etc.'[55]

Significantly, many of the characteristics of the Asiatic mode of production continue to operate today. In China, for example, there is a two-track system of landownership. The Land Administration Law of the People's Republic of China provides that all land belongs collectively to all the people of China. Within this context, a two-track system of landownership exists where ownership of rural land belongs to the village ('rural collective economic organisations') while ownership of urban land belongs to the state.[56]

Conclusion

What does this exploration of Marx's writings on the indigenous, ancient and Asiatic modes of production say about his theory of urban land, rent and cities? Six lessons can be drawn from the analysis so far.

First, Marx recognised that land was to be broadly understood as nature, and not narrowly as a natural 'resource' for production. Humans have always lived in, and with, nature. Nature includes complex natural processes such as climatic conditions causing famines, or the loss of soil fertility being revived over several years by the use of natural methods (such as plant recycling and the reuse of animal manures) as well as the application of artificial methods (such as fertilisers).[57] He was also aware that production by humans (especially in capitalism) was destroying nature: for example, of the destruction of freshwater fish and their habitat that occurred when 'the river is made to serve industry, as soon as it is polluted by dyes and other waste products and navigated by steamboats, or as soon as its water is diverted into canals where simple drainage can deprive the fish of its medium of existence'.[58] Marx's understanding of nature included issues that today we call ecosystems, biodiversity, the environment and climate change.

Furthermore, in some communities, there is a strong objective unity between community members and nature (where indigenous people live off the land as the source of food, clothing, shelter and so on, and use indigenous land management practices to sustain and provide stewardship of the land) and a strong subjective unity between community members and nature (where the community sees its identity and its political, legal, economic, social, cultural and spiritual institutions as integrated with nature). This includes the development of 'natural religion'[59] (as distinct from a religion based on one or more human-like gods) which continues to provide meaning and an identity for many people and communities around the world. In these circumstances, there is a social relationship of community members to nature based on land use combined with land care, sustainability and stewardship. Marx's insights into the 'unity' of many communities and their land (nature) are today recognised as 'the inherent rights of indigenous peoples which derive from their political, economic and social structures and from their cultures, spiritual traditions, histories and philosophies, especially their rights to their lands, territories and resources'.[60]

Second, from the point of view of production, land and labour are the two essential factors of production in all communities and societies. Nature (land) played, and continues to play, a crucial role for all communities and societies by being the source of the 'natural' resources that humans need for their food, fibre, fuel, shelter, minerals and all other materials which are essential for the sustenance and reproduction of people. Nature on its own, however, does not meet human needs: people must work on nature both directly (applying their labour to nature through hunting, foraging, pastoralism, agriculture, animal husbandry, irrigation, harvesting, mining, aquaculture and so on) and indirectly (transforming natural resources using the tools and techniques of handicrafts, cottage industry, smelting, manufacturing and so on). Labour, often with the aid of tools created from nature by labour, converts natural materials into consumption goods for people and intermediate goods needed for the use of industry. As a result, the two universal factors of production are land and labour: it is only with the development of the capitalist mode of production that capital developed as the third factor of production.

Third, land becomes a factor of production when it becomes landed *property*. With the development of the ancient and Asiatic modes of production, 'It is not the *unity* of living and active humanity with the natural, inorganic conditions of their metabolic exchange with nature, and hence their appropriation of nature, which requires explanation or is the result of a historic process, but rather the *separation* between these inorganic conditions of human existence and this active existence.'[61] Here, for the first time, community members are not living in unity with the land but are *proprietors* of land in the sense that their existence as a community requires them to occupy a territory or region (peacefully or violently), and by occupying the land, they make that territory their communal property. Community members have privileged use of this land because they are members of the community, and non-community members are excluded.

Fourth, the development of land as property also establishes various classes. Ownership of landed property by some but not others established social relations between the class of landowners (with their interests to use, benefit from and dispose of their land as they see fit) and the class of land non-owners (who need to use the land for their own sustenance but who are blocked from doing so by the landowners). In the ancient and Asiatic modes of production, '*property appears in the double form of state and private property* alongside one another, but so that the latter is posited by the former',[62] with the result that contradictory social (political economic) relations are established between people owning private (agricultural) land and people working the land, and between people owning private land (for agriculture) and people holding public land in the city. In the Asiatic mode of production, for example, the major contradictory social relation exists between the landowner (the emperor, monarch or other despot who personifies the community and owns all land on behalf of the community) and the land users (the local peasants and villagers who use the land in return for the payment of rent to the landowner).

This contradictory social relation is expressed in many ways: for example, rural peasants (wanting protection or infrastructure by the cities) have taxes levied on them and are controlled politically by the cities which, nonetheless, are dependent on the rural landowners and direct producers (peasants) for the surplus products the city needs to survive and prosper.

Fifth, the development of land as property was directly connected with the formation of the first cities. The ancient mode of production created a new form of landed property, public land, for the development of cities. In ancient communities, cities are established to defend the community's land, and the remaining communal land is held by peasants to produce sustenance for themselves and surplus goods for the cities. In Asiatic communities, cities are established as centres of administration, tax collection, infrastructure provision and political control. In other words, cities did not appear spontaneously in human history, or as a result of population growth or economic factors such as economies of scale,[63] but were established explicitly to carry out particular economic and political functions that were necessary to protect and perpetuate each particular community's mode of production and its form of political governance.

The development of cities also established new social groups with antagonistic economic interests. The ancient mode of production established a contradictory social (political) relation within the city-state between the land-holdings and slave-owning patricians and the urban-based manufacturers, traders and financiers. As with all contradictory social relations, each party relied on the existence and success of the other, but each party also had contradictory interests which were inconsistent with the interests of the other party. In democratic city-states, a contradictory social (political) relation was created between the city-state's ruling oligarchy and the urban citizenry who would occasionally arry out citizen revolts against tyranny, corruption and other resentments, for example, in the case of the revolt by the people of Athens in 508–507 BCE that overthrew the ruling oligarchy and established the almost century-long period of rule by participatory democracy. Similarly, in the Asiatic mode of production, rural peasants and villagers would occasionally revolt against the emperor's tax collectors, bureaucrats, military officers and other functionaries living in the cities.

Finally, over time, the contradictory social (political economic) relations between landowners and land non-owners, and between the holders of public land and of private land, caused major social, technological, political, military, demographic, cultural and other changes that affected the communities as a whole. Historically, the longest-lasting and most stable communities in the world have been those resting on the indigenous mode of production – Australia's First Nations people, for example, have continuously lived off their land for some 65,000 years. However, the contradictions within ancient communities contributed to the breakdown of those communities after many hundreds of years (e.g. the ancient Roman civilisation, in various forms, continued for around 1,300 years) while, within Asiatic communities, the nature of the political economic contradictions meant that dynasties ruled for almost two millennia.

The findings of this chapter are useful for understanding the political and economic nature of land, rent and cities in general, and give insights into those nations and cities which are currently organised on the basis of common kinship, ethnicity and language (listed in Table 1.3). In addition, the discussion of indigenous land and Asiatic land is directly relevant to contemporary policy debates over indigenous land rights and land nationalisation, respectively, which are discussed in detail in Chapter 7.

The next chapter focuses on Marx's exploration of how urban landed property, rent and cities take different forms in societies that are structured by feudal, capitalist and communist modes of production.

Notes

1. K. Marx, 'Forms Which Precede Capitalist Production', *Grundrisse*, London, Penguin Books in association with *New Left Review*, 1973, https://www.marxists.org/archive/marx/works/1857/grundrisse/ch09.htm
2. K. Marx, *The Poverty of Philosophy*, pt 2.D, Moscow, Progress Publishers, 1955, https://www.marxists.org/archive/marx/works/1847/poverty-philosophy/ch02d.htm
3. Over the decades, some have suggested revisions to Marx's categories. For example, Barry Hindess and Paul Q. Hirst added a sixth category, 'the slave mode of production' in their 1977 classic *Pre-Capitalist Modes of Production*, Abingdon, Routledge, 2018; and Soviet scholars proposed the Asiatic mode of production was a variant of the feudal mode of production (e.g. A. Pisarev, 'Soviet Sinology and Two Approaches to an Understanding of Chinese History', *China Review*, vol. 14, no. 2, 2014, pp. 113–30).
4. Marx, 'Forms Which Precede Capitalist Production', *Grundrisse*, ch. 9, https://www.marxists.org/archive/marx/works/1857/grundrisse/ch09.htm
5. C. Gailey, 'Community, State and Questions of Social Evolution in Marx's "Ethnological Notebooks"', *Anthropologica*, vol. 45, no. 1, 2003, pp. 43–55.
6. For example, K. Marx, *Pre-Capitalist Economic Formations*, New York, International Publishers, 1964, https://www.marxists.org/archive/marx/works/1857/precapitalist/index.htm
7. K. Marx and F. Engels, *The German Ideology*, Moscow, Progress Publishers, 1968, https://www.marxists.org/archive/marx/works/1845/german-ideology/index.htm
8. Marx, *Pre-Capitalist Economic Formations*.
9. R. Hatfield and J. Davies, *Global Review of the Economics of Pastoralism*, Nairobi, International Union for the Conservation of Nature, 2006, https://www.iucn.org/sites/dev/files/import/downloads/global_review_ofthe_economicsof_pastoralism_en_1.pdf
10. L. Rodriguez, *A Global Perspective on the Total Economic Value of Pastoralism: Global Synthesis Report Based on Six Country Valuations*, Nairobi, World Initiative for Sustainable Pastoralism, 2008, https://www.iucn.org/sites/dev/files/import/downloads/tev_report.pdf
11. Marx, *Pre-Capitalist Economic Formations*.
12. Ibid.
13. Marx, *Grundrisse*, ch. 9, https://www.marxists.org/archive/marx/works/1857/grundrisse/ch09.htm
14. United Nations Office of the High Commission for Human Rights, *Briefing Note Indigenous Peoples' Rights and the 2030 Agenda*, Geneva, Office of the High Commission for Human Rights, 2017, https://www.un.org/development/desa/indigenouspeoples/wp-content/

uploads/sites/19/2016/10/Briefing-Paper-on-Indigenous-Peoples-Rights-and-the-2030-Agenda.pdf

15. Marx, *Grundrisse*, ch. 9, https://www.marxists.org/archive/marx/works/1857/grundrisse/ch09.htm

16. Ibid.

17. Ibid.

18. K. Marx, *Capital*, vol. I, ch. 32, Moscow, Progress Publishers, 1887, https://www.marxists.org/archive/marx/works/1867-c1/ch32.htm

19. Marx and Engels, *The German Ideology*, pt 1.A, https://www.marxists.org/archive/marx/works/1845/german-ideology/ch01a.htm

20. K. Marx, *Capital*, vol. III, 1894, New York, International Publishers, 1959, https://www.marxists.org/archive/marx/works/1894-c3/ch48.htm

21. J. Locke, *Second Treatise of Government* [1690], Cambridge, MA, Hackett Publishing Company, 1980.

22. K. Marx, *A Contribution to the Critique of Political Economy*, App. 1, Moscow, Russia, Progress Publishers, 1977, https://www.marxists.org/archive/marx/works/1859/critique-pol-economy/appx1.htm

23. For example, P. Cartledge and D. Konstan, 'Marxism and Classical Antiquity', *Oxford Classical Dictionary*, Oxford, Oxford University Press, 2016.

24. E. M. Wood, *Peasant-Citizen and Slave: The Foundations of Athenian Democracy*, London, Verso, 1988 and *Democracy against Capitalism: Renewing Historical Materialism*, Cambridge, Cambridge University Press, 1995.

25. For example, M. Lazarus, 'Marx's Concept of Class and the Athenian Polis', *Eras Journal*, vol. 18, no. 1, 2016, pp. 21–37.

26. Marx, *Capital*, vol. III, ch. 47, https://www.marxists.org/archive/marx/works/1894-c3/ch47.htm

27. Marx and Engels, *The German Ideology*, pt 1.A, https://www.marxists.org/archive/marx/works/1845/german-ideology/ch01a.htm; K. Marx, *A Contribution to the Critique of Political Economy*, Moscow, Russia, Progress Publishers, 1977, https://www.marxists.org/archive/marx/works/1859/critique-pol-economy/preface.htm; and K. Marx, *The Ethnological Notebooks of Karl Marx*, Assen, Van Gorcum & Co., 1974, https://www.marxists.org/archive/marx/works/1881/ethnographical-notebooks/notebooks.pdf. This topic is also covered extensively in G. E. M de Ste. Croix's 1980 masterpiece, *The Class Struggle in the Ancient Greek World from the Archaic Age to the Arab Conquests*, Ithaca, NY, Cornell University Press, 1981. See also E. M. Wood's classic *Democracy against Capitalism: Renewing Historical Materialism*, Cambridge, Cambridge University Press, 1995.

28. Marx, *Ethnological Notebooks*.

29. British Broadcasting Corporation, 'Episode 25 – Gold Coins of Croesus', transcript of radio programme, *A History of the World in 100 Objects*, London, British Broadcasting Corporation and British Museum, 2010, https://web.archive.org/web/20100227235939/http://www.bbc.co.uk/ahistoryoftheworld/about/transcripts/episode25/.

30. M. Roberts, 'Modern Monetary Theory: A Marxist Critique', *Class, Race and Corporate Power*, vol. 7, no. 1, 2019, pp. 1–17.

31. C. Lapavitsas and N. Aguila, 'Monetary Policy Is Ultimately Based on a Theory of Money: A Marxist Critique of MMT', *Developing Economics*, 17 Mar. 2021, https://developingeconomics.org/2021/03/17/monetary-policy-is-ultimately-based-on-a-theory-of-money-a-marxist-critique-of-mmt/

32. Marx, *Capital*, vol. III, ch. 36, https://www.marxists.org/archive/marx/works/1894-c3/ch36.htm

33. Marx, *Capital*, vol. I, ch. 14, https://www.marxists.org/archive/marx/works/1867-c1/ch14.htm

34. Marx, *Capital*, vol. III, ch. 36, https://www.marxists.org/archive/marx/works/1894-c3/ch36.htm

35. Marx, *Capital*, vol. I, ch. 27, https://www.marxists.org/archive/marx/works/1867-c1/ch27.htm#n23

36. Ibid., vol. I, ch. 24, https://www.marxists.org/archive/marx/works/1867-c1/ch14.htm

37. Marx, *Capital*, vol. III, ch. 47, https://www.marxists.org/archive/marx/works/1894-c3/ch47.htm

38. K. Marx, 'Forms Which Precede Capitalist Production', *Grundrisse*, London, Penguin Books in association with *New Left Review*, 1973, https://www.marxists.org/archive/marx/works/1857/grundrisse/ch09.htm.

39. Ibid.

40. Ibid.

41. Marx's writings on Asiatic forms of property have been controversial. Scholars from the former Soviet Union understood that Lenin had taken the view that the *feudal* mode of production was the basis for the system of social-economic relations in all parts of the world prior to the emergence of the capitalist mode of production, and therefore Marx's writings on the Asiatic mode of production had to be interpreted as some variant of feudalism. The development of China was therefore but a variant of the development of European feudalism, and not a distinct, different mode of production. This interpretation of Lenin's comments is now contested: for example, J. Li, *Chinese Civilization in the Making, 1766–221 BC*, London, Palgrave Macmillan, 1996 and A. Pisarev, 'Soviet Sinology and Two Approaches to an Understanding of Chinese History', *China Review*, vol. 14, no. 2, 2014, pp. 113–30.

42. Ibid.

43. K. Marx, 'The British Rule in India', *New-York Daily Tribune*, 25 June 1853, https://www.marxists.org/archive/marx/works/1853/06/25.htm

44. Marx, *Capital*, vol. I, ch. 15, https://www.marxists.org/archive/marx/works/1867-c1/ch15.htm

45. Ibid.

46. Marx, 'The Chapter on Capital (cont.)', *Grundrisse*, ch. 9, https://www.marxists.org/archive/marx/works/1857/grundrisse/ch09.htm

47. Ibid.

48. Wood, *Democracy against Capitalism*.

49. Marx, 'Forms which Precede Capitalist Production', *Grundrisse*, ch. 9, https://www.marxists.org/archive/marx/works/1857/grundrisse/ch09.htm

50. Marx, *Capital*, vol. III, ch. 47, https://www.marxists.org/archive/marx/works/1894-c3/ch47.htm

51. Marx, *Pre-Capitalist Economic Formations*, pt 1, https://www.marxists.org/archive/marx/works/1857/precapitalist/ch01.htm

52. Marx, 'Forms Which Precede Capitalist Production', *Grundrisse*, ch. 9, https://www.marxists.org/archive/marx/works/1857/grundrisse/ch09.htm

53. Pisarev, 'Soviet Sinology'.

54. Marx, 'Forms Which Precede Capitalist Production', *Grundrisse*, ch. 9, https://www.marxists.org/archive/marx/works/1857/grundrisse/ch09.htm
55. Ibid.
56. Z. Liu and M. Liang, 'Study on Dual-Track System of Chinese Land Ownership', *Cross-Cultural Communication, vol.* 11, no. 9, 2015, pp. 24–8.
57. K. Marx, 'Letter to Nikolai Danielson in St Petersburg, 19 February 1881', *Marx and Engels Correspondence*, Moscow, International Publishers, 1968, https://www.marxists.org/archive/marx/works/1881/letters/81_02_19.htm
58. Marx and Engels, *The German Ideology*, pt 1.B, https://www.marxists.org/archive/marx/works/1845/german-ideology/ch01b.htm
59. Ibid., pt 1.A, https://www.marxists.org/archive/marx/works/1845/german-ideology/ch01a.htm
60. United Nations, *Declaration on the Rights of Indigenous Peoples*, New York, United Nations, 2007, https://www.un.org/development/desa/indigenouspeoples/wp-content/uploads/sites/19/2018/11/UNDRIP_E_web.pdf
61. Marx, 'Forms Which Precede Capitalist Production', *Grundrisse*, ch. 9, https://www.marxists.org/archive/marx/works/1857/grundrisse/ch09.htm
62. Ibid.
63. B. O'Flaherty, *City Economics*, Cambridge, MA, Harvard University Press, 2005.

CHAPTER 4

Feudal, Capitalist and Communist Land

> The bourgeoisie has subjected the country to the rule of the towns. It has created enormous cities, has greatly increased the urban population as compared with the rural ...[1]

Introduction

This chapter gives an overview of the characteristics of the feudal, capitalist and communist modes of production; their particular forms of urban landed property, rent and the state; and the contradictory social relations within these modes of production that cause them and their cities to change. It challenges the views of economists and political scientists who claim that Marx's findings are only relevant to capitalist societies, that he under-theorised the nature of communist societies and/or he had little to say about the relation between economics and cities. In part, this misunderstanding has arisen because of the general tendency of scholars and activists to focus only on Marx's writings on labour and capital and their relations within capitalism. This is understandable given Marx's main objective was to develop a critique of the political economy of capitalism. However, as this book shows, when Marx's considerable writings on *land* are included, it is clear he provided a far more sophisticated critique of capitalist and non-capitalist modes of production, especially feudalism and communism, than is normally appreciated.

The distinction between communities and societies

It may be recalled from Chapter 2 that Marx's methodology recognises there is no single general theory of economics or politics and no universal concepts (such as land and rent) that have unchanging characteristics irrespective of the society within which they play a part. These concepts, institutions and practices always vary depending on the particulars of the society under investigation: they are always context-dependent.

One of the important particulars identified by Marx is the difference between *Gemeinschaft* – communities where community membership is based on shared ancestry and communal ownership of land (as was shown with the indigenous, ancient and Asiatic communities) – and *Gesellschaft* – societies where societal membership is based on a shared geography and there is individual ownership of land. Societies, Marx argued, with their particular modes of production, types of governance and social values originated in central Europe in the Middle Ages and, over the centuries, developed into social formations based on feudal, capitalist and communist modes of production. Incidentally, one of the founders of German sociology, Ferdinand Tönnies, subsequently took Marx's concepts of *Gemeinschaft* and *Gesellschaft* and developed them,[2] as did his colleague Max Weber.

Societies in Europe originated from indigenous groups such as the Celtic, Slavic and Germanic-speaking peoples who conquered much of the Roman Empire and ended its ancient mode of production. These groups destroyed many Roman-built buildings, machinery and other productive forces; oversaw the decline in agriculture; and witnessed the decay of industry, transport and trade. As a result, the former Roman regions of central and northern Europe saw a decrease in the size of their rural and urban populations.[3] Dispersed thinly across a large geographical area,[4] these populations lived in self-sufficient, scattered peasant families and groups of families that were not necessarily related. These groups were led by a warrior chief who also lived in the same forests and worked the same agricultural land as the others.[5] These groups comprised people from many different ethnic backgrounds, all of whom had an equal right to a proportionate share of the land occupied by the group – a situation that 'created a sense of individual self-respect and mutual dependence'.[6]

Given the extended geographical reach of these societies, the isolation of its inhabitants and their dependence on strangers, these early societies organised their governance, trade and other forms of social intercourse on the basis of written laws, impersonal contracts, societal institutions and democratic polities (unlike the reliance on personal trust, mutual obligations and kinship responsibilities expressed as impersonal agreements, oaths and promises between kin and clan members which were the basis of *Gemeinschaft* communities). Although he did not mention in his published writings how it was possible that the illiterate people of Europe of the time came to rely on formal, impersonal, legalistic and written documents, in his *Ethnological Notebooks* Marx speculated that the church (which dominated the lives of European Christendom at this time) may have been the source of the materials and skills needed to produce such documents given that 'The Will, the Contract, and the Separate Ownership were in fact indispensable to the Church as the donee of pious gifts'.[7]

These early societies have three distinctive characteristics. First, there is the obligation of all members of the society to help those from their own region who face difficulties. That is, the society arose, in part, through the establishment of mutual surety (collective responsibility for each other) and the establishment of the associations of mutual support. For example, Marx discusses the Dithmarschen, a district in Germany which, from the thirteenth century to 1559, was an independent peasants' republic with a strong culture and practice of both self-sufficiency and communal obligations to help others who were disadvantaged.[8]

Second, the society has an *ager publicus*, communal or people's land, which took the form of land used by the society members for hunting, timber production, fishing and so on. This public land differs from the individual land owned and used by peasants in that the communal land could not be subdivided and could be used by all society members. In other words, the *ager publicus* is 'a complement to individual property, and figures as property only to the extent that it is defended militarily as the common property of one tribe against a hostile tribe'.[9]

Third, and a defining characteristic of these societies, is that they had a participative form of governance. The politically equal members of the society would meet together in communal meetings to make communal decisions about matters that affected their society (such as war, legal deliberations, religious obligations and so on). This direct, participatory coming together of free and independent landholders (peasant farmers) to make communal decisions is very different from *Gemeinschaft* communities where city-states or a unitary ruler made political decisions for the community on behalf of the community. In societies, instead of establishing polities that were institutionally separate from its members, politics consisted of participatory democratic practice where there was 'the periodic gathering-together [*Vereinigung*] of the commune members ... a *coming-together* [*Vereinigung*], not as a *being-together* [*Verein*]; as a unification made up of independent subjects, landed proprietors, and not as a unity'.[10] The main differences between feudal, capitalist and communist societies and the indigenous, ancient and Asiatic communities are summarised in Table 4.1.

Marx only briefly discusses how, over time, these small groupings of self-sufficient, scattered peasant families and groupings of households came to establish the feudal mode of production.[11] The small family groups, households and clans were forced by war and political alliances into larger groups living in and ruling over larger territories. The leaders, through war and marriage, established themselves as the landed nobility with a monarch at its head. The once self-sufficient peasantry came to be dependent on the (monarch's) land and became serfs, agricultural workers who worked on the land and were legally 'tied' to the land such that, if the land was conquered or transferred to another landowner, responsibility for the serfs on that land was transferred to the new landowner.

Feudal mode of production

The feudal mode of production is stereotypically considered to be structured by two social relations based on the ownership and rent of land: vassalage and manorialism.[12] The ruling monarch (the personification of the feudal state) is the owner of all land in the realm, often on the justification of holding the land on Earth on behalf of God. However, because the feudal ruler is militarily, economically, politically and fiscally *weak*,[13] the ruler had little choice but to seek the

Table 4.1 Communities (*Gemeinschaft*) and Societies (*Gesellschaft*)

	Communities (*Gemeinschaft*)	Societies (*Gesellschaft*)
Communal origins	Ancestry (common ancestors, kin and clan relations, language and customs)	Locality (peoples with diverse ethnic backgrounds living in common regions)
Landed property	The community has collective ownership of, and responsibility for, community land. In ancient and Asiatic communities, communal land is divided into land for private use and public use	Individuals have private ownership of small areas of the communal land, except for some large expanses of common land used for collective purposes
Major economic contradictions	None in indigenous communities. In ancient and Asiatic communities, the social relation between landowners and direct producers (peasants and slaves) and between rural and urban production	The social relation between landowners and direct producers (feudal serfs, slaves and capitalist farm labourers) who produce the surplus
Rent	None in indigenous communities. Limited in ancient communities. Fundamental to Asiatic communities (where peasant land users pay rent to the collective landowner, the emperor)	Landowners lease land to land non-owners in return for the payment of rent
Landowning class	None in indigenous communities. Private owners of large land estates and slaves in ancient communities. The imperial ruler in Asiatic communities	The private owners of land, which, in particular modes of production, are the landowning nobles, capitalist land and property owners and developers, or the state
The state	None in indigenous communities. The city-state in ancient communities. The imperial ruler (and associated bureaucracy) in the Asiatic mode of production	Originally an assembly of all members, the periodic coming together of members to discuss, deliberate and make collective decisions that apply to themselves and their society. Later, a polity with elected or unelected rulers
Examples	Indigenous communities, ancient city states, Asiatic communities	Feudal, capitalist and communist societies

Sources: Marx's comments on communities (*Gemeinschaft*) and societies (*Gesellschaft*) in *The German Ideology*, *Grundrisse*, *The Ethnological Notebooks of Karl Marx* and volumes I and III of *Capital*

support of other members of the feudal aristocracy. To bolster their position and their political and fiscal strength, feudal rulers often (but not always)[14] establish a social relation (of vassalage) with lesser nobles, where the ruler grants large estates of land (fiefs) to the lesser nobles to rule over *in return for* fealty (a formal acknowledgement of loyalty to the ruler), military support to the ruler when needed, and the payment of rent for the land.

The second social relation of landed property that structures the feudal mode of production and feudal societies is manorialism. Manorialism is the economic relationship between landlords (the noble vassals) and the direct producers (the serfs). In this social (economic) relation, the landlord provides the serf with protection, justice and the 'privilege' to cultivate certain fields within their manor in exchange for the payment of rent.[15] The landlord would keep part of that rent for their own use (or wealth) and remit the remainder to the feudal ruler as part of their vassalage obligations.

Both these social relations of vassalage and manorialism are contradictory. For example, the interests of the ruling monarchs (who need to defend their territorial boundaries, maintain their position in society, exert power over their vassals and maximise the extraction of military service and rent from their vassals) conflict with the interests of the vassals (who need to exercise their own power over their fiefs, manage their relations with competitive vassals, control their enserfed workforce and maximise the appropriation of rent from that workforce, and minimise the payment of military service and rent to their rulers). Similarly, there is a clear economic dependence and antagonism between the owners of landed property and their direct producers. Landlords rely on the serfs to work their large estates, and serfs need the landlord to allocate land to them so they can live. Likewise, the landlord is under pressure from their vassalage obligations to maximise the amount of rent they can appropriate from the direct producers while the serfs want to keep all the surplus they produce for themselves.

Over the centuries, these contradictory social relations expressed themselves in different ways. The contradictions within the social relations of vassalage promoted landowner revolts against the ruling monarch, royal retaliation against traitorous nobles, and, in jurisdictions such as England, the use of Parliament to limit the taxation and other powers of the kings over their vassals. Similarly, the contradictions in manorialism could be seen with serfs and landlords taking each other to court, labour strikes by the serfs (especially in times of war or plague when there were labour shortages), lockouts by landlords, and the development of new agricultural technologies to make labouring easier, reduce labour costs and improve productivity.

This general picture of the feudal mode of production, a self-reinforcing land-based system of economic manorialism and political vassalage, is now understood to be too simplistic to capture all the particulars of feudalism in the real world.[16] It is beyond the scope of this book to assess the many variants of feudalism, but it should be noted that feudalism has existed in various forms around the world including in China (*fēngjiàn*) beginning around 1,000 BCE, India (fourth to eleventh century),[17] Europe (ninth to thirteenth centuries) and medieval Japan (twelfth to seventeenth century), and continues to exist in several of today's Middle Eastern nations (see Table 1.2).

Furthermore, in Europe at least, there were multiple other social relations of production between many different stakeholders (rather than just vassalage and manorialism). For example, the church was a major landowner: the church 'is said to have owned between one-fourth and one-third of the land of western Europe' which it used for its own agricultural, manufacturing and commercial enterprises.[18] In addition, as will be discussed below, medieval cities were centres of economic and political power that often had to defend their municipal territory, governing council, urban economy and their autonomy by developing strategic alliances with the ruling monarch and against the local ruling vassal.

Feudal rent

In feudal societies, there were three forms of rent. All rent is a portion of the unpaid surplus labour provided by the direct producer (peasant, serf, labourer, slave and so on) which is appropriated by the landowner for the use of their land. However, in the feudal mode of production, rent could be paid in three different forms – as surplus labour (labour-rent); as surplus product (also called rent in kind); and as money-rent. Marx discusses these at length in chapter 47 of volume III of *Capital*.[19]

Marx calls labour rent 'the simplest and most primitive form of rent'.[20] Typically, this form of rent (compulsorily provided, unpaid, surplus labour, or *corvée*) arises when direct producers (serfs and their families) use their own instruments of labour (plough, cattle, etc.), which actually or legally belong to them, to cultivate a plot of the landlord's soil which they lease as their own and in return, they must work upon the estate of the feudal lord, under the control of the feudal lord, and without any compensation from the feudal lord, for a period of time. A variation occurs when the direct producer provides unpaid labour intermittently and for limited periods of time (such as a number of weeks' work each season) for the landlord.

The direct producer is autonomous and independent when they apply their own labour to their own land with their own technology. They have control over their working hours and conditions; they determine what to produce for their own sustenance (and the sustenance of their family); and they own any surplus-to-sustenance products and decide how they will use or dispose of their property. On the other hand, all the obligatory, unpaid, additional labour that the direct producer provides for the benefit of the landowner is surplus labour in the sense that it is additional to the necessary labour the direct producer needs to apply for their own subsistence.

Marx noted a characteristic of labour-rent is that it is an *obligatory* payment made in return for the use of the landlord's *land* which is paid in the form of *labour time*. In these social relations between the direct producer and the landlord, insti-tutionalised in the lease arrangement, the direct producer has a relatively large degree of power. This power exists because, although the landowner owns the land, the direct producer possesses their own means of production (such as tools and equipment, seed and livestock). As a result, the direct producer is not tied to a single landowner and there is the potential for the direct producer to 'shop around' between competing landowners for a good land leasing agreement. In addition, by possessing their own tools, machinery and materials, the direct producer has a high degree of control over how they work to produce their own means of subsistence and how they manufacture their family-produced domestic handicrafts. The direct producer, in other words, can work and produce in ways that are independent of the control of the landowner, except when they must provide labour rent.

On the other hand, because the direct producer can work and produce inde-pendently of the landlord, the landholder needs the backing of various sources of power to enforce their economic interests. First, the landowner needs some political or other backing to strengthen their bargaining position and influence the *magnitude* of the labour rent being demanded by the landlord. Second, the landowner needs the power, where necessary, to ensure the direct producer com-plies with the lease arrangement and provides their surplus labour to the benefit of the landholder. In both cases, the landowner could enforce the lease arrange-ment through the use of economic powers (such as by establishing workplace controls and directly overseeing the work of the direct producer) and through the application of non-economic sources of power such as enforcement by the state (such as imprisonment for breaking the law); the promise of religious merit to be provided by cultural institutions; and, when necessary, the direct use of extraju-dicial violence by the landholder against the serf.

The second form of rent identified by Marx which developed in the feudal mode of production was *surplus-product rent*, also called rent in kind. Here, the direct producer pays the landlord for access to and the use of the landlord's land by providing a volume of surplus goods as rent. The surplus-product rent may consist of a quantity of agricultural produce grown on the land by the serf, products they have fabricated in their home as domestic industry or handicraft makers, or a combination of both.

There is a significant benefit for the direct producer if they can pay rent as sur-plus-product rent rather than labour rent. With surplus-product rent, the tenant works independently of the landowner. The tenant uses land directly to cultivate their own plants or livestock, and indirectly to convert their agricultural produce into manufactured handcrafts for their own use, for barter or for sale. The serf keeps what is needed for their own sustenance and the sustenance of their family, and to replace the tools and stores of materials they need for the following sea-sons; and provides a portion of the remaining, surplus-to-requirements products as unpaid, compulsory surplus-product rent to the landowner.[21] If the tenant is able to grow, raise or manufacture an amount of surplus products that is in excess of what is needed for the rent, then that excess of surplus products that remain after the rent is paid (which in the capitalist mode of production will be called 'profit') can be accumulated by the peasant as wealth or be sold in the market for money.

Most importantly, although there is compulsion in both surplus-product rent and labour-rent, with surplus-product rent, how the work is carried out by the direct producer is determined by the direct producer and without the supervision or interference by the landlord or their representatives. With labour-rent, on the other hand, the landowner directly supervises the tenant farmer to ensure the labour-rent hours of work are performed in full. Marx explains the difference by wryly saying that the seemingly independent direct producer is still forced to pay rent but 'through legal enactment rather than the whip'.[22]

The third form of land-based rent that developed in the feudal mode of production is rent paid as money: money-rent. Money-rent is 'merely a changed form of rent in kind' where, instead of paying the landlord with a number of hours of unpaid, surplus labour-time or an amount of unpaid surplus-products, the direct producer provides the landlord with an equivalent amount of cash.

Cities and class

A new form of property – unlike landed property or personal property – was developed in the feudal mode of production, one that was inherently associated with towns and cities.

Guilds (associations of tradespeople, professionals and merchants) were created in towns at a time when skilled labour was facing competition from the arrival of unskilled labour (escaped serfs) from the countryside. The legal rights, privileges and obligations of guilds were given and guaranteed by the municipal law of the city government and, in some instances, by the ruling monarch (through letters patent or other, similar royal imprimatur). Essentially, guilds were monopolistic economic associations established to protect its members (shareholders) from competition: they were 'sworn brotherhoods whose members were bound by their oaths to protect and serve one another'.[23]

Guilds established a new form of property called corporative or company property. Corporative property 'consisted chiefly in the labour of each individual person'.[24] However, although guilds were made up of individual members, these corporations were legal entities which had an existence which was independent of their members. As corporations, guilds had rights to own property, make contracts, employ labour, sue others (and be sued), have representatives carry out legal acts and be bound by obligations (such as to pay taxes) on behalf of the guild. The legal rights, privileges and obligations of guilds were often given and guaranteed under the municipal law of the city government where they were situated. In some instances, corporations were empowered and authorised by the ruling monarch (through letters patent or other, similar royal imprimatur) in return for their support of the crown.

Guild members were the wealthier town citizens, the burghers. These citizens typically were master artisans, tradespeople and craftsmen (such as weavers, dyers, masons, painters, metalsmiths, blacksmiths, armourers, bakers, butchers, leather-workers and cobblers); merchants (including retail and wholesale merchants); and traders (including inter-city traders). These urban-based traders, professionals and industrialists operated on a much larger scale than the domestic-scale industry carried out in peasant households, and unlike the peasant households that generally produced goods for their own needs, urban artisans and manufacturers (who were often also merchants) produced products for sale (rather than for their own use).

Corporative property brought four major benefits to the wealthy burghers that they could not achieve as individuals. First, it allowed guild members to protect their buildings, tools and technology, materials and products from theft or appropriation by the landed nobility who dominated feudal societies. Uniting together into a legal association with a legal status, rights, privileges and duties gave the guilds (and their members) a degree of state protection which they could not necessarily achieve as individuals. For this legal status and protection by the state, in a quid pro quo, the guild paid corporate taxes imposed by the municipal council or, if the guild was formed under letters patent, the guild paid corporate taxes to the monarch. Second, as an association of employers, guilds helped members to protect their own livelihoods. By taking a unified approach to the regulation of wages and working conditions of their employees, guilds could undermine the industrial claims of employees (by setting uniform minimum or maximum prices and hours of work) and prevent competition between members within the city. In addition, guilds monopolised control over the number of entrants who could enter into the trade, profession or industry; their training (as apprentices); and their accreditation as journeymen.[25]

Third, because the powerful artisan and merchant guilds were based in towns and supported by town governments, the guilds gave towns (and themselves) a degree of economic power and political independence that helped prevent the town from being attacked or threatened by the nobility (landlords) or the monarch.[26] One of the consequences was that towns ceased being extensions of, or supports for, the countryside and increasingly became a competitor with the countryside. Economically, for example, urban-scale manufacturing, trade and finance industries could produce more, cheaper and better-quality goods and services than was possible by the rural handicraft and domestic-scale industries that existed in the rural regions.

Fourth, guilds had the capacity to influence city governments in ways that individual members could not – not just to defend guild members from the imposition of high municipal taxes by the city-state, but to also influence urban planning, the provision of urban infrastructure and any city regulations that could affect the conduct of markets and trade. Fifth, membership of guilds helped develop inter-city or inter-regional trade. Membership of a local guild gave to its members a degree of legitimacy and commercial security that assisted them when they were developing agreements with traders and merchants from other cities or countries who were effectively strangers. Finally, guilds made it possible for members to act as a cartel, setting fixed prices, ensuring no member could undercut the price of other members with the result that customers in the city had little choice but to pay the monopolistic prices set by the guild.

Marx notes that the creation of corporate property also helped develop what in capitalism would become the capitalist class. Guilds assisted those who were the owners of tools, machinery, buildings and raw materials (and other forces of production) to unify and work together to protect their common economic, commercial and industrial interests. These wealthier town citizens recognised they had common political interests and defended themselves against political pressures from the municipal council, estate-based landowners and the monarch. In addition, through their inter-city and inter-regional trade and communications, the burghers of separate towns worked together to defend their common economic interests across cities. Guild members also worked together within and across cities to develop common wage and work conditions and other agreed industrial relations practices to reduce competition among themselves and to have a common front in the control of their workforces. The burghers, working together within and between separate towns and cities, acted as a proto-class to change societal-wide conditions to benefit their economic and political interests. As they organised and acted collectively, they slowly developed into a new bourgeois class in the face of two simultaneous pressures: one external ('The separate individuals form a class only insofar as they have to carry on a common battle against another class; otherwise they are on hostile terms with each other as competitors') and the other internal ('the class in its turn achieves an independent existence over against the individuals, so that the latter find their conditions of existence predestined, and hence have their position in life and their personal development assigned to them by their class, become subsumed under it').[27]

Primitive accumulation

The development and growth of the feudal mode of production occurred over centuries through social processes that were sometimes political, legalistic and bureaucratic, and at other times were bloody and violent. These changes occurred as a result of the power struggles within the contradictory social relations between monarchs and vassals, landlords and direct producers, cities and vassals, and guild master artisans and journeymen and apprentices. These economic and political struggles also drove the development of technology, changes to working conditions, rural to urban migration, urban development, and changes to trade and finance. It took centuries to establish new types of property ownership and new societal and workplace divisions of labour, new law and other institutions, and new workforce skills.

The crucial stage of economic change called primitive accumulation was to dispossess self-sufficient peasants from their land and their tools. There was 'the complete separation of the labourers from all property in the means by which they can realise their labour'.[28] This separation of the direct producers from their means of production was accompanied by the dissolution of all the traditional 'guarantees of existence afforded by the old feudal arrangements'. As a result, almost all ex-agricultural workers, property-less and no longer able to live by working on rural land, became a new mass labour force that had no choice but to migrate to cities in search for work. These asset-less 'free' workers were left with no economic choice but to sell their labour power to the owners of the means of production. In other words: 'The so-called primitive accumulation, therefore, is nothing else than the historical process of divorcing the producer from the means of production. It appears as primitive, because it forms the pre-historic stage of capital and of the mode of production corresponding with it.'[29] Primitive accumulation also involved consolidating economic and political power in the hands of the owners of land and capital. In Western Europe, for example, some landowners consolidated their landholdings into ever larger estates, while others used their land for industrial purposes by building factories, warehouses, transport infrastructure and other industrial facilities that could be used for mining, forestry, flour milling, tanneries, toolmaking, transport and so on.

In addition, the state's role expanded, especially through the availability of credit and finance. Public debt was crucial: 'with the stroke of an enchanter's wand, [public debt] endows barren money with the power of breeding and thus turns it into capital, without the necessity of its exposing itself to the troubles and risks inseparable from its employment in industry or even in usury.'[30] Public debt, new laws to facilitate new forms of credit and mortgages, new international trading and shipping organisations protected by the state's naval forces, the establishment of great banks, the growth of stock exchanges and other new financial institutions and practices were all enabled by the state either directly (through the fiscal practices of the state) or indirectly (through the creation of legislation, policing and courts to provide security and certainty to capitalist investment, trade and operations).

Primitive accumulation in Western Europe also involved stripping people and communities of their traditional livelihoods; land grabbing; the forced movement of people from rural communities to overcrowded, polluted and dangerous cities; and the establishment and enforcement of new forms of control over the urban workforce by capitalists. It was often a violent process: 'the history of this, their expropriation, is written in the annals of mankind in letters of blood and fire.'[31] There was always resistance by the dispossessed workers,[32] and the state often expanded, trained and armed its police force and its military to enforce the dispossession of working people at home, defend colonialisation, protect new trade routes, and enforce the new capitalist laws over private property, employment, trade, commerce and credit.

The process of primitive accumulation was not limited to seventeenth- and eighteenth-century Europe. It continues today, especially in the Global South. This can be seen in the large-scale land acquisitions that take place through the buying, leasing, bribery or outright theft of land; the dispossession of self-sufficient First Nations people, agricultural workers, peasants and others from their customary or communal homelands, water reserves, forested areas, fishing reserves and mining areas; the immigration of people from their traditional lands in the search of paid work; and the growth of cities. This contemporary process of primitive accumulation has been actively promoted by the World Bank and the International Monetary Fund, among others. They have produced policies and provided funding to countries to dispossess people living in self-sufficient, customary or feudal communities; to privatise land and institute administrative 'reforms' to document the changes in land title; to encourage landless workers to move to cities to find work; to establish 'free' markets and international trade (rather than fair markets and trade); to limit government regulation of the economy and markets; and to undermine resistance or collective action against these 'reforms'.[33]

In short, primitive accumulation is a stage of economic development where the feudal mode of production in Europe slowly transformed into the capitalist mode of production, and which in contemporary times is being deliberately fostered and funded on many Global South nations as if it were some novel 'national development strategy'. Whether in feudal Europe or today's Global South, 'The expropriation of the agricultural producer, of the peasant, from the soil, is the basis of the whole process.'[34]

Capitalist mode of production

The capitalist mode of production is even more distinctive in the way it establishes and uses land, rent and cities to produce the goods and services needed for the sustenance of people and the reproduction of the capitalist society.

There are four essential features of the capitalist mode of production.[35] First, the factors of production (land, labour and capital) are owned privately. Second, production is for profit; that is, companies invest their capital (to purchase natural resources, labour and other forms of capital such as tools or machinery) to produce commodities (goods and services that are useful for consumers) but only if those goods and services can be sold for a profit. Third, companies are compelled by economic pressures to reinvest that profit into additional production (or face a loss in the value of their capital because of competition from other capitals, struggles by labour for higher wages, demands of financiers for higher payments of interest and landlords for higher rent, improvements in productivity from new technologies, depreciation, inflation, demands from the state for higher taxes, and so on). Reinvestment of capital is not a choice; it is an economic (capitalist) imperative. Fourth, in this continuous cycle of investment, production, profit-making and reinvestment, the source of all profit, and economic growth more generally, is the *unpaid* surplus labour that workers provide during the phase of production, but which is appropriated by capitalists.

This cycle of investment, profit-making and reinvestment is often summarised as a three-phase cycle with the investment, production and realisation of capital. Symbolically, these phases are summarised as:

$$M - C \dots P \dots C' - M'$$

The first phase, investment, is the $M - C$ phase. Here banks (or capitalists, shareholders and other investors) advance an amount of money (of value M) to a capitalist who uses it to purchase commodities with an equal value C. These commodities, which will be inputs to production, include raw materials, technology, premises and the labour power of workers.

The second phase is production: the $\dots P \dots$ phase. Here, the direct producers (workers) use their labour to manufacture the input commodities (C) into new commodities which have an *expanded* value (C'). The value of the final commodities (C') has expanded because although each direct producer gets paid a wage in return for the labour they added in production, the direct producer does not get paid for the full amount of the value they added; that is, the value of the final commodities (C') has expanded from the value of the original C because labour is only partly compensated for, and unpaid, surplus labour (embodied in the value of the new commodities) is captured by the capitalist.

In the third phase, realisation (the $C' - M'$ phase), the capitalist sells their commodities (C') for an equal value of money (of value M') and keeps the profit (represented by $M' - M$). This cycle is then repeated.

The circuit of capital accumulation can be described in more concrete terms by considering the activities of industry sectors. Banks provide loans of a certain amount (M) to productive industry sectors (agriculture, mining, manufacturing, construction and the communication and transport)[36] which invest the money, exchanging it for an amount of commodities of the same value (C), which are transformed by labour in production (P) into higher-value commodities (C'), which are sold for money-plus-profit (M').

The exploitation of labour, the exchange of unequal value, is at the heart of capitalism. In capitalism, workers expect an equal exchange where they provide their labour to produce commodities of a certain value and in return get paid a wage that equals the value they created. On the other hand, the capitalist wants to maximise the value of the commodities produced and minimise the value of the wages paid. What *appears* to be an equal exchange, where the value of the wages paid to the workers equals the value of the commodities they produced, is in fact an unequal exchange because the workers are compensated with a value of wages which is less that the value they produced. The significant difference between the capitalist mode of production and the ancient, Asiatic and feudal modes of production is that in capitalism the extraction of the unpaid surplus labour (surplus value) occurs in production, anonymously and without discussion, while in the other modes of production unpaid surplus labour is extracted in a public, transparent and political process where the landowners, emperor and landlords explicitly and visibly command the direct producers to provide surplus labour and threaten legal consequences or other retribution if they do not.

The model of $M - C ... P ... C' - M'$ may suggest a smooth, circular and cumulative flow of capital from M to M'. In reality, capitalist economies are not harmonious, balanced or continuous but crisis-ridden. Breakdowns, disruptions and uneven development can occur at any point along the $M - C ... P ... C' - M'$ cycle, and within firms, between industries and across the economy as a whole.

For example, at the level of the individual firm, capitalists struggle against their workforce to cut costs by reducing the size of the workforce, cutting wages and/or replacing labour with new labour-saving technology. At the level of an industry sector, 'each individual capital strives to capture the largest possible share of the market and to supplant its competitors and exclude them from the market',[37] and if they can't succeed, firms have no choice but to cut costs, restructure or merge with other companies to improve productivity, replace their labour with technology, or enter bankruptcy. Across the economy as a whole, capital invested in industry sectors with low rates of profit will exit and move to more profitable sectors, causing economic restructures. Capitalism is continually disrupted by overproduction, underconsumption and class struggle, and the tendency across the economy for the rate of profit to fall[38] causes frequent cycles of unemployment, bankruptcies, recessions, financial crises and economic restructuring which *necessarily* arise from the everyday operation of capitalism.[39] Capital does all it can to maximise its profitability by increasing the exploitation of its labour, stifling competition (and establishing monopolies) and undertaking foreign trade,[40] not to forget lobbying governments to 'protect' favoured industries, cut company taxes, provide subsidies and take other action to increase the profitability of industry.

The model of capitalism summarised above is merely Marx's first version of the capitalist mode of production. Marx made several changes to make it a closer approximation to reality. One change was to introduce the influence of land. As will be shown in the discussion of absolute rent and differential rent in Chapter 5, capital circulation (M — C ... P ... C' — M') takes place on land, and so the model is made more sophisticated to incorporate the fact that land is leased from landlords in return for rent.

Marx also made a second change to make the model a closer approximation to reality. When money capital is loaned to capitalists (the phase of M – C), the capitalists must eventually repay that loan in full and with interest. In this more sophisticated version of the general model, when the capitalist sells their commodities, a portion of the revenue earned is used to repay the loan and the interest on the loan.

In this introduction to the capitalist mode of production, it must be added that this continuous circuit of capital accumulation cannot go on for ever. In each cycle, there is a tendency for the rate of profit to fall. That is, the amount of profit made each circuit, compared with the amount of capital being thrown into production, reduces over time. When the economy gets to the point where capital can no longer expand, capital is devalued or destroyed, there are economic restructures and an economic crisis. It is beyond the scope of this book to explore the theories of capitalist crises, among which are those based on the falling rate of profit (originally developed by Henryk Grossman, Paul Mattick and Rosa Luxemburg), underconsumption (associated with Paul Baran and Paul Sweezy and the *Monthly Review* magazine) and class struggle (such as Harry Cleaver[41] and Antonio Negri). However, what is significant for this book is that all these theories of crisis focus on the social relations between labour and capital and are silent on how land, rent and the landowning class contribute to, or counteract, capitalist crises.

Finally, it should be clear from this exposition of the cycle of capital accumulation that – unlike other modes of production – landed property is independent of, and not involved in, either the production of unpaid surplus value or its appropriation by capital. Instead, landed property can act as a barrier to the creation and circulation of unpaid surplus value; and landowners appropriate a portion of the unpaid surplus value (as rent, in return for the temporary use of their privately owned land). The ways landed property intervenes in the cycle of capital accumulation, through the processes of differential and absolute rent, are discussed in detail in Chapter 5.

Land and the capitalist mode of production

As indicated in the section on primitive accumulation above, dispossessing the majority of people of their property is essential for the establishment of capitalism: capitalism requires 'the expropriation of the labourer from the conditions of labour, the concentration of these conditions in the hands of a minority of individuals, [and] the exclusive ownership of land by other individuals'.[42] That is, the direct producers become 'free' (in the sense they earn an income by selling their own labour-power), while landowners acquire an income from their owner-ship of landed property, and capitalists acquire an income from their ownership of money, machinery, tools, materials, buildings and other capital assets.[43]

Much of Marx's analyses of landed property in capitalism referred to the dominant land use of his time, agricultural land. He noted that capitalism encouraged land to be privatised and aggregated into large farms owned by a small number of landowners who then used the land to produce agricultural products for profit (rather than for use). For example, land in England that had once provided employment and sustenance for agricultural peasants and their families, and wealth for the landlord, was converted to enable the mass produc-tion of wool for sale for profit in the new commodity markets.[44] The capitalist imperatives to make ever more profit forced these large farms to introduce indus-trial-scale, intensive production methods (such as chemical fertilizers, mechanised agricultural processes and other technologies) that could maximise the returns from, and minimise the costs of, agricultural production.[45] With the introduc-tion of labour-saving machinery, agricultural workers were expelled en masse from the land. Both these actions, investing in new technologies on the land and expelling agricultural labour, had a direct impact on the growth of towns and cities: 'They conquered the field for capitalistic agriculture, made the soil part and parcel of capital, and created for the town industries the necessary supply of a 'free' and outlawed proletariat'.[46]

Although most of Marx's analyses of landed property in capitalism referred to agricultural land, he did make some references to urban land. In capitalist cities, Marx wrote, the capacity of urban landownership to appropriate rent from leasing out the use of the land to others for a limited period of time, was based on the same social relations and economic processes that applied to private own-ership of agricultural land:

> Wherever natural forces can be monopolised and guarantee a surplus-profit to the industrial capitalist using them, be it waterfalls, rich mines, waters teeming with fish, or a favourably located building site, there the person who by virtue of title to a portion of the globe has become the proprietor of these natural objects will wrest this surplus-profit from functioning capital in the form of rent.[47]

In his analysis of urban land, Marx distinguished between rent (paid for the use of land) and interest and amortisation on capital (which arose from investment in buildings and other forms of capital). This was illustrated by 'a big building spec-ulator in London' who Marx discovered had told a Parliamentary Committee in Britain:

> 'I think a man who wishes to rise in the world can hardly expect to rise by follow-ing out a fair trade … it is necessary for him to add speculative building to it, and that must be done not on a small scale; … for the builder makes very little profit out of the buildings themselves; he makes the principal part of the profit out of

the improved ground-rents. Perhaps he takes a piece of ground, and agrees to give £300 a year for it; by laying it out with care, and putting certain descriptions of buildings upon it, he may succeed in making £400 or £450 a year out of it, and his profit would be the increased ground-rent of £100 or £150 a year, rather than the profit of the buildings at which ... in many instances, he scarcely looks at all.'[48]

One of the key theoretical challenges of land in capitalism is to explain the source of the rent that is captured by landowners. Recall from Chapter 2 that the value of something is 'the labour time socially necessary for its production'.[49] Urban land (nature) is not produced by labour and therefore has no (economic) value, and cannot add any value to the final value of commodities.[50] Thus, when an urban landowner leases a block of land for some urban purpose in exchange for rent, what is the source of that rent, and how does the landowner appropriate the rent from the capitalist and/or the direct producer? How this occurs is discussed in detail in the next chapter.

The landed property class
A recurrent theme in Marx's writings on land concerns the existence and activities of the landed property class. He continually referred to the activities of landowners, individually and collectively, in the ancient, Asiatic and feudal modes of production, and, in particular, to their exploitative social relations with the direct producers (slaves, serfs, peasants and so on), and their involvement within the polities of those communities and societies.

Marx also wrote a little about the activities of the landed property class in capitalist societies. This was most explicit in his political writings on the French revolutions in *The Class Struggles in France, 1848 to 1850*; the longer analysis of this period, *The Eighteenth Brumaire of Louis Bonaparte*; Marx's study of the first proletarian government in *The Civil War in France* of 1871 as well as publications such as *The German Ideology*.

Marx planned to write much more on the issue of class in capitalism. He began a chapter on class with the following sentence: 'The owners merely of labour-power, owners of capital, and land-owners, whose respective sources of income are wages, profit and ground-rent, in other words, wage-labourers, capitalists and land-owners, constitute the three big classes of modern society based upon the capitalist mode of production.' It breaks off at this point.[51]

In one of his earlier writings, Marx made a distinction between a class-in-itself and a class-for-itself. Commenting on the situation in England in the mid-nineteenth century, he noted the economic conditions had given a large number of working people some common economic interests and a common opponent to struggle against. In their collective struggle (as a class-in-itself) to address their economic grievances, the mass of people began to unite into a class-for-itself, defending their common interests, and acting in a concerted and class-conscious way with a political struggle:

> Economic conditions had first transformed the mass of the people of the country into workers. The combination of capital has created for this mass a common situation, common interests. This mass is thus already a class as against capital, but not yet for itself. In the struggle, of which we have noted only a few phases, this mass becomes united, and constitutes itself as a class for itself. The interests it defends become class interests. But the struggle of class against class is a political struggle.[52]

That is, as capital expanded and increasingly interfered in the lives of ever more people, the shared experience of economic struggles against capital would develop within working people a self-conscious awareness of their circumstances: that is, 'with the accumulation of capital, the class-struggle, and, therefore, the class consciousness of the working men, develop'.[53]

This process was not automatic or guaranteed. For example, Marx noted that small-landholding peasants in France once formed an enormous mass of people who all lived in similar conditions with similar interests. However, they did not form into a class-for-itself.[54] Their mode of production isolated them from one another and limited their interaction and discussion of their common work circumstances. This situation was reinforced by the poor communication infrastructure at the time, and the lack of resources (the poverty) of the peasants. Each individual peasant family was almost self-sufficient, directly producing most of its sustenance needs, living off the land with limited social relationships, rather than through interactions with others in society. To the extent that the peasants and their families did work together with others, it was in local markets or local towns rather than in cities, regions or nationally. Millions of families living under these common conditions of existence had a common mode of life, economic and political interests, and culture: they had many of the conditions for the existence of a class-in-itself. However, their potential to form a class was undermined by the merely local interconnection among these small-holding peasants, their separation from others across the region or nation, and their often-hostile opposition to each other (as market competitors and political rivals). Life seemed accidental, something over which they, as separate individuals, had no control. The result was this class-in-itself did not constitute itself as a class-for-itself with its own common collective causes, a sense of solidarity with others and a political organisation. They were unable to assert their class interest in their own name, and instead of representing themselves, were represented by politicians who sought their vote and spoke in their name.

Given Marx's limited discussions about class, it is not surprising that class has been a contested concept in both Marxist and non-Marxist scholarship ever since. For example, Marx's statements suggest class could be defined on the basis of ownership of property (such as land) or the source of income (such as rent). Marx often refers to class as the power of one class over another ('the unlimited despotism of one class over other classes').[55] In some writings, each mode of production has only two classes ('Freeman and slave, patrician and plebeian, lord and serf, guild-master and journeyman, in a word, oppressor and oppressed') but in others there are three classes with additional fractions of classes ('The lower middle class, the small manufacturer, the shopkeeper, the artisan, the peasant, all these fight against the bourgeoisie, to save from extinction their existence as fractions of the middle class').[56] Class is sometimes considered to be an objective phenomenon defined in terms of who produces and who appropriates surplus value ('Only the agricultural labourers, not the landowners, appear as a productive class, as a class which creates surplus-value'),[57] and at other times class has also a subjective character ('Upon the different forms of property, upon the social conditions of existence, rises an entire superstructure of distinct and peculiarly formed sentiments, illusions, modes of thought, and views of life').[58]

However, since the 1970s, almost all scholarly discussion on class in capitalism has assumed the existence of only two classes: the class of the unpaid surplus value producing direct producers (the working class) and the class of the unpaid surplus value appropriating capitalist (the capitalist class).[59] The landed property class, continually referred to by Marx, has been all but ignored. This book suggests the study of class would be deepened if more was understood about the origins, economic interests, organisational structures and actions of the urban landed property class in cities.

Marx's writings on landed property suggest a general framework that can be used to investigate the landed property class and its influence over cities. The framework considers the urban landed property class, its stage of development, and the strength of its influence in terms of its private ownership of land for income purposes; collective economic action (class-in-itself); collective political action (class-for-itself); and reactions to the actions of the landed property class.

First, the analysis of any urban landed property class begins by identifying those who generate income from the lease, or buying and selling, of land. This includes identifying the individuals and corporate bodies which privately own landed property (for income-generating purposes) or directly rely on these landowners for their own income. In capitalist cities, core members of the landed property class include those who own urban land from which they generate income from the lease of their land, the buying and selling of their land, or real estate agents and others who act as middle operators to facilitate these exchanges. The members of the urban landed property class include large-scale property developers (including those operating on newly available urban land on the edge or cities and those involved in urban regeneration of existing urban land) and land speculators; real estate organisations involved in the buying, selling and leasing of land; and small-scale landowners (including 'mum and dad' landowners) who own one or more properties which they rent out to others. Although there are various fellow travellers of the landed property class (such as mortgage providers and other financial bodies that fund various land transactions, and the construction industry that builds or renovates buildings on the land), they are not directly involved in the capture of rent from the leasing of land and therefore may be allies but not members of the urban landed property class.

Second, the analysis of the urban landed property class focuses on what its members do, individually or collectively, to protect and promote their economic interests against its opponents (including capital, tenants and the state). This is where the urban landed property class acts a class-in-itself. These actions may include colluding together to set fixed prices and limit price-cutting competition in the real estate industry; lobbying or bribing state officials to release (or rezone) land for commercial use; petitioning lawmakers to change laws and regulations to strengthen their property rights over their land (and limit incursions on landowners' rights by tenants or environmental protection obligations); making commercial deals to promote stability and limit competition within the real estate sector; and applying political pressure on the state to maximise government-funded provision of land-price-enhancing urban infrastructure (such as roads, utilities and recreation areas) and to limit or abolish the imposition of land taxes and charges by the state. The actions taken at this basic stage of class sophistication, organisation and consciousness are usually actions on or against the state, financial institutions, the construction industry and other stakeholders who are affecting the property ownership rights and the rental income capacity of the class.

Third, the urban landed property class becomes visible through its actions as a class-for-itself. Here the members of the class act proactively within non–real estate institutions. It establishes industry and professional bodies to lobby, develops training organisations, and works with the state (and others such as financial institutions) to establish acceptable industry regulations and real estate workforce wages and conditions. Instead of acting from the 'outside' on relevant bodies (such as the city council, land and environment courts, financial institutions, universities and the media), members of the urban landed property class promote their economic interests by directly participating in these bodies. For example, landowners and their supporters get elected to city councils and other arms of the state; become lawyers who are appointed to the land and property courts; become financial professionals involved in mortgage, investment and other land-specific financial institutions; establish real estate research and education organisations within institutions of higher education; and join the media as journalists and editors to promote news and views favourable to the economic interests of the landed property class.

If successful, a conscious urban landed property class becomes an effective fraction of the ruling class, promoting its values and interests, along with all the other fractions of the ruling class. As Marx noted, mockingly, after the failure of several working-class uprisings:

> Soon after this the June insurrection in Paris and its bloody suppression united, in England as on the Continent, all fractions of the ruling classes, landlords and capitalists, stock-exchange wolves and shop-keepers, Protectionists and Freetraders, government and opposition, priests and freethinkers, young whores and old nuns, under the common cry for the salvation of Property, Religion, the Family and Society.[60]

Finally, the influence of the urban landed property class can be ascertained through the study of the resistance to the actions of the class. There can be popular resistance against the class's attempts to make land grabs, to rezone land for their own financial benefit rather than the benefit of the urban population, or to acquire private control over new holdings of land in other ways. There can also be resistance by commercial and residential tenants and the local state when the landed property class attempts to strengthen property ownership rights and to maximise rental revenue at the expense of the land rights and economic interests of commercial and residential tenants, the construction industry, the state and the landless.

In summary, it is possible to use Marx's insights into the landed property class to identify characteristics of the urban landed property class in capitalist cities. The framework discussed here can be used as a guide for further empirical research and case studies.

The financialisation of land and fictitious capital

One of the assumptions Marx made about land in capitalism was that money is invested in land and capital for productive purposes; that is, to produce more capital. The alternative was usury, where money is lent for consumption or other purposes in return for interest which must be paid on a definite date; credit that does not make any contribution to the reproduction of capital.[61] However, with the financialisation of land, the assumptions of land being used for production, and of money only being invested in capitalist production, must be revised.

The financialisation of land came to prominence with the international financial crisis that originated in the US economy in 2007–8, a financial crisis which is also known as the global financial crisis (GFC) or the subprime mortgage crisis. It is beyond the scope of this book to analyse the GFC.[62] However, a little history is needed to show how the financialisation of land developed within the capitalist mode of production.

Beginning in the 1990s in the United States, billions of dollars were diverted from investment in commercial land and productive industries. Instead, money was funnelled into mortgages to assist many working-class people to buy their own home. Bankers formed an alliance between the finance, insurance and real estate sectors to encourage working people (and even people who did not have a job) to take out a mortgage to buy a house-and-land package. The rationale was that land and house prices would continually increase and/or taxes on land and homes would reduce. In either case, buying a house made good financial sense. When the Federal Reserve cut interest rates, mortgage rates fell and home refinancing surged in the United States from $460 billion in 2000 to $2.8 trillion in 2003, despite stagnant wages.[63]

The financial sector calculated it could not lose. If people successfully paid off their home, the mortgage providers would be repaid their loan plus interest. If borrowers defaulted on their mortgage repayments, the financial institutions would foreclose, repossess the 'asset', sell it at its higher price, and recoup the cost of the mortgage. The finance sector also packaged individual mortgages into residential mortgage-backed securities, which were repackaged into 'collateralised debt obligations' (CDOs). These were given triple-A ratings by credit rating agencies and sold to investors who believed these were high-quality, safe investments. There was a burgeoning global demand for these residential mortgage–backed securities that offered seemingly safe and high returns which were based on American real estate with apparently ever-rising prices.

When house prices fell, it created trillions of dollars of problematic securities, debt and derivatives resting on real estate assets, the collapse of financial institutions, thousands of people losing their homes, a large rise in unemployment and economic losses that affected countries around the world. It was 'the worst financial crisis since the Great Depression', and the subsequent global recession with its contraction in annual real per capita global GDP (and broad-based weakness in other key indicators of global economic activity) was the deepest and most synchronised in almost a hundred years.[64]

A key factor in the GFC was a new capitalist phenomenon: treating land as a financial asset. For example, banks capitalised land rent into interest-bearing loans;[65] land was treated as mortgage-backed security issued by real estate financing institutions;[66] and markets were created to buy and sell these mortgage-backed securities.[67]

In the Global South, a different road was taken to 'financialise' land. In 2017, the United Nations Human Rights Commission (UNHCR) reported on the 'financialisation' of housing that was taking place in the Global South.[68] In some instances, large companies (often with the support of governments) were carrying out mass forced evictions of people from their traditional housing suburbs to make way for new luxury developments. In other instances, corporations would purchase real estate in cities and, expecting a return on their 'investment', would raise house prices and rent charges with the effect that local people were pushed out of their communities because they could no longer afford to live there. In Ethiopia, for example, the development of the financial sector did not stimulate the growth of industrialisation but instead stimulated real estate companies and the construction sector, leading to an inflated real estate market, inequality and higher debt burdens.[69]

Land finalisation in the Global South was facilitated by market liberalisation and deregulation in the 1980s which removed strong protectionist trade policies, making it easy for global financial institutions to buy up land in the Global South, especially after decades of colonial rule or strong protectionist trade policies in Africa.[70] With legislation favouring foreign investment, private markets and the use of land for profit (rather than for social benefits such as housing), urban development was led by markets rather than government, which led to the uncoordinated development of cities, and mismatches between urban population growth and the use of urban land.

The financialisation of land also encouraged land grabs by centralised multinationals or decentralised transnational companies aiming to profit from commercial land transactions. While many of these large companies are involved in the production and export of food, animal feed, biofuels, timber and minerals, most have expanded operations to include the appropriation of land. In Brazil, for example, speculative land acquisitions have historically played a role in the portfolio of many large companies, but with the deregulation of financial markets and the financialisation of land acquisition became more intensive.[71] In many instances, the financial beneficiaries of these land grabs are private equity funds, pension funds and special-purpose vehicles in the Global North.[72]

The financialisation of land in the Global North and South was not something Marx considered, but his approach to land can help to explain these phenomena.

Marx expected banking to be subordinated to the needs of industrial capitalism.[73] That is, capital would invest in productive industries. With the financialisation of land, however, money capital (M) was 'invested' into consumption goods (workers' housing). Financiers treated real estate as if it was an asset, like capital, capable of generating new, expanded wealth. In fact, land and housing were 'fictitious capital'.

Fictitious capital is a form of credit where money-capital is 'invested' in *non-existent capital* (assets which use money without producing any additional capital stock). There are three forms of fictitious capital: credit money, government bonds, and shares.[74] Specifically, fictitious capital 'consists of claims (bills of exchange), government securities (which represent spent capital), and stocks (drafts on future revenue)'.[75] In all these cases, money is 'invested' to earn more money (interest, bond yields, mortgage fees and so on) but without expanding capital. Fictitious capital, in other words, 'represents nothing more than accumulated claims, or legal titles, to future production whose money or capital value represents either no capital at all, as in the case of state debts, or is regulated independently of the value of real capital which it represents'.[76]

These cases of the financialisaton of land have clear ramifications for urban policy, and in particular, for urban housing. First, in capitalism, if policymakers wish to see housing provided by the private sector, these examples provide strong evidence that the finance, insurance and real estate sectors need to be strongly regulated to ensure they provide mortgages and housing at affordable prices. The evidence is clear that the alternative, of 'free' (unregulated) markets, will unshackle capitalist incentives which will drive people to maximise financial returns rather than produce affordable housing to those in need. Second, if cities wish to promote economic growth, regulatory and financial incentives to expand the construction of new houses will also result in urban jobs and capital growth. The alternative, of providing incentives for people to buy and sell existing housing stock, may generate short-term revenue for, and employment in, the finance, insurance and real estate sectors, but there will be no appreciable growth in the economy in the longer term. Third, and more radically, the cases of the financialisation of land raise questions about whether the private sector can ever provide housing for low-income residents, and whether such housing can only be provided by state or by community-owned organisations. This matter will be returned to in Chapter 7.

Land and the spatial turn

Marx always wrote about land in capitalism as landed property, referring to the social relations between the landowner and those who were not landowners. He almost never wrote about land as 'space'.[77] Beginning in the 1970s, however, the concept of space became a characteristic of much Marxist urban political economic scholarship.

Henri Lefebvre introduced the spatial turn to political economy. He argued that every mode of production creates its own 'space'. In his *The Production of Space*,[78] Lefebvre argued that the physical layout of cities is structured by the prevailing mode of production (and the state), and that, in turn, the physical layout of cities helps to reproduce the mode of production, the control of the ruling class, and the society itself. By 'space' he referred to 'absolute space' (the division between urban and non-urban regions, the physical layout of cities, and the suburban patterns of residential, industrial, commercial and other land uses that are established by zoning) and 'social space' (the values, meanings and understandings that are inferred from the physical arrangement of cities). Lefebvre's argument that *cities* were crucial for the reproduction of capitalism, of the hegemony of the ruling class and of societies suggested that future revolutions would take place in, and require struggles for the control of, cities.[79]

Independently of Lefebvre, David Harvey was investigating the links between space and urbanisation and in 1982 published his important and influential *The Limits to Capital*.[80] *The Limits to Capital* showed how capitalism (and specifically capital) continuously reshapes the built environment, urban planning, transport routes, communication and related infrastructure in cities with the objective to speed up the circulation time of capital. Businesses, for example, wishing to cut costs, reduce delays in their supply chains, and have a pool of skilled workers in close proximity are likely to agglomerate into particular localities, hubs or 'industrial districts'.[81] One of the most important and novel insights of *The Limits to Capital* is that, while capital may change the urban environment (or colonise other nations or shift from national to global-scale operations) in the hope of increasing profits and preventing the tendency of the rate of profit to fall, these 'spatial fixes' ultimately fail, and capitalism continues to swing from crisis to crisis.

Harvey subsequently referred to three interrelated concepts of 'space, place and the environment' to describe the physical settings where human activity occurs.[82] Places refers to 'regions' or 'locality'; the environment encompasses 'the physical and biological landscape of the earth'; and both are different from 'space'. Space is *relationally* constructed.[83] By this he means spaces arise when 'external influences get internalised in specific processes or things through time.'[84] For example, Harvey discussed how distinct changes in urban structures in industrialised nations emerged under the influence of the different phases in the development of capitalism.[85] Fordist accumulation, with its basis in mass production and mass consumption of low-cost goods, stimulated urban planning that promoted the development of relatively homogenous suburbs on the fringes of cities which would consume mass-produced, standardised housing, cars and other consumer goods. This Fordist-inspired urban planning was reinforced by the development of credit-based finance that facilitated the move of people out of CBDs and into this form of suburbanisation.

Marx's writings on land provide some valuable criteria which can be used to evaluate this spatial turn in urban political economy. First, the insight that the capitalist mode of production (with the state) actively structures the location, size, layout, physical appearance and density of the buildings, housing, infrastructure and so on within cities is totally consistent with Marx's comments about how other modes of production also restructured their cities. For example, as shown in Chapter 3, the ancient mode of production established the city-state with an important function of defending the community, the city and the agricultural land in its hinterland. On the other hand, the Asiatic mode of production structured the location and function of cities so that they would be effective in taxing the peasants and villagers and in providing infrastructure (such as irrigated water). Marx did not discuss how the capitalist mode of production has structured its cities, or how the spatial features of cities facilitate the capitalist mode of production. Lefebvre, Harvey and many others have done a valuable service in filling this gap.

Second, the discussions of urban design and urban development processes often refer to how the actions and interests of labour and capital affect the geography of cities, but there is mostly a silence on the role of land and the landed property class. Marx's writings showed that land actively interferes in the accumulation of capital, blocks some developments and facilitates others, and how its appropriation of rent directly contributes to the centralising or decentralising of production are missing. In short, a more comprehensive understanding of urban design and urban development would emerge by incorporating the interests, activities and influence of land, landownership and the landowning class.

Finally, the tendency to reduce a city's physical layout, patterns of zoning, design of its built environment, location of transport routes and other infrastructure, and so on, to a discussion of space undermines the political potential of urban studies that was identified by Lefebvre. Discussions of urban space as a general category blurs the differences between privately owned land and buildings, community-owned land and public land and their potential as a lever for change. Rather than analysing or critiquing 'space', Marx's focus was always on the social relations of landownership, the potential of changing the laws and practices that reinforce the social relations of property, and the role of classes (including the landowning class) in defending or promoting urban change. In terms of concrete political action, it is more useful to know who owns which particular sites of land, how the land is being used, and how the state is zoning, taxing, planning and in other ways influencing the use of the land, rather than analysing sites as disembodied categories of 'space'.

In short, although there have been some benefits in the spatial turn in urban political economy, Marx's focus on the social relations of land, that is, land as property, will be more fruitful in explaining and critiquing the location, geographical arrangements, architectural design and patterns of land use in cities, and all other aspects of urban design and urban development.

Urban processes under capitalism – a framework

Marx made no direct comments about the urban process under capitalism. He was clear that cities were established in the ancient mode of production to provide military protection from attack, and in the Asiatic mode of production to provide water and other infrastructure to villages and to collect taxes for the emperor. However, by looking at Marx's approach to cities in these modes of production it is possible to glean a framework that can be used to investigate urban processes as they occur in particular ways in different cities operating within the capitalist mode of production.

In general, urban processes are those processes that establish and change the functions and size of cities; the growth or decline of cities over time; and the nature and location of human activities within cities. In capitalism, these are determined by four, contradictory processes driven by capital, labour, land and the state. Capital accumulation often drives the centralisation and concentration of investment, production, consumption and accumulation within a limited region. Labour, dependent as it is on capital for income, also concentrates in cities; a process that requires cities to be structured in such a way that workers (and their families) can access sustenance (food, clothing, shelter and so on) and a quality of life (including health, education, recreation and leisure). The power of private property landowners to capture rental income from capital and labour in cities is high (compared to those in rural regions) but the imperative to capture rent is contested by both capital and labour. Finally, as a result of the contradictions and conflicts between capital, labour and land, an urban-focused capitalist state is established to regulate and adjudicate the economic interests of capital, labour and land in the long-term interests of capital accumulation, and to acquire resources from capital, labour and land so it can maintain its own effectiveness and legitimacy.

For example, if a city produces and retains capital (surplus value), or if the city appropriates capital produced from other cities, it will become wealthier; or, alternatively, if it loses the capital it produces in the urban region to other cities, it is likely to become poorer. The quality of life in the city for residents will depend on the extent to which the surplus value is distributed to all residents or whether it is retained, unequally, by the wealthiest residents. House prices may rise or fall depending on numerous factors such as changes in the size and age of the population, interest rates and the wealth of the population. Depending on the quantity of resources the urban polity can appropriate through taxes and charges, it may develop new human services, upgrade community infrastructure and buildings, and generally improve the quality of the urban environment, or, alternatively, see these services and infrastructure fall into disrepair. Depending on the quality of life, migrants may travel to the city for work and other opportunities and create a population boom with its associated pressure for housing, education and other services, or, alternatively, the workforce may leave in search of better opportunities elsewhere.

Two further refinements are needed of this framework. First, and depending on the circumstances of each city, urban processes may be shaped by the international, national and/or urban forms of capital, labour, land and the state. Urban processes are *not* driven solely by factors within the city. For example, the urban processes of a city may radically change if investment by international finance capital displaces the previously dominant sector of capital within the city. Similarly, the quality of life of urban workers may be disrupted (for better or worse) by an influx of immigrants. In addition, the role, resources and practices of the city government may be changed significantly not only by political pressures from capital, labour or land within the city but also by legislative or funding interventions by the provincial or national government.

Second, this framework for urban processes recognises that the functions, size, growth or decline of cities, and the nature and location of human activities within cities, are always the outcome of contested, contradictory and complex political economic processes. These conflicted processes slowly and persistently act to reinforce or reshape the apparent permanence of urban institutions (such as property, corporation and labour law, the activities of employer and labour unions, and the bureaucracy of the state) and the apparent immovability of urban buildings (such as roads, rail, water and communication infrastructure, and office, housing and other buildings). However, given that the capitalist mode of production is inherently unstable (with contradictions and class struggle in the social relations between labour, capital and land) and continually striving to increase profits and counteract the tendency of the rate of profit to fall (with its subsequent restructurings), the urban processes of cities will always slowly change. Significantly, the direction and pace of urban change will also be affected by the actions, power, resources and organisation of stakeholders (such as the working class, non-government organisations, or trade and professional bodies).

In the long run, Marx expected that the internal pressures, contradictions and class struggle within the capitalist mode of production would lead to its eventual restructure and replacement by a democratic, accountable and effective mode of production which would meet the needs of people. It is to that mode of production we turn in the next section.

In summary, although Marx did not explicitly discuss the urban development process in societies structured by the capitalist mode of production, his comments on the urban development process in other modes of production can be used to develop a framework for analysing capitalist cities. The framework suggested here, based on the conflicted social relations between land, labour, capital and the state, provide a realistic basis for explaining and intervening in the urban processes which in capitalist societies structure the functions and size of cities, the growth or decline of cities, and the nature and location of human activities within cities.

Communist mode of production

Marx wrote relatively little about the communist mode of production and the type of society that could be structured on its economic foundations. Interestingly, the role of land (as both nature and as landed property) figure highly in his writings on communism.

Marx wrote his early works about communism at a time when, across Europe, there were high levels of poverty, unemployment and urban pollution; cities and population were in decline; and democratic institutions were under attack.[86] Widespread political conflict engulfed Europe, between those wishing to overthrow the old feudal-based governments and replace them with modern (capitalist) governments, and those wishing to maintain the status quo. Marx argued many of the actions to emancipate people had been limited merely to political change rather than full emancipation: 'It is not the *radical* revolution, not the *general human* emancipation which is a utopian dream for Germany, but rather the partial, the *merely* political revolution, the revolution which leaves the pillars of the house standing.'[87] True human emancipation, on the other hand, required political *and* economic freedom. A critique of the capitalist political economy was needed to identify strategies people could use to liberate themselves from the undemocratic strictures of the capitalist mode of production.

One problem of the capitalist mode of production raised in 'A Contribution to the Critique of Hegel's Philosophy of Right', 'On *The Jewish Question*' and *Economic and Philosophic Manuscripts of 1844*, is that the laws of capitalism turn workers into mere *objects* who are organised by capital to transform nature into other objects (commodities) which then confront the direct producer 'as *something alien*, as a *power independent* of the producer' and which are *estranged* from the direct producer (and appropriated by capital).[88] A second problem was the 'intrinsic connection between private property, greed, the separation of labour, capital and landed property; the connection of exchange and competition, of value and the devaluation of man, of monopoly and competition, etc. – the connection between this whole estrangement and the money system'.[89]

In other words, capitalist accumulation separated people from nature ('Man lives on nature ... with which he must remain in continuous interchange if he is not to die ... for man is a part of nature')[90] and 'estranged' people from each other.[91] Capitalist institutions, especially private property, controlled, enslaved or oppressed people: primogeniture, for example, was an institution where '[l]anded property always inherits, as it were, the first born of the house'.[92] Marx's point was that, in capitalism, people did not control private property: private property controlled the life opportunities of people. True human emancipation required the establishment of new non-destructive relations of production with nature, and the creation of political and economic practices and institutions under democratic control. What was needed were strategies to stop human beings from being objectified, alienated and estranged, or, in other words, strategies to bring about 'the emancipation of society from private property, etc., from servitude'.[93] There needed to be the 'negation of private property' to establish a new economy and society where there 'is the complete unity of man with nature'.[94]

Three stages of revolutionary change were needed to develop a communist society: to abolish private property; to abolish the state based on private property; and to develop a society where there would be the 'transcendence of *private property* as *human self-estrangement*' (emphasis in the original). These changes would overcome the destructive conflicts caused by the division of people from nature, and of people from each other: 'the *genuine* resolution of the conflict between man and nature and between man and man – the true resolution of the strife between existence and essence, between objectification and self-confirmation, between freedom and necessity, between the individual and the species'.[95]

In *The Communist Manifesto*, Marx and Engels called for the abolition of (private) property and the classes who defend private property: 'The distinguishing feature of communism is the abolition of bourgeois property.'[96] Five of the ten measures identified in the *Manifesto* as transition steps to bring about communism refer to land, three of which could be applied to urban land:

- Abolition of property in land and [the] application of all rents of land to public purposes
- Abolition of all rights of inheritance
- Extension of factories and instruments of production owned by the State; the bringing into cultivation of waste-lands, and the improvement of the soil generally in accordance with a common plan
- Equal liability of all to work. Establishment of industrial armies, especially for agriculture
- Combination of agriculture with manufacturing industries; gradual abolition of all the distinction between town and country by a more equable distribution of the populace over the country.

The Communist Manifesto recognised that a slow democratisation of the capitalist state was occurring to varying degrees around the world but that, at the same time, the capitalist economy was becoming increasingly despotic and less under the democratic control of people. For example: 'Political emancipation was, at the same time, the emancipation of civil society [the economy] from politics …'[97] Citizens may be winning a greater degree of political freedom in capitalism, but their economic lives continued to be tightly controlled by the private owners of property and by the laws of the capitalist mode of production.

Based on this critique of privately owned property, Marx and Engels developed a solution that aimed to supersede private rights over property (which divided people into groups of owners and non-owners and which gave property owners the power to control the lives and livelihood of the property-less). The alternative was to develop communities where people were no longer estranged (or alienated) from each other, property, the production of goods and services, their community or nature.[98] The communist mode of production made it possible for all people to have the resources and opportunities they need to flourish individually, to contribute to society, and to live in harmony with nature. Interestingly, many of these qualities of a communist society are those Marx identified as existing in the indigenous communities (discussed in Chapter 3) but with the significant difference that communist societies would be technologically advanced.

Community-owned property would replace capitalist, privately-owned

property and establish a mode of production based on cooperation and the production of goods with use-values that benefit individuals, families and the broader
community (rather than production for profit).[99] People would work in such a
way that working people would have democratic control over their working lives,
and, more generally, a new democratic mode of production would be established
which produced goods and services for the benefit of people and in ways that did
not exploit or subjugate direct producers for the private benefit of others.[100]

Small cooperatives and worker-run collectives would have an important role
to play in the transition to a communist mode of production. The cooperative
movement of the day was seen to be one of the transforming forces of capitalism. Its merit was to show, in practical ways, that it was possible to establish
associations of free and equal producers. With the ownership of land and the
instruments of production in the hands of urban, regional and national organisations of working people, it would be possible for these models of productive
enterprises to be expanded across the society to establish a communist mode of
production made up of 'one large and harmonious system of free and co-operative labour' managed by the producers themselves.[101]

The communist mode of production would allocate goods and services to
individuals, families and the broader community according to their needs (rather
than to those who could afford to buy them). For example, the allocation of the
total social product (a concept similar to gross domestic product) would include:
the provision of general consumption to meet the sustenance needs of all; funds
for the replacement of all means of production used up in production and for
investment to expand production; an insurance fund to provide against calami-
ties or other risks to production; funds to meet community needs (such as schools,
health services and public housing); funds to support those unable to work (such
as the elderly); and funds to cover the general costs of administration not belonging to production. In other words, the direct producers in a society would receive
exactly what they produced (less deductions for the maintenance and development of production, the reproduction of the population, the support of those
unable to contribute to production, and public administration). One of the roles
of the public administration agencies of the state would be to verify that workers
furnished particular amounts of labour and received an amount of consumption
goods according to their individual and family needs.[102]

Marx made a significant change in his last writings on communism. The early
writings of Marx suggested the existence of capitalism was necessary for the
development of a communist society. A Russian radical, Vera Zasulich, asked
Marx in 1881 whether this was the only route to communism. She argued Russia's
economy was based on rural communes which also were 'capable of developing
in a socialist direction, that is, gradually organising its production and distribution on a collectivist basis'.[103] Marx wrote five drafts of a reply to Zasulich, eventually concluding capitalism was not the only route to communism, and that it

was possible to build a communist mode of production based on the democratic, worker-controlled social relations of communes:

> To save the Russian commune, there must be a Russian Revolution ... If the revolution takes place in time, if it concentrates all its forces ... to ensure the unfettered rise of the rural commune, the latter will soon develop as a regenerating element of Russian society and an element of superiority over the countries enslaved by the capitalist regime.[104]

In summary, one important characteristic of the communist mode of production as conceived of by Marx was its policies on production (production to be placed under democratic control, production to occur without the exploitation of labour, and production to meet the needs of people and the maintenance of the society rather than the production of profit). Second, communism would be based on new relations between people and nature, a relation that in capitalism had resulted in pollution, the unsustainable use of natural resources, and the destruction of nature of which, existentially and economically, people are a part. In the few writings Marx made about communist societies, no mention was made of the role and structure of cities in the communist mode of production.

Conclusion

This chapter has documented Marx's comments about urban landed property, rent and cities as they occur in the feudal, capitalist and communist modes of production. These modes of production developed in Europe from land or geography-based *Gesellschaft* societies (unlike the indigenous, ancient and Asiatic modes of production that developed from kin-based *Gemeinschaft* communities).

The feudal economy and society were structured by a complex network of social relations of contradictory interdependencies. These included relations of land control in return for fealty between the monarch and royal vassals (vassalage), of land use in return for rent between landlords and peasants (manorialism), and of land control in return for fealty and/or rent between the monarch and city governments. Within the limits of these 'external' social relations, urban development in feudal times was often influenced 'internally' by the development of urban industrialists, tradespeople and their guilds with their control over land, tools and equipment, and the training, wages and working conditions of skilled labour (journeymen and apprentices).

Most of Marx's writings concern the origins, operations, growth and crises of the capitalist mode of production. For the first time, urban development processes are primarily driven by the owners of capital (and not landed property). However, urban landed property continued to play an important role in urban development through the power of landownership to control the use of land (until payment of rent is made) and through the organisation of the urban

Table 4.2 Historical modes of production, landed property and rent

Mode of production	Main economic use of land	Form of land tenure (property rights)	Main economic relations	Producer of the unpaid surplus	Form of rent	Main role of cities
Indigenous	Hunting and gathering, pastoralism	Indigenous (customary)	People–Nature	Nil	Nil	Almost no cities in this mode of production
Ancient	Rural agriculture	Private (rural land) and public (city-state)	City state–peasant	Slaves	Labour, goods	City-states defend community territory
Asiatic	Rural agriculture	State	Emperor–peasant	Peasants	Labour, goods and/ or money	Provincial cities administer, tax and provide regional infrastructure
Feudal	Rural agriculture	Feudal and commons	Landlord–tenant	Serfs, farm labourers	Labour, goods and/ or money	Municipal cities are artisanal, trade and religious centres
Capitalist	Lease land for capitalist production in return for rent; profit from providing housing for workers	Private	Capitalist–worker and landlord–capitalist	Industrial workers	Differential rent; Absolute rent	Metropolises, global cities and megacities are centres of production, consumption and capital accumulation
Communist	Urban production and consumption	Communal	People-People; and People-Nature	Nil (all surplus labour is paid for)	Nil	Metropolises, global cities and megacities are centres of production, consumption and human development

Sources: Summary of Marx's writings discussed in Chapters 3 and 4

landed property class which acts to defend its economic interests and, in the right circumstances, to promote its economic interests and legitimacy as a fraction of the ruling class.

Although Marx wrote very little about the communist mode of production, two issues which continually recurred concerned production and land (nature). In the communist mode of production, the division of working people from the ownership and management of production would be overcome so that production would be democratically controlled and would be organised for the needs of people and the maintenance of society (not for profit). Similarly, the division of people from nature (which in capitalism was destroying nature in the incessant search for profit) would be resolved so that people, existentially and economically, would be once again live in a sustainable and healthy relation with nature. Marx made no comments about the characteristics of cities in societies based on the communist mode of production.

Some of the most important characteristics of land, rent and cities in all six of Marx's modes of production are compared in Table 4.2. It reinforces that the same concepts, in different modes of production, take on different characteristics and need to be understood in their own context. There is no single economic law or mathematical model of the economy that can capture the diversity of political economics. When interpreting the table, it needs to be kept in mind that the dynamism inherent in the contradictory social relations of production and of landed property are not captured in a static table.

Finally, this chapter has noted that, in the capitalist mode of production, landed property is a barrier to capital accumulation, a capacity that makes it possible for landowners to appropriate rent from capitalists. Exactly how this occurs requires a detailed assessment of how rents arise in capitalism. This is the subject of the next chapter.

Notes

1. K. Marx and F. Engels, *Manifesto of the Communist Party*, *Marx/Engels Selected Works*, vol. I, Moscow, Progress Publishers, 1969, https://www.marxists.org/archive/marx/works/1848/communist-manifesto/ch01.htm

2. N. Bond, 'Ferdinand Tönnies' Appraisal of Karl Marx: Debts and Distance', *Journal of Classical Sociology*, vol. 13, no. 1, 2013, pp. 136–62.

3. K. Marx and F. Engels, *The German Ideology*, pt 1.A, Moscow, Progress Publishers, 1968, https://www.marxists.org/archive/marx/works/1845/german-ideology/ch01a.htm

4. K. Marx, *The Ethnological Notebooks of Karl Marx*, Assen, Van Gorcum & Co., 1974, https://www.marxists.org/archive/marx/works/1881/ethnographical-notebooks/notebooks.pdf

5. K. Marx, 'Forms Which Precede Capitalist Production', *Grundrisse*, ch. 9, London, Penguin Books in association with *New Left Review*, 1973, https://www.marxists.org/archive/marx/works/1857/grundrisse/ch09.htm

6. Marx, *Ethnological Notebooks*.
7. Ibid.
8. Marx, 'Forms Which Precede Capitalist Production', *Grundrisse*, ch. 9, https://www.marxists.org/archive/marx/works/1857/grundrisse/ch09.htm
9. Ibid.
10. Ibid.
11. Marx and Engels, *The German Ideology*, pt 1.A, https://www.marxists.org/archive/marx/works/1845/german-ideology/ch01a.htm
12. M. Bloch, *Feudal Society*, London, Routledge, 2014.
13. K. Marx, 'Revolutionary Spain', *New-York Daily Tribune*, 20 Nov. 1854, https://www.marxists.org/archive/marx/works/1854/revolutionary-spain/ch06.htm
14. J. R. Major, '"Bastard Feudalism" and the Kiss: Changing Social Mores in Late Medieval and Early Modern France', *Journal of Interdisciplinary History*, vol. 17, no. 3, 1987, pp. 509–35.
15. A. Jones, 'The Rise and Fall of the Manorial System: A Critical Comment', *Journal of Economic History*, vol. 32, no. 4, 1972, pp. 938–44.
16. For example, S. Reynolds, *Fiefs and Vassals: The Medieval Evidence Reinterpreted*, Oxford, Oxford University Press, 1996, and T. Byres and H. Mukhia, *Feudalism and non-European Societies*, Bristol, Stonebridge Press, 1985.
17. R. S. Sharma, *Indian Feudalism*, 3rd edn, Delhi, Macmillan, 2005.
18. H. J. Berman, *Law and Revolution*, Cambridge, MA, Harvard University Press, 1983, p. 237.
19. K. Marx, *Capital*, vol. III, ch. 47, https://www.marxists.org/archive/marx/works/1894-c3/ch47.htm
20. Ibid.
21. An option not discussed by Marx is that the peasant farmer could also employ other labourers to work the fields, requiring them to pay labour-rent to the peasant farmer.
22. Marx, *Capital*, vol. III, ch. 47, https://www.marxists.org/archive/marx/works/1894-c3/ch47.htm
23. H. J. Berman, *Law and Revolution: The Formation of the Western Legal Tradition*, Cambridge, MA, Harvard University Press, 1983.
24. Marx and Engels, *The German Ideology*, pt 1.A, https://www.marxists.org/archive/marx/works/1845/german-ideology/ch01a.htm
25. Journeymen were skilled and experienced tradespeople or artisans who had completed their apprenticeship but who did not yet have approval from the guild to be self-employed or to employ others. They were employees who had a right to charge a fee for each day's work: 'journey' is derived from *journée*, meaning 'day'.
26. R. J. Barendse, 'The Feudal Mutation: Military and Economic Transformations of the Ethnosphere in the Tenth to Thirteenth Centuries', *Journal of World History*, vol. 14, no. 4, 2003, pp. 503–29.
27. Marx and Engels, *The German Ideology*, pt 1.D, https://www.marxists.org/archive/marx/works/1845/german-ideology/ch01d.htm
28. Ibid.
29. K. Marx, *Capital*, vol. I, ch. 26, Moscow, Progress Publishers, 1887, https://www.marxists.org/archive/marx/works/1867-c1/ch26.htm
30. Ibid., vol. I, ch. 31, https://www.marxists.org/archive/marx/works/1867-c1/ch31.htm

31. Ibid., vol. I, ch. 33, Moscow, Progress Publishers, 1887, https://www.marxists.org/archive/marx/works/1867-c1/ch33.htm

32. The classic work by E. P. Thompson, *The Making of the English Working Class*, Harmondsworth, Penguin Books, 1968, gives multiple examples of how this process occurred in England.

33. F. Fukuyama, 'The End of History?', *The National Interest*, no. 16, Summer 1989, pp. 3–18.

34. Ibid.

35. This section on the metamorphoses of capital and their circuits is primarily based on *Capital*, vol. II (https://www.marxists.org/archive/marx/works/1885-c2/index.htm), as well as on the process of capitalist production as a whole discussed in volume III of *Capital* (https://www.marxists.org/archive/marx/works/1894-c3/index.htm). Ben Fine and Alfredo Saad-Filho's *Marx's Capital* provides an excellent summary of these volumes.

36. Marx, *Grundrisse*, ch. 10, https://www.marxists.org/archive/marx/works/1857/grundrisse/ch10.htm

37. K. Marx, *Theories of Surplus Value*, ch. 17, Moscow, Progress Publishers, 1969, https://www.marxists.org/archive/marx/works/1863/theories-surplus-value/ch17.htm

38. K. Marx, *Capital*, vol. III, ch. 13, https://www.marxists.org/archive/marx/works/1894-c3/ch13.htm

39. S. Clarke, 'The Marxist Theory of Overaccumulation and Crisis', *Science & Society*, vol. 54, no. 4, Winter 1990–1, pp. 442–67.

40. Marx, *Capital*, vol. III, ch. 14, https://www.marxists.org/archive/marx/works/1894-c3/ch14.htm

41. P. Bell and H. Cleaver, 'Marx's Theory of Crisis as a Theory of Class Struggle', *Research in Political Economy*, vol. 5, 1982, pp. 189–261.

42. Marx, *Capital*, vol. III, ch. 51, https://www.marxists.org/archive/marx/works/1894-c3/ch51.htm

43. K. Marx, 'Marx-Zasulich Correspondence', in T. Shanin (ed.), *Late Marx and the Russian Road: Marx and the 'Peripheries of Capitalism'*, New York, Monthly Review Press, 1983, https://www.marxists.org/archive/marx/works/1881/zasulich/index.htm

44. Marx, *Capital*, vol. I, ch. 27, https://www.marxists.org/archive/marx/works/1867-c1/ch27.htm

45. Marx, 'The Chapter on Capital (cont.)', *Grundrisse*, ch. 5, https://www.marxists.org/archive/marx/works/1857/grundrisse/ch05.htm

46. Marx, *Capital*, vol. I, ch. 27, https://www.marxists.org/archive/marx/works/1867-c1/ch27.htm#16a

47. Marx, *Capital*, vol. III, ch. 46, https://www.marxists.org/archive/marx/works/1894-c3/ch46.htm

48. Quoted in ibid.

49. Ibid.

50. Marx, *Capital*, vol. I, ch. 1, https://www.marxists.org/archive/marx/works/1867-c1/ch01.htm

51. Marx, *Capital*, vol. III., ch. 52, https://www.marxists.org/archive/marx/works/1894-c3/ch52.htm

52. K. Marx, *The Poverty of Philosophy*, Moscow, Progress Publishers, 1955, https://www.marxists.org/archive/marx/works/1847/poverty-philosophy/ch02e.htm

53. Marx, *Capital*, vol. I, ch. 25, https://www.marxists.org/archive/marx/works/1867-c1/ch25.htm

54. K. Marx, *The Eighteenth Brumaire of Louis Bonaparte*, ch. 7, Marx/Engels Internet Archive, 1995, https://www.marxists.org/archive/marx/works/1852/18th-brumaire/ch07.htm

55. Ibid., ch. 1, https://www.marxists.org/archive/marx/works/1852/18th-brumaire/ch01.htm

56. Marx and Engels, 'Manifesto of the Communist Party', https://www.marxists.org/archive/marx/works/1848/communist-manifesto/ch01.htm

57. Marx, *Theories of Surplus Value*, ch. 2, https://www.marxists.org/archive/marx/works/1863/theories-surplus-value/ch02.htm

58. Marx, *The Eighteenth Brumaire of Louis Bonaparte*, ch. 3, https://www.marxists.org/archive/marx/works/1852/18th-brumaire/ch03.htm

59. For example, '"Causes That Were Lost"? Fifty Years of E. P. Thompson's *The Making of the English Working Class* as Contemporary History', special issue of *Contemporary British History*, vol. 28, no. 4, 2014, reviews the 1970s clash between E. P. Thompson's humanist and historical approach to class and Louis Althusser's structural view of class.

60. Marx, *Capital*, vol. I, ch. 10, https://www.marxists.org/archive/marx/works/1867-c1/ch10.htm

61. Unlike interest-bearing money (capital) that is invested in capitalist production and the creation of unpaid surplus labour, usury is more associated with borrowing that 'takes place as a result of individual need, as at the pawnshop; where money is borrowed by wealthy spendthrifts for the purpose of squandering; or where the producer is a non-capitalist producer, such as a small farmer or craftsman, who is thus still, as the immediate producer, the owner of his own means of production; finally where the capitalist producer himself operates on such a small scale that he resembles those self-employed producers' (Marx, *Capital*, vol III, ch. 3, https://www.marxists.org/archive/marx/works/1894-c3/ch36.htm).

62. For example, Financial Crisis Inquiry Commission, *The Financial Crisis Inquiry Report: Final Report of the National Commission on the Causes of the Financial and Economic Crisis in the United States*, Washington, DC, US Government Printing Office, 2011, https://www.govinfo.gov/content/pkg/GPO-FCIC/pdf/GPO-FCIC.pdf.=

63. The Financial Crisis Inquiry Commission, *The Financial Crisis Inquiry Report*, p. 5.

64. M.A. Kose, N. Sugawara and M. E. Terrones, *Global Recessions: Policy Research Working Paper 9172*, Washington, DC, World Bank, 2020, https://documents1.worldbank.org/curated/en/185391583249079464/pdf/Global-Recessions.pdf

65. H. Ticktin (ed.), *Marxism and the Global Financial Crisis*, London, Routledge, 2013, p. 80.

66. For example, F. H. Taques, H. P. B. De Souza and D. A. Alencar, 'The 2007–08 Financial Crisis from a Marxist View', *Modern Economy*, no. 8, 2017, pp. 1069–81; and J. Rasmus, 'The Deepening Global Financial Crisis: From Minsky to Marx and Beyond', *Critique*, vol. 36, no. 1, 2008, pp. 5–29.

67. J. He, J. Qian and P. E. Strahan, 'Credit Ratings and the Evolution of the Mortgage-Backed Securities Market', *American Economic Review*, vol. 101, no. 3, 2011, pp. 131–5.

68. United Nations Human Rights Commission, 'Financialization of Housing' https://www.ohchr.org/EN/Issues/Housing/Pages/FinancializationHousing.aspx

69. A. Löscher, 'Financialisation and Development: A Case Study of Ethiopia', *Qualitative Research in Financial Markets*, vol. 11, no. 2, 2019, pp. 138–96.

70. J. Clapp, 'Land and Financialization: Role of International Financial Actors in Land Deals in Africa' [online video], *Exploring Economics*, Heidelberg, Germany, 2013, https://www.exploring-economics.org/en/discover/land-and-financialization-role-of-international/

71. B. P. Reydon and V. B. Fernandes, Financialization, Land Prices and Land Grab: A Study Based on the Brazilian Reality', *Economia e Sociedade*, vol. 26, Dec. 2017, n.p. https://www.scielo.br/j/ecos/a/tvNZNZT4CXk9zpLw7wswLcH/?lang=en

72. T. Ferrando, 'The Financialization of Land and Agriculture: Mechanisms, Implications and Responses', ID 2916112, SSRN Scholarly Paper, Rochester, NY, Social Science Research Network, 2017, https://papers.ssrn.com/abstract=2916112

73. M. Hudson, 'From Marx to Goldman Sachs: The Fictions of Fictitious Capital, and the Financialization of Industry', *Critique*, vol. 38, 2010, pp. 419–44.

74. C. Durand, *Fictitious Capital: How Finance is Appropriating our Future*, London, Verso, 2017.

75. Marx, *Capital*, vol. III, ch. 29, New York, International Publishers, 1959, https://www.marxists.org/archive/marx/works/1894-c3/ch29.htm

76. Ibid.

77. A rare example is 'The demand for building sites raises the value of land as space and foundation, while thereby the demand for elements of the terrestrial body serving as building material grows simultaneously' (Marx , *Capital*, vol. III, ch. 3, https://www.marxists.org/archive/marx/works/1894-c3/ch46.htm#r40).

78. H. Lefebvre, *The Production of Space*, Hoboken, NJ, Wiley-Blackwell, 1991.

79. Ibid.; D. Harvey, *The Limits to Capital*, Oxford, Basil Blackwell, 1982; C. Cockburn, *Local State: Management of Cities and People*, London, Pluto Press, 1977; D. Massey, *Spatial Divisions of Labour: Social Structures and the Geography of Production*, 2nd edn, New York, Routledge, 1995; F. J. B. Stilwell, *Economic Crisis, Cities and Regions: Analysis of Urban and Regional Problems in Australia*, Oxford, Pergamon Press, 1980.

80. D. Harvey, 'Reflections on an Academic Life', *Human Geography*, vol. 15, no. 1, 2021, pp. 14–24.

81. F. Belussi and K. Caldari, 'At the Origin of the Industrial District: Alfred Marshall and the Cambridge School', *Cambridge Journal of Economics*, vol. 33, no. 2, 2009, pp. 353–5.

82. D. Harvey, 'The Social Construction of Space and Time: A Relational Theory', *Geographical Review of Japan*, Ser. B, vol. 67, no. 2, 1994, pp. 126–35.

83. D. Harvey, 'Space as a Key Word', Paper for Marx and Philosophy Conference, London, Institute of Education, 29 May 2004, http://frontdeskapparatus.com/files/harvey2004.pdf

84. Ibid.

85. D. Harvey, 'The Urbanisation of Capitalism', *Actuel Marx*, vol. 35, no. 1, 2004, pp. 41–70.

86. K. Marx, *Communism and the Augsburg* Allgemeine Zeitung, Marx/Engels Internet Archive, n.d., https://www.marxists.org/archive/marx/works/1842/10/16.htm

87. K. Marx, *A Contribution to the Critique of Hegel's Philosophy of Right*, Marx/Engels Internet Archive, n.d., https://www.marxists.org/archive/marx/works/1843/critique-hpr/intro.htm

88. K. Marx, *Economic and Philosophic Manuscripts of 1844*, Moscow, Progress Publishers, 1959, https://www.marxists.org/archive/marx/works/1844/epm/1st.htm

89. Ibid.

90. Ibid.

91. Ibid.
92. K. Marx, *Critique of Hegel's Philosophy of Right*, s. 307, ed. J. O'Malley, Cambridge, Cambridge University Press, 1970, https://www.marxists.org/archive/marx/works/1843/critique-hpr/ch05.htm
93. K. Marx, 'Estranged Labour', *Economic and Philosophic Manuscripts of 1844*, Moscow, Progress Publishers, 1959, https://www.marxists.org/archive/marx/works/1844/manuscripts/labour.htm
94. K. Marx, 'Private Property and Communism', *Economic and Philosophic Manuscripts of 1844*, Moscow, Progress Publishers, 1959, https://www.marxists.org/archive/marx/works/1844/manuscripts/comm.htm
95. Ibid.
96. K. Marx and F. Engels, *The Manifesto of the Communist Party*, pt II, in *Marx/Engels Selected Works*, vol. I, Moscow, Progress Publishers, 1969, https://www.marxists.org/archive/marx/works/1848/communist-manifesto/ch02.htm
97. K. Marx, *On the Jewish Question*, Marx/Engels Internet Archive, 2000, https://www.marxists.org/archive/marx/works/1844/jewish-question/
98. Marx, 'Estranged Labour'.
99. K. Marx, 'The Second Draft' (of Marx's reply to a letter from Vera Zasulich), in T. Shanin. (ed.), *Late Marx and the Russian Road: Marx and the 'Peripheries of Capitalism'*, New York, Monthly Review Press, 1983, https://www.marxists.org/archive/marx/works/1881/zasulich/draft-2.htm
100. Marx and Engels, *The Manifesto of the Communist Party*, pt II, https://www.marxists.org/archive/marx/works/1848/communist-manifesto/ch02.htm
101. K. Marx, 'Instructions for the Delegates of the Provisional General Council', pt 5, *The International Courier*, nos. 6/7, 20 Feb. 1867 and nos. 8/10, 13 Mar. 1867, London, International Workingmen's Association, 1867, https://www.marxists.org/archive/marx/works/1866/08/instructions.htm
102. K. Marx, 'Critique of the Gotha Programme', in *Marx/Engels Selected Works*, vol. III, Moscow, Progress Publishers, 1970, https://www.marxists.org/archive/marx/works/1875/gotha/ch01.htm
103. V. Zasulich, 'Letter to Karl Marx', in T. Shanin (ed.), *Late Marx and the Russian Road: Marx and the 'Peripheries of Capitalism'*, New York, Monthly Review Press, 1983, https://www.marxists.org/archive/marx/works/1881/zasulich/zasulich.htm
104. K. Marx, 'The First Draft' (of Marx's reply to a letter from Vera Zasulich), in Shanin (ed.), *Late Marx and the Russian Road: Marx and the 'Peripheries of Capitalism'*, https://www.marxists.org/archive/marx/works/1881/zasulich/draft-1.htm

CHAPTER 5

Capitalist Rents

Just as the operating capitalist pumps surplus-labour, and thereby surplus value and surplus-product in the form of profit, out of the labourer, so the landlord in turn pumps a portion of this surplus-value, or surplus-product, out of the capitalist in the form of rent …[1]

Introduction

Rent is central to many current crises in capitalist cities.

The power of rent is often associated with a variety of social issues such as the long-term rises in property prices,[2] the uneven development of housing prices in cities,[3] and restructuring of publicly funded seniors' care in Canada.[4] The price of a house or other real estate property is directly affected by rent because property prices are essentially capitalised rent. For residential tenants, government initiatives such as capital gains taxes, negative gearing policies and investment incentives can distort the rental housing market by causing 'more high-value, high-rent stock being brought into the rental sector, and low-cost, low-rent properties dropping out',[5] exacerbating homelessness. The authority of rent also controls commercial tenants, as was shown during the COVID-19 pandemic in the early 2020s, when businesses around the world found they were obliged by the terms of their lease to pay rent even if they had no income (due to lockdowns).[6]

Marx proposed there are three main forms of rent in capitalism. Absolute rent determines whether capital will invest on land at all. There are two forms of differential rent which, in different ways, influence the extent to which capital will invest in city centres or in suburban regions.

However, Marx also recognised rent caused a theoretical problem for his theory of value. Capitalist rent, as with other modes of production, is always a portion of the surplus labour provided by workers. However, rent is not a portion of the profit captured by capitalists but additional to profit: rent 'is always a surplus over and above profit'.[7] The problem then arises: if capitalists appropriate all the unpaid surplus value as their profit, what is the source of the additional surplus value that comprises rent?

This chapter addresses these issues. It analyses the economic mechanisms whereby landed property captures differential rent (DR) and absolute rent (AR) from capital. It will show that DR arises when land interferes in the process that establishes the market value of a commodity; and AR arises when land intervenes in the process that establishes the price of production for a commodity. The magnitude of rent that can be captured from capital by landed property, however, is not limitless; the very nature of the rent appropriation process puts limits on how much can be captured.

To understand how DR and AR arise and drive crises in contemporary capitalist cities, therefore, it is necessary to delve deep into the processes of how the market value of a commodity is determined, and how the price of production of a commodity is established. First we consider the case of how market value is formed, thus making it possible for landowners to extract DR from capitalists.

Market value

As noted in Chapter 2, capitalism consists of a continuous, relentless and crisis-ridden cycle of capital accumulation. In general terms, an amount of capital (of value M) is invested to buy commodities (with an equivalent value, C); the commodities are then transformed by labour in production (P) where they gain an enhanced value (C') arising from the unpaid surplus value (profit) provided by workers; and the new commodities with their enhanced value (C') are then sold for an equivalent amount of value (M'). As a result, the capitalist realises a larger magnitude of value (M') than was originally invested (M). The general formula for this cycle of investment, production and realisation of capital is summarised as:

$$M - C \dots P \dots C' - M'$$

Within this general formula are numerous detailed economic processes. To solve the problem of rent, of where surplus value for rent originates when all surplus value (created by labour) is captured as profit by capital, it is necessary to focus on the way commodities are realised for money; that is, what occurs in detail in the C' — M' phase of the overall process for the production and realisation of capital.

The first process which is necessary for the creation of rent, differential rent (DR), is the establishment of the market value of a commodity.

Consider any industry sector where multiple capitalists are producing the same commodity in competition with each other. Each capitalist produces a commodity which embodies a particular quantity of value. The value embedded in commodity is made up of the value of the physical commodities used up to produce the commodity (called constant capital, c_i); the value of the employees' labour used up to transform the materials into the new commodity and which is paid for with a wage (called variable capital, v_i); plus the value provided by labour that was not paid for (surplus value, s_i). The value of each new individual commodity, therefore, is $(c_i + v_i + s_i)$.

No capitalist in this industry sector is the same. Each capitalist uses a different combination of physical commodities and technologies (c) and different magnitudes of labour-time (v) and extracts different amounts of unpaid surplus value (s) from its workers. As a result, the commodities made by each capitalist have different magnitudes of value embodied in them. For example, Capitalist A may produce a commodity that has a value of $(c_a + v_a + s_a)$ while Capitalist B, producing the same commodity, may have a commodity that has a value of $(c_b + v_b + s_b)$, and so on.

Having produced their commodities, the capitalists within each industry then have to realise the value of these individual commodities $(c_i + v_i + s_i)$ as money. To do so, each capitalist puts their commodities into the market to sell. It is here in this competitive marketplace, with its many buyers and sellers, that the market value of the commodity is established.

Our capitalists present their commodities to the market for sale. As happens in all markets, capitalists who ask too high a price for their commodities will not sell them all; and capitalists who ask too low a price will sell them all but at the risk of not making as large a profit as is possible. Through this market bidding and correction process, an agreed market price (or, in value terms, an agreed market value) is established for each particular commodity. This market value is 'the average value of commodities produced in a single sphere [industry sector]' or, more accurately, 'the individual value of the commodities produced under average conditions of their respective sphere and forming the bulk of the products of that sphere'.[8] The market value of this particular commodity, established by the average conditions of production used to produce the commodities, is symbolised as $(c_m + v_m + s_m)$ to distinguish it from the value of the individual commodities $(c_i + v_i + s_i)$ produced by each capitalist in the industry.

Conceptually, the 'market value' of a commodity is similar to the contemporary concept of the Wholesale Price Index, a measure of the average selling price of a representative basket of wholesale goods. This is a common measure of the wholesale price of each commodity which is used by many contemporary bureaux of statistics around the world.

For example, consider an industry sector where two capitalists, Capitalist A and Capitalist B, produce the same commodity. Capitalist A produces commodities very efficiently (using labour-saving technologies that require far less labour) or more productively (where a set amount of capital and labour inputs produced a larger-than-industry-average number of commodities). In this case, Capitalist A discovers their commodities, which have an *individual* value of $(c_a + v_a + s_a)$, is lower than the industry-average *market* value that this commodity sells for $(c_m + v_m + s_m)$. That is, symbolically, $(c_m + v_m + s_m) > (c_a + v_a + s_a)$. As a result, Capitalist A sells the commodities in the market at the going market value $(c_m + v_m + s_m)$, even though it cost only $(c_a + v_a + s_a)$ to produce. The outcome of the sale is that Capitalist A realises the surplus value (s_a) they captured in production plus an *extra* amount of surplus value (symbolised as $(c_m + v_m + s_m) - (c_a + v_a + s_a)$). Marx calls this additional amount of surplus value, captured from the sale of the commodity in the market, the 'surplus of surplus value' or 'surplus profit'.

On the other hand, Capitalist B produces the same commodity in a relatively inefficient or less productive way. In this case, when Capitalist B sells their commodities in the market at the average, market-determined value for the commodity, they lose value. Capitalist B's commodities, which have an *individual* value of $(c_b + v_b + s_b)$, is higher than the industry-average *market* value that the commodity sells for $(c_m + v_m + s_m)$. Symbolically, $(c_b + v_b + s_b) > (c_m + v_m + s_m)$. As a result, when Capitalist B sells their commodities at the going market value, Capitalist B loses value. Depending on how inefficient or how unproductive is Capitalist B's production process, when Capitalist B sells their commodity in the market, they may lose all their profit (s_b) and only receive an amount of money to pay for the cost of the commodities $(c_b + v_b)$ used up in production. In a worst-case scenario, Capitalist B will receive payment for their commodities $(c_m + v_m + s_m)$ which does not even cover their cost to produce those commodities $(c_b + v_b + s_b)$ and they will go into debt or bankruptcy.

In this simple industry sector, with Capitalist A and Capitalist B making the same commodity in different ways, the average, market-determined selling price for the commodity (the market value) produces a result that is similar to a zero-sum game, where the magnitude of Capitalist B's loss of value equals the magnitude of Capitalists A's value gain.

For clarity, it is worth briefly considering a different example expressed in monetary terms. Consider an industry where Capitalist A and Capitalist B make the same number of the same commodities, using the same constant capital and exploit their workers at the same rate (they both make a profit of 100 per cent of the cost of their workforce). The more efficient and productive Capitalist A uses relatively little labour to produce each commodity at a cost of, say, $100 per commodity (made up of $40 + $30 + $30 for commodities, wages and profit, respectively). The less efficient and less productive Capitalist B uses relatively more labour to produce the same commodity but at a cost of, say, $130 (made up of $40 + $45 + $45 for commodities, wages and profit, respectively). Both firms enter the market to sell their commodities and discover the commodity sells at the average market price of $115. As a result, efficient Capitalist A makes a profit in production of $30 and an additional *surplus* profit of $15 in the market (because the commodity it made for $100 is sold at the market value of $115). As a result, efficient Capitalist A makes a total profit of $45 per commodity. On the other hand, the inefficient Capitalist B, which produced the same commodities but at a cost of $130, finds their commodities sell in the market at the going market price of $115, incurring a loss of $15 per commodity. Capitalist B's loss of $15 per commodity is Capitalist A's gain of $15 per commodity. For this industry sector as a whole, Capitalist A will continue to produce successfully, while Capitalist B will be forced to modernise their technology, reduce labour costs, change work practices and take other actions so it can compete against the more efficient Capitalist A.

With this explanation of the process which establishes market value and makes it possible for more efficient firms to capture surplus profit, it is now possible to explain the source of the differential rent (DR). To foreshadow Marx's argument, it is the surplus profit captured by the efficient firms which is the value that is potentially available to be appropriated by landowners as differential rent.

Differential rent I

There are two types of differential rent (DR). The first, differential rent I (DR I), arises when *equal amounts of capital* are invested on *different types of lands* (lands with different locations, orientation, terrain or other natural features that are attractive to capital and are not made by labour). Differential rent II (DR II) arises when *different amounts of capital* are invested on *equal lands*. In both cases, differential rent arises because the intervention of landed property in production changes how *market value* is established. This section considers DR I, and the next, DR II.

In all modes of production, an investment on land with the best situation will be more productive than an equal investment on the same size of land in a poorly situated site. Consider, again, a simple example using the industry sector with two capitalists, Capitalist A and Capitalist B. Assume both capitalists are equally efficient in their use of capital and labour: the only difference is that Capitalist A is located on the best-situated site (e.g. housing is being built on terrain that is flat) while Capitalist B is located on the worst-situated site (housing is being built on terrain with a strong incline).

As noted above, the market value for a commodity is established by the commodities produced under *average conditions* and *forming the bulk of the products* of an industry. In this present example, Capitalist A and B have the same materials, technology, labour force and rate of profit: the only difference is Capitalist A is situated on the best land for production and Capitalist B is situated on the worst land for production. In this case, it is not *average conditions* that establish the market value for the commodity but the *worst land* establishes the market value and therefore determines how much surplus profit the capitalists on the better located land will be able to capture.

Why does the worst land determine the market value of commodities? In non-land-based industries, market value is at first determined by the differences between the capitalist firms within the sector, but over time, competitive pressures over the short to medium term will force efficiencies within each firm in the industry sector and force the least efficient capitals to become more efficient and eventually all firms within the sector produce commodities at the same market price. On the other hand, with land-based industry sectors, competitive pressure cannot change the features of land; there will be a permanent advantage to capital investing on the best land, and a permanent disadvantage to capital investing on the worst land. As a result, the worst land – in this case, the sloping land – which reduces the productivity of the capital invested on the land establishes the market value of commodities. When Capitalist A and Capitalist B sell their commodities in the market, the value of the commodities produced by Capitalist B on the worst land establishes the market value for those commodities.

Differential rent (DR I) arises from the difference between the value of the commodities produced on the worst land compared with the value of the commodities produced on the best land. Consider a more complex (and realistic) example where there are four equal sites of urban land (with the same size, terrain and so on) except for one difference: their location. The first site, Site A, has the best location for a firm within its industry (it is located in the centre of its market in the central business district, CBD); the second site, Site B, is located in the middle suburbs; Site C is in an outer suburb, and Site D is located on the urban fringe, far from its markets in the CBD. In this example, the capitalists investing on the urban sites are specialised design offices producing CAD/CAM design and 3D printing but this example could equally apply to many other businesses such as those in construction; textiles and fashion which designs and produces clothing, footwear and jewellery; publishing (including digital publishing and websites); accommodation; and food production (such as restaurants and cafés).

The four capitalist firms invest on their sites an equal amount of constant capital (c, such as buildings, raw materials and technology) and variable capital (v, labour power), and all produce the same commodities with the same use value and with the same rate of profit.

The capitalist invested on Site A located in the CBD benefits from its location: there are urban agglomeration effects such as lower transport and communication costs, a large supply of skilled labour, close and cheap access to customers and suppliers, and higher knowledge spill over rates.[9] Site D, by comparison, located on the urban fringe, has limited access to a skilled workforce and its customers, has high transport and other costs, and does not benefit from knowledge spill overs. The middle suburban sites, Sites B and C, will have some benefits arising from their location, fewer than Site A but more than Site D. As a result, although all sites are equal in terms of the quantities of capital invested on them, the firm on the CBD land is more productive, producing more commodities for the same capital inputs than Sites B and C, with Site D being the least productive.

When the commodities are sold on the market by the four firms, the market value for the commodity is established. Ordinarily, if there had been no intervention by landed property, the market value would be the value set by the average conditions of production for the bulk of the commodities. However, with the intervention of a natural feature of land, 'the worst soil, i.e., which yields no rent, is always the one regulating the market-price',[10] or, in other words, the 'market-price is regulated … by the capital invested in the worst soil'.[11]

Returning to our example of the four sites, Table 5.1 shows the four firms mobilise an equal magnitude of capital ($c + v + s = 60$) but on different sites. Site A, on the best-located land, is able to use its capital to produce four commodities. On the other hand, Site D, the worst-located site, uses an equal amount of capital but it can produce only one commodity. In the suburban sites, the better-situated Site B, uses an equal amount of capital to produce three commodities and the less well-located Site C uses its equal amount of capital to produce two commodities. (Note: each number of commodities can be thought of as dozens, scores, hundreds, thousands or some other multiple of the number of commodities.) In other words, the capitals invested on the more advantageous sites are more productive and therefore capture more surplus profit, whilst the capital invested on the worst land, which sets the market value, captures no surplus profit. It is this surplus profit, which capitalists have captured because of the features of the land where they are located, that landed property then demands as rent while the capitals invested on the less advantageous sites are less productive.

Table 5.1 shows numerically what happens when the commodities are sold in the market. Site D, the worst-located site, produces one commodity with a value of 60; and this value sets the going rate, the market value, that is used to sell all the commodities. Site D, therefore, which produced one commodity with a value of 60, sells it at the market value of 60 and, by doing so, covers the cost of production ($c + v$ plus a surplus value, s) but does not create any 'surplus of surplus value' or 'surplus profit'. On the other hand, Site A sells its four commodities at the going market value (of 60) with the result that it earns a revenue of 240; and given that the value of the capital it invested was 60, the capital on Site A captures a surplus profit of 180. Similar calculations apply to the capitals on Sites B and C, which generate a surplus profit of 120 and 60, respectively. As Table 5.1 shows, the landowner of site A can potentially capture all the surplus profit of 180, with the differential rent paid to the landowners of sites B, C and D being 120, 60 and 0, respectively.

	Capital ($c + v + s$)	Product	Value (capital per product)	Market value (per product)	Revenue (Products × Market value)	Surplus profit (Revenue – Capital)	DR I
Site D (Worst)	60	1	60	60	60	0	0
Site C	60	2	30	60	120	60	60
Site B	60	3	20	60	180	120	120
Site A (Best)	60	4	15	60	240	180	180

Table 5.1 DR I: equal capitals invested on different lands

This example assumes, for the sake of simplicity, that there is demand for all the commodities supplied, and there are no barriers to the competitive operation of the market, with the exception of that caused by the location of the land. Similarly, although this example assumes the distinguishing natural feature of the urban sites is their location, the same results would be achieved even if the land was affected by other natural features which advantage, or disadvantage, the capital invested on them: for example, the orientation of the sites towards or away from the sun (which would affect, for example, the productivity of the capitals invested in the production of solar energy, gardening or urban farming), or the slope of the site's terrain (which would affect, for example, the productivity of the capitals invested in building construction).

This example of equal capital invested on different lands explains two essential features of differential rent. First, differential rent (and the surplus profit which is its basis) does not appear magically in the economy from nowhere: it emerges from the process that establishes the market value at which commodities are sold. Specifically, the potential for differential rent arises from the 'surplus of surplus value' or 'surplus profit' that is captured by capitalists who have greater productivity because of the advantageous natural features of the land. Second, the owner of land, as always, will demand a tribute, a rent, from the capitalist for the lease of the site. However, there are clear limits on what can be captured as differential rent. Marx's analysis of DR I shows there is always a *maximum limit* on the amount of value that can be captured as DR I which is determined by the magnitude of surplus profit that is appropriated by the capitalist. Similarly, the potential maximum rent that can be captured by landlords varies from site to site depending on the extent to which the features of the land facilitate or hinder the production of surplus profit.

In practice, does the landowner automatically capture all of the capitalist's surplus profit, or only some of the surplus profit? Economics cannot predict the outcome of the struggle within the social relation between each landowner and capitalist. Within the limits set by the economic processes, how much surplus profit the landowner captures depends on historically specific contextual factors such as the power differential in the social relation between the landowner and the capitalist, the negotiating skills of the parties, and, more generally, the status of the class struggle between landowners and capitalists in particular cities and at particular times.

Differential rent II

Thus far we have considered the differential rent that arises when *equal* capitals are invested on *unequal* lands, where DR I is determined by the difference between the yield from capitals operating on the best land and the yield of capital on the worst land. By its nature, DR I arises from how the natural features of land enable (or hinder) the productivity of capital, not from the characteristics of the land itself.

Differential rent II (DR II), on the other hand, arises when *unequal* capitals are

	Capital (c + v + s)	Product	Value (capital per product)	Market value (per product)	Revenue (Products × Market value)	Surplus profit (Revenue – Capital)	DR II
Site A	60	1	60	60	60	0	0
Site B	70	2	35	60	120	50	50
Site C	80	3	26.6	60	180	100	100
Site D	90	4	22.3	60	240	150	150

Table 5.2 DR II: different magnitudes of capital on equal lands

invested on *equal* land. When this occurs larger capitals (invested on equal lands) will generate larger quantities of surplus value and hence larger surplus profits which can be appropriated by landowners as rent.

Consider, for example, four equal urban sites with different magnitudes of capital invested on them which are producing the same commodities (see Table 5.2). This could be a land site that has different amounts of capital invevsted in it over time, or one which is subdivided into four lots, with different magnitudes of capital invested on each of the four lots. Site A has 60 units of capital invested on it which produces one commodity (or one dozen, score, hundred or other multiple of one). Sites B, C and D are invested with 70, 80 and 90 units of capital respectively, and produce two, three and four commodities, respectively. As usual, when the capitals sell their commodities, the market value for each commodity is established by the average conditions of production that apply to the majority of the products. As the lands are equal, they have no impact on the formation of the market value. Assume Site A sets the market price and therefore generates its usual profit but no surplus profit, while the other sites generate a surplus profit of 60, 120 and 180 units. Some or all this surplus of surplus value, the surplus profit, could be appropriated by the landlord as DR II.

In 'Transformation of Surplus-Profit into Ground-Rent', Marx considers multiple variations for how DR II may arise (such as a case where the additional capital on the equal land has a constant, decreasing or an increasing effect on the productivity)[12] and in all cases there is a relative rise in DR II with the addition of capital.

DR II has a number of qualities. First, DR II is not independent of DR I, because the existence of DR II is not possible without the presence of DR I. Second, DR II is not permanent. As occurs with any industry sector in capitalism, a larger-than-normal investment of constant capital (in new equipment, machinery, technology and so on) gives a capitalist a short-term productivity advantage over their competitors which allows them to capture the additional surplus value. However, over the longer term, competition between capitalists causes a general diffusion of equipment and technologies across the industry sector and the additional surplus value (and DR II) arising from the first-mover advantage is lost.

Third, DR II and DR I have an interactive, not a cumulative, effect on each other. For example, the best sites (generating more **DR I**) will also be the ones selected for greater investment (generating more **DR II**) because they afford the best promise that the capital invested on that site will be more profitable. On the other hand, the worst sites (which generate no or little **DR I**) are also less likely to have capital invested on them (and therefore will generate no or little **DR II**).

Differential rent is a reminder that capitalists who invest higher-than-industry-normal quantities of capital on the best land are not guaranteed to capture higher-than-industry returns because some or all of the benefits of the investment on that land will be captured by the landowner as rent. It is in this sense that landowners block capital. Landowners are a clear disincentive to capitalist investment on land. Capitalists who invest extra capital on land in the hope of producing greater profits face the certainty that some or all of the surplus profit they create will be captured by the landowner as differential rent.

As a result, over time, the rate of investment in land-based industries slows (relative to investment in other industries) and the diffusion of productivity-increasing investment into land-based sectors slows. In the best-case scenario, capital technology continues but at a slower rate over time (all other factors being equal). In the worst case, investment ceases, technology is no longer modernised, the land-based industry stagnates and unemployment increases.

Prices of production

As just discussed, differential rent is made possible when *intra-industry* competition (competition within each industry sector) establishes the market value for each commodity. However, *intra-industry* competition is just one factor in determining the final price of each commodity. The final price of a commodity (produced in one industry sector) also depends on the competitiveness and productivity of capital in that industry compared with the profitability of capitals in all other industry sectors across the whole economy. That is, the final price of a commodity is also affected by *inter-industry* competition which creates each commodity's price of production. This section considers how prices of production are formed, and the following section shows how these prices of production make it possible for landowners to capture absolute rent (**AR**).

Recall all capitalist economies are divided into various specialised industry sectors (such as agriculture, manufacturing, transport, wholesale and retail, and finance). Each industry sector has its own rate of profit (r') calculated as the ratio of the surplus value (s) produced by the industry in proportion to the constant capital (c) and variable capital (v) used up to create that surplus value. That is, each industry has its own rate of profit summarised as $r' = \dfrac{s}{c + v}$.

Each industry sector is in competition with the others to maximise their rate of profit. If one industry sector is more profitable than another, capital from low-performing sectors will exit the low-profit industries and move into the more profitable sectors. This continuous flow of capital out of the least profitable sectors into more profitable sectors in search for greater profits leads to constant industry restructuring, innovation, and the growth and decline of employment in the more profitable and less profitable industries, respectively.

As investment moves into high-profit industries, competition increases, profit falls and the rate of profit in the high-profit sector will fall towards the general, 'average' economy-wide rate of profit (R'). Conversely, low-profit industry sectors lose investment as some capital exits and moves to sectors where it can get a higher return. This decline continues up to the point where the remaining capitals are able to increase their rate of profit to levels towards the general, 'average' economy-wide rate of profit (R').

The general rate of profit (R') therefore refers to the general return on the investment of all capital in a capitalist economy. It is calculated as the ratio of total surplus value or 'total social capital' (S) produced in the economy divided by the capitals that were advanced to create and realise that total surplus value; that is, total constant capital, C, and total variable capital, V: that is, $R' = \dfrac{S}{C+V}$. In a similar way to how competition between capitals within an industry sector establishes a commodity's market value, so, too, does competition between capitals across the whole economy establish the economy-wide rate of profit that is used to finalise the commodity's price of production:

> What competition, first in a single sphere, achieves is a single market-value and market-price derived from the various individual values of commodities. And it is competition of capitals in different spheres, which first brings out the price of production equalizing the rates of profit in the different spheres.[13]

In essence, capitalist firms in the least efficient (more labour-intensive) industry sectors that produce commodities with higher-than-average magnitudes of surplus value find some or all of that value is transferred by the general rate of profit (R') to the industry sectors where capitalist firms produce their commodities with lower-than-average value. The result is that when commodities sell, they sell not at their market value (established within their industry sector) but at their price of production – a price that includes the market value established within the industry but also incorporating the allocation of surplus value across the economy.

Recall that when commodities, produced with and for capital, are exchanged in the marketplace for money, they are not exchanged simply as commodities, as objects with a use value that are sold at any price determined by the invisible hand of the market that balances supply and demand. Instead, there are distinct limits on what price capitals can sell their commodities for because all capitals are under relentless economic pressure (from their financiers, employees, shareholders and competitors) to sell their commodities at prices that will realise 'as much surplus-value, or profit, on capital advanced for production, as any other capital of the same magnitude, or pro rata to its magnitude'.[14] In other words, all sellers exchange their products of capital (their commodities) at a price which will capture their share of the total surplus value (*S*) produced in the economy *in proportion to the magnitude of the capital used to produce it.*[15]

The price at which commodities are sold then, the price of production, is the price that allocates a portion of the total *S* in the economy to all the individual capitals in the different industry sectors consistent with the economy-wide general rate of profit (*R'*). In other words:

> When a capitalist sells his commodities at their price of production, therefore, he recovers money in proportion to the value of the capital consumed in their production and secures profit in proportion to this advanced capital as the aliquot part in the total social capital. His cost-prices are specific. But the profit added to them is independent of his particular sphere of production ...[16]

Table 5.3 gives an example of how the price of production allocates the total *S* to individual capitals in all industries (while making the usual simplifying assumptions to make calculations easier but which are nevertheless consistent with the labour theory of value and with the reality of the production and circulation of capital).[17] Consider a simplified economy made up of four different industry sectors, each of which has the same total quantity of capital (100 units). Each sector has its own particular mix of constant capital (*c*) and variable capital (*v*): for example, Sector 1 has a capital of $80_c + 20_v$ and Sector 3 has a capital of $40_c + 60_v$. For simplicity, assume each industry sector has the same rate of exploitation of labour; that is, the amount of unpaid surplus value produced by labour is 100 per cent in all sectors. As a result, all the industry sectors, some of which are more labour-intensive and some more technology-intensive, use the same total capital (100) and the same rate of labour exploitation (100 per cent) but produce commodities with different individual prices (which in value measures are 120, 140, 160 and 180, respectively).

For this four-sector economy, the total amount of the constant capital is 200_c, the total amount of variable capital is 200_v and the total magnitude of surplus value (*S*) is 200_S. As discussed above, inter-industry competition forces this total surplus value (*S*) to be allocated equally to all sectors *in proportion to the magnitude of capital advanced* to produce the total surplus:

> Prices of production arise from an equalisation of the values of commodities. After replacing the respective capital-values used up in the various spheres of production, this distributes the entire surplus-value, not in proportion to the amount produced in the individual spheres of production and thus incorporated in their commodities, but in proportion to the magnitude of advanced capitals.[18]

In Table 5.3, the general rate of profit is $R' = \dfrac{S}{C+V}$ (or 50 per cent), and therefore the price of production, the price paid for the commodities when bought

Table 5.3 Formation of prices of production

Industry sector	Capital $(c + v)$ advanced in production	Surplus value (s) (E.g. at a rate of 100 per cent)	Total value (The individual price of commodities) $(c + v + s)$	General rate of profit (The economy-wide average rate of profit) $R' = \dfrac{S}{C + V}$	Price of production (Capital + its portion of the economy-wide surplus value) $(c + v) + R(c + v)$	Excess profit (Price of production – Total value)
Sector I	$80_c + 20_v$	20_s	120	Total S = 200 Total $(C + V)$ = 400 $R' = \dfrac{200}{400}$ = 50%	150	30
Sector II	$60_c + 40_v$	40_s	140		150	10
Sector III	$40_c + 60_v$	60_s	160		150	(10)
Sector IV	$20_c + 80_v$	80_s	180		150	(30)
Total economy	$200_c + 200_v$	200_s	600		600	0

and sold throughout the economy, consists of the value needed to replace the advanced capital $(c + v)$ plus a profit equal to the *general rate of profit* allocated in proportion to the amount of the advanced capital $(R'(c + v))$. In this example, capitalists receive a price of production for their commodities equal to $(c + v = 100) + (R'(c + v) = 50)$, or 150.

The commodities sell in the market at their price of production. When this occurs, the capital in Sector I, which used labour-saving technology to produce its commodities at an individual cost (or total value) of 120, receives the price of production for its commodities (150), thus making an *excess profit* of 30. On the other hand, the capital in Sector IV produced its commodities relatively inefficiently (with much labour) with an individual price (total value) of 180. When this capital sells its commodities in the market, it receives the economy-wide price of production (150), thus making a loss of profit of 30. The inefficient industry Sector IV, which had captured a large amount of unpaid surplus value in production, is paid a price of production for its commodities that results in it losing a portion of its surplus value which is transferred, through the price of production, to the more efficient and productive Sector I. As we shall soon see, this excess profit captured by Sector I is the source of the Absolute Rent which is appropriated by landowners.

In summary, Marx uses the labour theory of value at three levels of analysis: the individual capitalist firm; the firm within its industry sector; and the industry sector within the economy. At the level of an individual capitalist firm, each capitalist produces individual commodities with a *cost of production* $(c_i + v_i)$ plus a profit (unpaid surplus value, s_i); that is, with an individual *value* of $(c_i + v_i + s_i)$. Having produced a commodity with its individual value, each capitalist in the industry uses the market to determine the market value of the particular commodity. By benchmarking the commodity against the same commodity produced by other firms in the industry, the capitalist ascertains the 'average' *market value* of the commodity of $(c_m + v_m + s_m)$. Finally, having established its market value, the capitalist determines the commodity's actual selling price, its price of production. All the unpaid surplus value produced in each industry sector makes up the total surplus value (S) in the economy. Due to inter-industry competition, which establishes the general rate of profit in the economy (R'), the commodity sells at its *price of production* of $(c_i + v_i) + R'(c_i + v_i)$.

Establishing the general rate of profit and the price of production in the market is never a smooth, technical exercise based on perfect information, market harmonisation and general equilibrium. In reality, each capitalist market is one of constant, unrelenting and historically specific forms of competition between capitals; disruptions in the flow of technology within industry sectors and across the economy; class struggle as employees and shareholders struggle to capture a larger portion of the firm's profit for themselves; and other crises. This relentless search to maximise profit causes individual firms to shed labour, introduce labour-saving technologies, increase the rate of exploitation of the labour force (to produce more commodities using fewer labour costs) and/or move their capital to more profitable industry sectors; and causes individual industries to restructure and innovate in ways that are often chaotic and wasteful. As discussed in Chapter 2, many industries take action to reduce competition and/or seek government 'protection' from competitive pressures. Occasionally, 'disruptive' industries emerge that capture very high excess profits for a period of time. However, in general, competition slowly brings the rate of profit of all industry sectors back to the economy-wide average rate of profit. Incidentally, when the rate of profit in all industries settles around the economy-wide average rate of profit (R'), this does not result in economic stability or economic 'equilibrium'; instead, competition and other political economic forces create a tendency for this general rate of profit to fall over time, which forces the capitalist economy to undergo its characteristic cycles of growth and crisis.[19]

With this explanation of the process which establishes prices of production, it is now possible to explain how landed property intervenes in this price of the production-setting process and, by doing so, captures absolute rent (AR).

Absolute rent

Absolute rent (AR) is a one-off payment made to landowners for the use of 'new' land. Unlike differential rent, which arises from the capacity of the natural features of land (such as location, orientation, terrain and so on) to boost the productivity of capital invested on the land, absolute rent arises purely from the power of landowners to demand a one-off payment of absolute rent before capital can invest on the land. The magnitude of absolute rent is determined when land provides a barrier to the process that establishes the price of production.

There are many potential sources of new land. For example, a landowner can make available to capital land that was previously used or zoned for non-economic purposes. Absolute rent is a one-off payment because once the land has been rezoned (or released for capitalist investment) and capital is invested on the land, the landlord will be able to calculate the magnitude of differential rent to charge in the lease from that day forward.[20] A classic example of where AR intervenes in production is on the fringes of cities where the owners of 'undeveloped' land can demand a one-off tribute (absolute rent) to make the land available for the use of capital for purposes such as housing:

> In general, housing construction meets a barrier in the ownership by a third party of the land upon which the houses are to be built. But, once this land has been leased for the purpose of housing construction, it depends upon the tenant whether he will build a large or a small house.[21]

AR is a particular challenge for the labour theory of value because Marx needed to explain how new, undeveloped land can have a rent and a price when it has no value (because value arises only from labour) and no capital invested on it (and hence no surplus value that could be used to establish a price). Furthermore, Marx wanted to show how and why there is always an upper limit on the amount of absolute rent that can be appropriated for undeveloped land.

Landowners holding new land want a payment of rent (absolute rent) to release the land for use. Capitalists wanting to invest on the new land can examine the economy and estimate the price of production they will receive for their commodities when they invest. The payment they are required to make, to bring the land into production therefore, must be in addition to the price of production.

Consider the example in Table 5.4. It shows an economy where all capitalists, except the capitalist wishing to invest on new land, produce commodities using a composition of capital of $85c + 15v$ and a surplus value of 100 per cent (or $15s$), produces commodities with a value of $(c + v + s)$ or 115. On the new land, the capitalist invests in such a way to produce commodities using a composition of capital of $75c + 25v$ and a surplus value of 100 per cent (or $25s$) and therefore produce commodities with a market value of $(c + v + s)$ or 125, which means the commodities produced on the new land have a value that is 5 higher than the economy-wide price of production of 120. Ordinarily, the excess of value (above the price of production) produced by a labour-intensive sector is re-allocated by the price of production process to the more productive sectors. However, new land obstructs this process. New land demands a payment irrespective of the existence of competition between capitals. As a result, the land-renting capitalist sells their commodities at their value (not the price of production), and the difference between the value and price of production is appropriated by the landowner (as AR). In the case of Table 5.4, the excess of value embedded in the commodities of the new land-based capitalist (of value 5) is paid to the landowner as AR rather than it being allocated to the more productive capitalists.

Table 5.4 Formation of absolute rent (full appropriation)

	Capital advanced (c + v)	Surplus value (s)	Value (c + v + s)	General rate of profit $R' = \dfrac{S}{C+V}$	Price of production (c + v) + R'(c + v)	If no AR (PoP – Value)	If AR = 5
Existing capitalists	$85_c + 15_v$	15_s	115	20%	120	5	0
New land capitalist	$75_c + 25_v$	25_s	125	20%	120	(5)	AR = 5
Total economy	$160_c + 40_v$	40_s	240	20%			

Table 5.5 Formation of absolute rent (partial appropriation)

	Capital advanced $(c + v)$	Surplus value (s)	Value $(c + v + s)$	General rate of profit $R' = \dfrac{S}{C+V}$	Price of production $(c + v) + R'(c + v)$	If no AR (PoP − Value)	If AR = 3
Existing capitalists	$85_c + 15_v$	15_s	115	20%	120	5	2
New land capitalist	$75_c + 25_v$	25_s	125	20%	120	(5)	AR = 3
Total economy	$160_c + 40_v$	40_s	240	20%			

Table 5.6 Failure to form absolute rent

	Capital advanced $(c + v)$	Surplus value (s)	Value $(c + v + s)$	General rate of profit $R' = \dfrac{S}{C+V}$	Price of production $(c + v) + R'(c + v)$	If no AR (PoP − Value)	AR
Existing capitalists	$85_c + 15_v$	15_s	115	10%	110	(5)	
New land capitalist	$95_c + 5_v$	5_s	105	10%	110	5	0*
Total economy	$180_c + 20_v$	20_s	220	10%	110		

The difference between the value of commodities produced on new land and their price of production sets the upper limit of what can be captured as AR. Whether the AR equals the entire difference between the market value and the price of production, or only a part of it, will depend on the state of the market, supply and demand for land and so on.

Table 5.5 shows what happens when only a portion of the surplus value produced on new land is captured by the landowner as AR, with the remainder being allocated via the price of production to the rest of the economy. In Table 5.5, the landowner captures an AR of 3 from the new land-based capitalist while the remaining surplus value of 2 is transferred by the price of production to the other capitals.

One other example is useful to clarify the economic mechanisms that produce AR. What AR is possible if the capitalist investing on new land produces commodities in a highly productive way compared with the rest of the economy? As shown in Table 5.6, if a high-technology, low-labour investment is made on new land, then the value (105) of commodities produced on the new land is less than the price of production (110) and as a result there is no excess of surplus value created on the land that can be captured by land as AR.

How is it that landowners can capture the excess of surplus value as AR, or, to put it another way, why is it that the excess surplus value produced on the new land does not flow unimpeded (via the price of production) to the more productive capitals? The solution is that competition, which can force capitalists to cut costs in every other part of their business, cannot force the capitalist to reduce the AR on land. Commodities produced by land-based capital are sold at their value (and not at the price of production) because the legal and institutional *obligation* to pay the landowner rent overcomes (or overpowers) the forces of competition. As a result, the higher price of land-based commodities 'is not the cause of rent, but rather that rent is the cause of the increase in the price of the product'.[22]

Furthermore, whether the absolute rent equals the entire difference between the value and the price of production, or only a part of it, will depend on the power balance in the social relation between the landlord and the capitalist which is influenced by the state of the market, political factors (such as the strengths of landed property rights afforded by the state compared with the rights of capital) and economic factors (such as the strength of supply and demand for the land). Finally, the maximum limit of AR that can be appropriated by land is determined by the difference between the excess of the value of the new land commodities over their price of production.[23]

Monopoly prices

Rent can be confused with monopoly pricing.

A monopoly price is the price for a commodity that is set by a monopoly producer. As a result of the market power of the monopoly (and the lack of competition), the monopolist can set a price which is above the price of production and above the value of the commodity. Monopoly pricing therefore involves the transfer a portion of the profit of other commodity producers to the commodities having the monopoly price. The monopoly price requires either a reduction in the profit of capitalists or a deduction from the real wages of workers.[24] Monopoly prices therefore are distinctly different from, and capture surplus value from a totally different source than, differential rent which arises in intra-industry competition which establishes a surplus of surplus value over the market-price; or absolute rent which arises when the excess of value over the price of production is captured by land.

Marx's definitions of rent are a useful reminder that the 'filching' of surplus value through the power of landed property involves very different economic processes from monopoly pricing, lobbying and other political actions which have the intention to capture state finances for private interests.

House (and other building) 'rent'

Another common confusion in the understanding of rent arises when it is said housing tenants are paying 'rent', or other types of building lessors are paying 'rent'. Paying for access to and use of a building is a totally different economic process from the economic process of paying for access to and use of a land-owner's land. This confusion between 'ground-rent' and 'house-rent' is easily understood, especially when the landlord and the building speculator are the same person. However, it is important to clarify that rent is appropriated for the use of land while prices (for access and use of houses and other buildings) are a charge against the capital that was invested to build those buildings. The price paid for use of buildings is typically constituted by the interest and amortisation on the capital originally invested in the buildings (and not the land).

Although rent and paying for access to buildings are two different economic processes, they can and do operate together. Especially in cities, where popula-tion increases can create a high demand for commercial buildings and housing, the rent captured by the owner of urban land is often complemented by the prevalence of monopoly prices for the construction of buildings. Here property developers use the monopoly power of landed property together with construc-tion capital to extract monopoly prices for buildings as well as the land on which they are located.[25] This distinction between land rent and housing returns helps analyse the extent to which the supply and demand for land is the basis of prop-erty speculation – which it often is – and the extent to which the cost of construc-tion is the cause of house price and house rent inflation.

Other issues concerning capitalist rent

There are four outstanding issues raised in the above discussion that need to be clarified: how can rent be paid if there is no surplus profit; how is the price of land set; under what circumstances does the landowner capture all (or only part) of the available value as rent; and how does rent affect housing and homelessness in cities?

First, if a capitalist based on leased land is not operating profitably, how can the capitalist continue to pay rent even though they are not making enough surplus profit to cover the cost of the rent? This situation specifically arises for capitals invested on the worst land sites where, as a result, no differential rent is possible. In practice, there are three options. One is for the capitalist to try to renegotiate the lease to seek a 'rent holiday': this is an unlikely scenario as it would mean the landlord would need to forgo, or take a reduced level of, their own (rental) income.[26] Another option, and more common, is that the capitalist is forced by the market to improve their productivity by investing in labour-saving technology, reducing the size of their workforce, cutting costs and in particular cutting wages, and so on. Over time, the capital operating on the worst land may improve its productivity to the point where the capitalist is able to capture a surplus of surplus profit which can then be paid as differential rent.

Most often, however, capitalists on the worst land, who capture no surplus profit, have little choice in the short term but to pay their lease obligations by using some or all of their own profit (the surplus value, s, captured from their workers in production); by going into debt and borrowing additional capital from financial institutions or shareholders to pay for the rent; or by reducing the wages of their workers. In all three situations, the money the capitalist pays the landlord is called 'lease money' because it is taken from the capitalist's pool of capital or wages. It is not rent, which can only arise from the intervention of land in the realisation of capital through market values or the price of production. Marx notes the payment of 'lease money' is a common practice in capitalist economies, such as in capitalist agriculture:

> If the farmer pays 'lease money' which constitutes a deduction from the normal wages of his labourers, or from his own normal average profit, he does not pay rent, i.e., an independent component of the price of his commodities distinct from wages and profit. We have already indicated that this continually takes place in practice.[27]

These short-term options facing capitalists on the worst land (of reducing their profits, going into debt and/or reducing the wages of workers) are often observed in cities, where poorly located suburbs are also the regions with rundown buildings, old technologies, workers with depressed levels of wages and firms earning less-than-the-industry-average level of profit. These suburbs or regions are not economically sustainable in the short run. In these economically depressed suburbs, typical actions that occur are: the labour force stays and continues to earn lower than average wages (or leaves for higher-paid jobs); capitalists continue to operate with no or very low rates of profit and typically with no new investment in technology, lack of building maintenance, and so on (or are bankrupted); the landowner evicts the capitalist and either replaces them with a profitable capitalist or leaves the land vacant for long periods until economic conditions improve; the state intervenes with infrastructure, rezoning or other strategies to revitalise the area; or there is gentrification as wealthy people move in, improve housing and attract new businesses, and displace the long-term inhabitants in the process.

A second outstanding issue arising from the discussion of rent is how the price of the land is set. In general, the price to buy a site of land is the capitalised rent on the land[28] (where the current value of land is estimated using future rental income over a period of time, for example thirty years for commercial land, and taking into account costs such as inflation, debt servicing, rates and taxes). Clearly, the best located sites with the highest rent revenue will sell at a price which is higher than the price of the less well-located (and lower-rent) sites.

However, how can the price of the worst land be calculated given there is no rent? In these situations, rent is estimated by comparing the land with a similar parcel of land that is paying (differential) rent. For example, the price could be calculated on assumptions about the likely total rent that would be paid by a similar, profitable site over, say, thirty years, plus the addition of an amount equivalent to the expected interest rate. This assumption, that unused (or non-rent paying) urban land is owed a price based on a rent similar to the returns from comparable urban land contributes to the urban land speculation that is rife in cities around the world.

The third issue raised above is the basis for the magnitude of rent a landowner can capture from capital, and under what conditions landowners are able to appropriate all (or only a part) of the available value. Marx's analysis of rent establishes an upper limit on the magnitude of differential and absolute rent that could be captured by the landowner. Within this limit, however, how much value is actually captured by land cannot be predicted or modelled mathematically. In the real world of the real estate market, whether the landowner captures some or all of the available value as rent, and how much the capitalist tenant retains for themselves, is subject to many factors.

The landowner and the capitalist exist in a classic example of a dialectical social (economic) relation where both are mutually dependent on the other for their own economic success *and* both have mutually opposed economic interests. Within this contradictory social relation, each struggles against the other to maximise their own income and minimise any losses without jeopardising the relation on which both depend. These struggles are structured by real-world factors such as the prevailing legal and regulatory conditions in the city or nation (where the legal framework or standard lease agreements and obligations may be balanced more in the favour of the interests of landed property or capital); economic conditions (such as the strength of the supply and demand for the land and the potential for profit-making by the capitalist); political conditions (where government parties may be more inclined to support landowners or capitalists); and individual-level factors (such as the financial resources of the protagonists, negotiation skills of the lease parties, and so on).

These land–capital struggles take many forms. For example, there are typically strong disagreements between the landlord and their corporate tenants over core issues such as the length of a lease, the right to break the lease, and who is responsible for repairs and insurance. Interestingly, 'international corporate occupiers are significantly more concerned about the length of lease and the incidence of break clauses than national occupiers'.[29] Another indicator of the clash of economic interests between the landlord and the commercial tenant expresses itself in debates over whether to establish a gross lease (where the tenant pays a flat rental amount and the landlord pays all the other property expenses such as taxes, insurance, maintenance and repairs) or a net lease (where the tenant pays rent plus some or all of the property expenses).[30] Recently, a new conflict has arisen over whether the landlord or the commercial tenant is responsible for the environmental performance of the building.[31]

Marx's focus on production, rather than consumption, helps explain why he rarely considered the situation of urban housing, and focused more on how land supports capitalist investment, production and realisation (and the related issue of how landowners appropriate value as differential and absolute rent). He may also have wished to avoid an issue that was being analysed differently by his colleague Engels.[32]

Urban housing is an example of production, where capitalists combine constant capital (such as building materials and equipment) and variable capital (building workers) to produce commodities (such as houses or apartment buildings). Housing, for Marx, could easily fit within his analysis of the cycle of capitalist investment, production and realisation. However, Marx also recognised housing is a consumption good that is essential for the sustenance of workers, where ordinarily the cost of housing is factored into the calculation of the wage needed for the sustenance of workers. Marx was scathing of the landowning class for claiming to be interested in the good of society while, in reality, acting for their own financial benefit:

> The landlord being interested in the welfare of society means, according to the principles of political economy, that he is interested in the growth of its population and manufacture, in the expansion of its needs – in short, in the increase of wealth; and this increase of wealth is, as we have already seen, identical with the increase of poverty and slavery. The relation between increasing house rent and increasing poverty is an example of the landlord's interest in society ...[33]

Conclusion

This chapter has focussed on three key issues. First, it has shown how rent directly affects the location and type of investment that capital makes in cities. Second, to do this it provided detail on how the labour theory of value can be used to explain the complexities of absolute rent and differential rent. Finally, it clarified that commonly used terms such as 'monopoly rent' or 'house rent' are phenomena that arise from economic processes that are distinctly different from the processes that cause absolute and differential rent, and that to assume all forms of rent are the same leads to confusion.

One of the underlying themes throughout this chapter is that the state plays a crucial role in determining the outcome of the struggles between landowners and capitalists who are mutually dependent but with diametrically opposed interests. These struggles occur in many fields including property rights, land taxes, urban planning and environmental standards. How the landowning class influences the state is the focus of the next chapter.

Notes

1. K. Marx, *Capital*, vol. III, ch. 48, New York, International Publishers, 1959, https://www.marxists.org/archive/marx/works/1894-c3/ch48.htm
2. K. Beitel, 'Circuits of Capital, Ground Rent and the Production of the Built Environment: A (New) Framework for Analysis', *Human Geography*, vol. 9, no. 3, 2016, pp. 27–42.
3. K. Smet, 'Housing Prices in Urban Areas', *Progress in Human Geography*, vol. 40, no. 4, 2016, pp. 495–510.
4. K. Strauss, 'Beyond Crisis? Using Rent Theory to Understand the Restructuring of Publicly-Funded Seniors' Care in British Columbia, Canada', *Environment and Planning A: Economy and Space*, 25 Jan. 2021.
5. Australian Council of Social Service, *An Affordable Housing Reform Agenda: Goals and Recommendations for Reform*, Canberra, Australia, ACOSS, 2015, p. 12, https://www.acoss.org.au/images/uploads/Housing_paper_March_2015_final.pdf
6. A. E. Ryan and A. B. Koch, 'COVID-19 and Lease Negotiations: Early Termination Provisions', *Law Journal Newsletters*, Jan. 2022, https://www.lawjournalnewsletters.com/2022/01/01/covid-19-and-lease-negotiations-early-termination-provisions/
7. K. Marx, *Capital*, vol. III, ch. 37, New York, International Publishers, 1959, https://www.marxists.org/archive/marx/works/1894-c3/ch37.htm
8. Ibid., vol. III, ch. 10, https://www.marxists.org/archive/marx/works/1894-c3/ch10.htm
9. For example, S. S. Rosenthal and W. C. Strange, 'How Close Is Close? The Spatial Reach of Agglomeration Economies', *Journal of Economic Perspectives*, vol. 34, no. 3, 2020, pp. 27–49.
10. Marx, *Capital*, vol. III, ch. 39, https://www.marxists.org/archive/marx/works/1894-c3/ch39.htm
11. Ibid., vol. III, ch. 41, https://www.marxists.org/archive/marx/works/1894-c3/ch41.htm
12. Ibid.
13. Ibid., vol. III, ch. 10, https://www.marxists.org/archive/marx/works/1894-c3/ch10.htm
14. Ibid.
15. Ibid.
16. Ibid., vol. III, ch. 9, https://www.marxists.org/archive/marx/works/1894-c3/ch09.htm
17. There is a detailed example in Marx, *Capital*, vol. III, ch. 9, https://www.marxists.org/archive/marx/works/1894-c3/ch09.htm
18. Marx, *Capital*, vol. III, ch. 45, https://www.marxists.org/archive/marx/works/1894-c3/ch45.htm
19. Ibid., vol. III, ch. 14, https://www.marxists.org/archive/marx/works/1894-c3/ch14.htm
20. Ibid., vol. III, ch. 45, https://www.marxists.org/archive/marx/works/1894-c3/ch45.htm
21. Ibid.
22. Ibid., vol. III, ch. 45, https://www.marxists.org/archive/marx/works/1894-c3/ch45.htm

23. Ibid., vol. III, ch. 50, https://www.marxists.org/archive/marx/works/1894-c3/ch50.htm
24. Ibid.
25. Ibid., vol. III, ch. 46, https://www.marxists.org/archive/marx/works/1894-c3/ch46.htm
26. In Australia, for example, when businesses were affected by the 2020–21 COVID-19 pandemic, requests for a 'rent holiday' were typically answered with 'no' (D. Wood, K. Griffiths and N. Blane, 'The Case for a Rent Holiday for Businesses on the Coronavirus Economic Frontline', *The Conversation*, 27 Mar. 2020, Australian edn, https://theconversation.com/the-case-for-a-rent-holiday-for-businesses-on-the-coronavirus-economic-frontline-134890).
27. Marx, *Capital*, vol. III, ch. 45, https://www.marxists.org/archive/marx/works/1894-c3/ch45.htm
28. Ibid., vol. III, ch. 39, https://www.marxists.org/archive/marx/works/1894-c3/ch39.htm
29. N. Crosby, V. Gibson and S. Murdock, 'UK Commercial Property Lease Structures: Landlord and Tenant Mismatch', *Urban Studies*, vol. 40, no. 8, 2003, pp. 1487–516.
30. D. Halvitigala, L. Murphy and D. Levy, 'The Impacts of Commercial Lease Structures on Landlord and Tenant Leasing Behaviours and Experiences', *Pacific Rim Property Research Journal*, vol. 17, 2015, pp. 560–83.
31. D. A. Prum, 'Commercial-Property Leases as a Means for Private Environmental Governance', *Georgia State University Law Review*, vol. 35, no. 3, 2019, https://readingroom.law.gsu.edu/gsulr/vol35/iss3/5
32. F. Engels, *The Housing Question*, Marx/Engels Internet Archive, https://www.marxists.org/archive/marx/works/1872/housing-question/ch02.htm
33. K. Marx, 'Rent of Land', *Economic and Philosophic Manuscripts of 1844*, Moscow, Progress Publishers, 1959, https://www.marxists.org/archive/marx/works/1844/manuscripts/rent.htm

CHAPTER 6

The State and the Landowner Class

The hitherto existing production relations of individuals are bound also to be expressed as political and legal relations.[1]

Introduction

Chapters 2–5 have mentioned in passing that almost every community or society has a fundamental and contradictory division within it between its mode of production (economy) and its political institutions (polity). The polity includes, at a minimum: elders or law makers, a military force to protect the social body from external threats and a police force to enforce its laws internally, and some sort of capacity to collect tribute from the community or society to resource the polity. The social relation between the economy and the polity is always contradictory, where the mode of production resources the polity and the polity in turn perpetuates the operation of the mode of production and the community or society as a whole.

This division of communities and societies into rulers (with the power, authority and resources to rule) and those who are ruled is not natural, neutral, technocratic, apolitical or organic but perpetuates artificial divisions between people that have been created by individuals, businesses and governments over centuries, often through violence; and great effort is applied continuously to justify, normalise, legitimise and, if necessary, enforce these divisions.[2]

Each mode of production has its own polities (such as councils of elders, city-states, monarchies and, in the case of capitalism, the state) which shape the economy in different ways depending on the underlying mode of production. However, in almost all modes of production, 'the State is the form in which the individuals of a ruling class assert their common interests, and in which the whole civil society of an epoch is epitomised'.[3]

This chapter reports on Marx's views on the origin, nature and role of the state with an emphasis on the relations between the landowning class and the state where landed property influences the state politically to protect its economic interests and the state extracts taxes from the ownership and development of land. These matters are discussed primarily in *The German Ideology*, A *Contribution to the Critique of Political Economy*, *Grundrisse*, *Theories of Surplus Value*, volumes I and III of *Capital*, and his *Ethnological Notebooks*.

Indigenous polities

The longest-lasting polities in the world are those organised in indigenous, clan and other kinship communities, many of which continue to lead their communities today. Marx wrote, with varying degrees of detail, on tribes, clans and other indigenous communities in countries as different as Mexica, Peru, India, Russia and Scotland.[4]

In indigenous communities, community governance, communally owned property and shared economic activity are integrated with each other and with the natural world. The exercise of power and authority over others in indigenous communities is diffused into the hands of many different people. Although there are no social divisions based on the ownership or non-ownership of land, there are social divisions within the community including between elders and non-elders, men and women, parents and children, and so on. To varying degrees, and depending on the culture, customs and traditions of the indigenous community, members participate directly or indirectly in making the decisions about their community governance, judicial requirements, defence and other issues affecting the maintenance and reproduction of the community's mode of production, customs, practices and identity.

In the productive sphere of the society, people have clear work roles, typically based on customary gender-based roles relating to hunting, gathering, cooking, childcare and so on. Labour by all members of the indigenous community is obligatory and enforced through customary and personal obligations and responsibilities (rather than any overseer). In communities where human labour is not alienated, all people contribute materially to the perpetuation of themselves, their kin groups and the broader community's material existence, as well as contributing through their labour to the immaterial identity, culture and customs of the community. Community members reach both their full *individual* potential as 'a natural, corporeal, sensuous, objective being' while also achieving their full *social* potential as conscious, active members of the community working together for 'the common good and the common comfort of their species.'[5]

Within this social context the formal polity of indigenous communities commonly consists of a group of indigenous leaders (such as elders who are senior initiated men and women from within the community); or an individual member (chief) of the community who is given a degree of authority to make crucial decisions on behalf of the community members. Elders and chiefs typically lead through consensus-building (rather than though occupying an ascribed or enforceable ruling position).

Indigenous elders and chiefs live as a part of, rather than 'above' or 'outside', their community. They are embedded in the everyday activities of the community including its language, culture, practices, customs and economic activities.

The general roles of indigenous elders and chiefs include ensuring stewardship of the earth, which is the community's source of production and, often, identity, and ensuring compliance by community members with the laws and customs laid down by their ancestors, culture and traditions. In addition, in indigenous communities that live in conflict with others, community leaders are responsible for organising community members into fighting groups to defend their land and their community.

Marx discussed Scottish Gaels as an example of the type of polity that exists in clans and other indigenous communities.[6] Members of the clan belong to one and the same 'family' and live in the district where the clan had established itself; the land in the district is the common property of the clan and not the property of individuals. The clan is led by a chieftain or laird, the symbolic father of the clan. Given success in war against other clans is a crucial requirement for the survival of the clan, a key role of the chieftain is to lead the clan members into battle. The chieftain divides and subdivides the land on the basis of the military functions carried out by individual members of the clan. In war-organised communities, 'the clan is nothing but a family organised in a military manner, quite as little defined by laws, just as closely hemmed in by traditions, as any family'.[7]

The clan chieftain has the power to entrust, cancel or enlarge land allotments on the basis of customary protocols or laws. It is also possible for those who are given land to redistribute individual plots of the land to their own vassals within the clan, a procedure that reinforces kin obligations and authority within families and throughout the clan more generally. In general, every plot of land is cultivated by the same family and inherited by the family from one generation to another. Landholding or landowning families pay a fixed but small impost to the clan chief (mainly for the common defence of the community), which is 'more a tribute by which the supremacy of the "great man" and of his officers [is] acknowledged, than a rent of land in a modern sense, or a source of revenue'.[8] In peacetime, the chieftain is also the chief magistrate who adjudicates disputes within the clan.

Ancient polities

As discussed in Chapter 3, governance of ancient communities takes the form of a city-state (based on public property) which defends, regulates and taxes the surrounding hinterland of communally owned (but privately held and used) agricultural land. In the contradictory social relation between the two, the city-state protects the hinterland and relies on it for resources, while the hinterland produces the resources and domestic-scale manufactures needed for the sustenance of the population plus surplus-to-sustenance resources which are appropriated by the city. The polity of the city-state also provides civil law making, policing and adjudicating on behalf of the community.[9]

Physically, this polity, the city-state, is a fortified city designed to house an army, manufacture weapons and other military resources needed to protect the surrounding agricultural *territorium*. In other words, an essential role of the city-state is to establish a monopoly of violence and exercise it over a territory. This is fundamental role of all polities irrespective of their modes of production.

Socially, the establishment of the city-state bifurcated ancient communities into the majority of the community's members (the peasant landowners who produced their own sustenance plus a surplus for the city) and the minority of the community's members (the urban residents who govern the community, house the military, develop urban industries such as manufacturing and trade, and tax the populace to collect the resources the state needs to carry out its functions). Despite the contradictory social relationship and clash of material interests between the peasant private land users and the urban public land users, these conflicts were always subsumed under the overall *communal* imperatives of supporting and defending the community and its (agricultural) economic base.

The archetypical city-states are those of ancient Athens and ancient Rome. In ancient Rome, for example, the polity was structured by the contradictory social struggles between the patricians (the long-standing, wealthy, ruling-class families with large agricultural estates) and the plebians (the 'free' citizens of Rome – that is, the majority of Rome's inhabitants who were not patricians and not slaves). The patricians and the plebians constantly struggled against each other to capture and control the *ager publicus*, a conflict over centuries known as the 'Struggle of the Orders' in which the plebeians sought political equality with the patricians. There were many ways to organise city-state: the Roman city-state, for example, took several different forms over the nearly three centuries of its existence, notably as a republic (with its annually elected magistrates and representative assemblies) and later as an empire (ruled with absolute powers by the Roman emperor).

The polity of the city-state has three historically unique economic characteristics. First, and as mentioned above, the city-state originated with the division of unified community-owned land into privately used agricultural land in the hinterland and public land, the *ager publicus*, used by the city-state. The *ager publicus* is used for military purposes (such as a garrison for the army and the manufacture of weapons and armour); related military services (such as diplomacy and espionage); economic purposes (including the regulation of coinage, markets and trade) and for the purpose of municipal governance itself (including a place for holding commune meetings, a judiciary, a bureaucracy to collect taxes, and possibly some urban planning to determine the location of palaces, temples, markets and other urban infrastructure.

Despite the powers of the city-state making it the political centre of a rural community, in ancient communities there was the ruralisation of the city (unlike the urbanisation of the countryside which occurs in capitalism).[10] The dominance of the rural over the urban in the city was reflected in the values of the ancient community (where people working in agriculture were highly respected and admired while those working in urban occupations and trades were little esteemed) and in the interests of many urban residents who were in fact private proprietors of, and workers on, the land that made up the agricultural hinterland. Politically, the members of the polity 'consist of working landed proprietors, small-owning peasants' and each peasant-producer 'relates to his private property as land and soil, but at the same time as to his being as commune member; and his own sustenance as such is likewise the sustenance of the commune, and conversely'.[11]

For the first time in human history, in city-states such as Athens in the sixth century BCE, this combination of the equality in status of (property-owning male, non-slave, non-foreigner) citizens and their direct participation in ruling their community introduced rule by democracy. The peasant-producers (in the economy) were also the peasant-citizens (in the polity) who determined policies such as defence, taxation and the regulation of slavery and urban industry for the good of the whole community. In other words, the members of the ruling aristocracy (in control of the city-state) were also members of the direct producing class; in other words, the peasant-producer (working) class controlled both the means of production and the state.[12] This 'unity between the worker and the conditions of production' and between the worker and the governing polity is one of the defining features of a communist society (discussed below).

The ancient Greece form of participative democracy changed over time. The larger landowning peasants were the only ones who had the time and the resources to both produce the goods needed for their own sustenance (or delegate the work to others) and govern the city-state. Peasants on smaller plots of land were too busy or too tired from working to participate as citizen-rulers, or they sold their lands and hence lost their eligibility to be a member of the polity. As a result, over time, communal priorities and community interests were increasingly determined and interpreted by the large landowners who controlled the polity and decided how the city-state would regulate, tax and police 'the community' for the common good. In reality, this meant that a small elite of the better-resourced, wealthier landed property owners became the patricians who ruled the city-state.

The third major characteristic of the ancient city-states was their reliance on slavery. The capture of slaves in war, or from raiding, divided the previously unitary community into the classes of peasant-citizens and slaves. With this division of the community, the peasant-citizens, the private holders of communal property established new associations to protect their interests, associations that were explicitly a 'form of association over [and] against their slaves'.[13]

The ancient city-states established new laws that supported the development of the institution of slavery. Slaves were considered to be moveable property (such as livestock, tools and equipment, manufactured goods and currency) and therefore slave owners had exclusive control over the use and disposal of their slaves.[14] The assumption that economic control required ownership of labour (such as slaves) would continue until the development of capitalism when capitalists realised they did not need to own workers but merely to buy their labour power: a capitalist 'does not appropriate the worker, but his labour – not directly, but mediated through exchange'.[15]

City-states also established laws on the master–slave relationship. Slaves, although a form of moveable property, were also human beings and clearly not equivalent to other forms of moveable property (such as livestock). The city-states developed an approach to master–slave laws that 'corresponds perfectly to the definition of modern economists who call it the power of disposing of the labour-power of others'.[16] The growth of slave labour (and the subsequent decline in peasant-based labour) led polities to establish and enforce new rights and obligations for slave owners (such as their rights to set hours of work, provide food and shelter, and release slaves consistent with the laws of manumission) and slaves (including the rights of slaves to own their own property, the rights of the children of slaves, and the rights of slaves to seek protection from cruel treatment). This new social relation of property, between the slave owner and slaves, was a precursor of what would, over time, evolve into the industrial relations laws that defined the rights of feudal and capitalist property owners to control and dispose of the use of labour in the workplace.

Asiatic polities

In Asiatic communities, the commune is represented by a single individual, the emperor (or some other form of political ruler). The emperor is a unity of roles needed for the defence of the community, the reproduction of the community's mode of production and the community's identity. The emperor rules the community through being simultaneously its political sovereign, its landlord holding all the community's land on behalf of the community, and its divine representative of heaven on earth. This form of government is 'despotic' in the sense that there is a single ruler who has absolute power and rules through consent, religious mandate[17] and/or force.

In the Asiatic state, all land is community property, owned by the monarch (on behalf of the community) and used privately by the direct producers (the peasants and villagers). The peasants and villagers are hereditary possessors and users of the emperor's state-owned land.[18] The peasants who produce on the land, and the villagers who use natural resources from the peasants to manufacture goods for domestic use or trade, are all required to pay rent to the emperor, 'the real landlord'.[19] However, the landlord who is also the community's political sovereign is also often the community's religious leader (e.g. in China the emperor is the 'Son of Heaven'). As a result of this unity of roles, peasants and villages are required to make three different forms of payment to the emperor (as head of the Asiatic state): land-based rent, political tribute, and religious offerings.

In the Asiatic state, villages have a large degree of local decision-making autonomy within the broader governance policies and priorities established by the monarch. Each village-based community manages its own local economic, political and communal priorities through village-level forms of governance. However, it is also well understood that the peasants and the villagers must always produce a surplus which is paid to the emperor, 'the comprehensive unity standing above all these little communities [who] appears as the higher proprietor or as the sole proprietor'.[20]

The Asiatic polity has many of the roles of other polities (such as the ancient city-states or the capitalist state). It must defend the territory from outsiders, support the reproduction of the mode of production, maintain the stability of the political status quo, and use education and religion to perpetuate the community's culture and identity. One unique feature of the Asiatic polity is that the emperor is the centralised provider and regulator of communal economic infrastructure (such as roads, waterways, dams and defence). In India, for example, 'One of the material bases of the power of the state over the small disconnected producing organisms [the villages] in India, was the regulation of the water supply.'[21] The Asiatic state often plans and delivers major works of economic infrastructure that cover large areas of its territory and which could not be afforded by individual, local villages. Given its power and authority, the Asiatic state often organises the local peasants and villagers to provide the labour and materials needed to build the infrastructure.

The Asiatic polity establishes, and relies on, two types of cities. Asiatic rulers typically live in imperial cities (such as the Japanese emperors' Imperial Palace in Kyoto, China's Forbidden City in Beijing, the Vietnamese imperial city of Huế, and in India, the capital of the Mughal Empire was Agra). The imperial cities are typically built to be separate from the lives of the local peasants and villagers, and are centres of wealth, learning, arts, commerce and religion, as well as the centre of the bureaucracy needed to govern, defend and tax the empire.

The Asiatic state also establishes regional or provincial cities that are essential for the operation of the state and the associated Asiatic mode of production. Provincial cities are established around the empire as urban centres for: regional garrisons against foreign invasions; public sector administration (such as tax collection, regional courts and regional infrastructure); communications and postal services; regional warehousing (to store goods produced by villagers for the state) and transport (to carry regional goods to the monarch); external trade (including the collection of duties and other charges from foreigners wishing to trade in the empire); and religion (where temples and other religious centres promote a worldview that has the emperor at the peak of the religious hierarchy).[22]

There was always internal pressure on the emperor to expand the territory of the empire as a way to keep the state's treasury flush with funds needed to maintain the community, strengthen the state and provide for the emperor's wealth. In addition, the Asiatic state often met its fiscal demands by extracting ever-larger surpluses from the peasants and villagers, a policy that led to impoverishment of the peasants and their villages and occasional peasant uprisings such as the Yellow Turban Rebellion in 184 CE when peasants rebelled against Emperor Ling because of an agrarian crisis (causing famine), labour exploitation by large landowners, high taxes and corruption, an uprising that hastened the collapse of the Han dynasty in 220 CE.[23]

The Asiatic polity was relatively stable over long periods of time. Although there were military struggles between different empires, power struggles within dynasties, new forms of warfare, new technologies and population change, the underlying Asiatic mode of production (based on village-level agriculture and manufacturing and the payment of a surplus to the ruler) was rarely disrupted.

Feudal polities

Marx argued the origins of feudal polities occurred when the members of geographically scattered, self-reliant family and larger societal groups would come together and participate in meetings. That is, the polity existed in the form of 'the periodic gathering-together [*Vereinigung*] of the commune members'.[24] Society members met for many functional reasons (such as to pledge allegiance to each other and make decisions on communal matters such as law and justice, war and religion).[25] Unlike ancient polities based on city-states and Asiatic polities made up of an absolute monarch and state officials, the origins of feudal polities lay in the self-aware, self-conscious and deliberative assemblies of societal members.

Over centuries, often due to wars and invasions, many small social groupings, villages and towns coalesced in larger associations and hierarchical kingdoms where the ruling monarch relied on the support of the independent leaders of these regional and local affiliations. The development of the feudal mode of production reinforced the hierarchical structure of power and authority throughout society: 'Hierarchy is the ideal form of feudalism; feudalism is a political form of the medieval relations of production and intercourse [economic social relations].'[26]

The feudal polity was based on the two main social relations of production: vassalage and manorialism (discussed in Chapter 4) where a relatively weak monarch distributed land estates and political jurisdiction over the estates to nobles (in return for their fealty and military support), and the nobles in turn provided land to serfs for their livelihoods (in return for the payment of rent). That is, the feudal polity consisted of a hierarchy made up of multiple layers of interdependent economic and political jurisdictions. In Europe, these political economic hierarchies of feudalism were reinforced by the church hierarchy where the powerful medieval church promoted the view that the monarchy represented God-on-earth (and, in return, the monarch protected the church and supported its collection of tithes).

In this devolved system of feudal governance, a monarch would delegate land and jurisdictional powers to vassals who, as landlords of the estate, ruled over the lord's demesne (and associated manor house) and the large expanse of agricultural, grazing, mining and other lands leased to tenants. The vassal/manorial landlord had legal jurisdiction over the use of the land including the wages and working conditions of the serfs and other direct producers; adjudicated over crimes committed against the land and its fixtures (such as trespass or theft); and had legal obligations to care for the servants employed in the manor house. The manor lord, in short, was landlord, employer, police officer, judge, tax collector and magistrate over most political, economic and customary matters occurring on their land.

The feudal state required constant negotiation between people with economic and political power. Allocations of land and their associated delegation of legal jurisdiction could be revoked. Richer, more powerful nobles would make demands of their monarch which monarchs would resist or comply with, depending on their authority, the extent of their support from other nobles and the size of their treasury. The scope of delegations between the monarch and the vassals could be unclear or ambiguous which could lead to conflict over the use and application of land and other rights. Uncoordinated imposition of taxation and rent could be onerous. The continuity of many feudal states was often interrupted by shifting alliances, wars of succession, revolutions, the overthrow of monarchs and peasant uprisings over onerous tax payments, oppressive conditions of serfdom and corruption.

On the other hand, some feudal states, such as the Ancien Régime in France, developed a polity that was centralised, strong, wealthy and structured on the basis of institutional systems (rather than personal patronage). It was one of the richest and most powerful empires of Europe. However, it also became immensely unpopular among peasants and, to a lesser extent, the emerging urban owners of capital (the bourgeoisie) who were required to pay high levels of taxation to support the absolute state and its wealthy aristocrats and their sumptuous lifestyles. It was not until the first French Revolution of 1789 that this feudal state began to be dismantled and replaced by a new, nation-based state; a process which required 'breaking all separate local, territorial, urban, and provincial powers in order to create the civil unity of the nation' while simultaneously promoting 'free competition and the beginning of big industry in the towns' overseen by a centralised but economically limited state.[27]

In defence of their property rights and livelihoods, the urban property-owning burghers (which included artisans, merchants, manufacturers, traders and usurers) took collective action to establish their cities as independent, self-governing municipalities. The burghers, despite the diversity of their industrial backgrounds, typically had a common urban, religious, commercial or industrial background which contributed to these city residents having a sense of common purpose and an inclination to collective action.[28] They objected to taxation and other imposts that benefited the royalty with few benefits returning to the cities and their citizens. The burghers, as employers, also had a common industrial cause against the town's laborers and other members of the urban workforce, especially with regards to limiting wage rises, setting workplace standards and conditions and blocking collective action against them by labour. Through their newly formed guilds and their influence over the municipality, the burghers worked together to protect their own private property rights and economic interests, defend themselves against both the feudal landed nobility[29] and exercise control over the town's labour force. As such, the burghers were the nascent capitalist class.[30]

City government was an essential component of the devolved and dispersed power in the feudal polity. In the late eleventh and the twelfth centuries, across Europe, thousands of new self-governing cities and towns came into existence.[31] The formation of these cities was hastened when citizens in urban centres united against political pressure from local landed nobles/manor lords who wished to control, tax or in other ways interfere in the rule of city. In the face of these attacks, feudal towns were true 'associations' which were 'called forth by the direct need, the care of providing for the protection of property, and of multiplying the means of production and defence of the separate members'.[32]

These cities had independent and self-governing autonomy, including legislative, judicial, taxing, regulatory and, in some instances, military capabilities. To achieve this, a new social (political) relation was established between the city government and the ruling monarch (or other noble or religious supporters) where the monarch delegated self-government to the city in return for fealty and the payment of taxes. With this high-level patronage, city governments could defend themselves from falling under the jurisdiction of less favourable manorial rule.[33]

On the other hand, the vast majority of urban residents were wage labourers, free peasants, property-less serfs, ex-slaves, ex-soldiers, domestic servants and apprentices or journeymen (who were skilled but, under the control of the master craftsmen and the guilds, could own no property and not employ staff). Other urban residents included foreigners who lived in cities as merchants and traders with other cities, and members of religious orders. These people, as property non-holders and non-citizens, were banned from voting for, or being representatives on, municipal councils.

The significance of cities in the feudal polity is twofold. Feudal cities provided city inhabitants with a degree of control over their economy and their lives that was not possible for serfs living under the jurisdiction of their feudal landlords. Some of these independent cities became the most powerful, largest and richest cities in Europe, and cities such as Florence, Venice and Rome in Italy, Bruges in Belgium and Toledo in Spain were the birthplace of the political, scientific, industrial, trade, cultural and artistic innovations that made up the 300-year-long European Renaissance. The second significance of feudal cities is that they established many of the political, legal and institutional arrangements that, over centuries, would be restructured into the capitalist state.

The capitalist state

In the development of the capitalist mode of production in Europe, the integrated, self-supporting and mutually dependent social (political) relations of vassalage and the social (economic) relations of manorialism that made up the feudal mode of production were divided into two separate spheres: one sphere based on privatised power over property, called 'the economy' (which Marx called 'civil society');[34] and the other sphere of societal activity based on public power, 'the state'. Marx wasn't the first to recognise that capitalism created this unique division of society into two mutually interdependent social spheres with contradictory interests: he acknowledged that 'Hegel's keenest insight lies in his sensing the separation of civil [economic] and political society to be a contradiction'.[35]

The separation of the complex, integrated and hierarchical webs of devolved power and authority and economic obligations and privileges that made up the feudal polity, and its replacement with a public-property polity and a private-property economy, took centuries. The owners of private property worked together to undermine the feudal legislation, institutions, regulations, infrastructure and forms of taxation that had been developed to support monarchies, estates, manors and local government and those who worked for them.

For example, feudal obligations of property owners based on laws that required them 'to provide work for those who do not own property or to pay them a wage which is at all times adequate, etc.'[36] were abolished, and these societal obligations to pay workers an 'adequate' wage and to employ the unemployed either ended or were transferred to the state. The owners of private property worked together to replace the feudal political economy and its social obligations with new institutional arrangements where '[e]veryone is free to exchange his possessions as he chooses, without any other consideration than his own interest as an individual' and where property owners are given 'the right to use and abuse the materials of all labour *i.e.*, to do as they wish with them'.[37] In other words:

Through the emancipation of private property from the community, the State has become a separate entity, beside and outside civil society; but it is nothing more than the form of organisation which the bourgeois necessarily adopt both for internal and external purposes, for the mutual guarantee of their property and interests.[38]

This process of transforming the feudal polity into a capitalist state that supported capitalist accumulation took place in different ways in different countries depending on their historical context – a process that often occurred only through bloody struggle. In France, for example, the first French Revolution had the effect of 'breaking all separate local, territorial, urban, and provincial powers in order to create the civil unity of the nation', while at the same time promoting 'free competition and the beginning of big industry in the towns' and developing a centralised but also economically limited state.

These changes were not inevitable. The form of each national state developed out of decades of struggles between those supporting the creation of a capitalist state and supporters of the old feudal system who wanted a return to an economy and society based on the wealth and obligations of large landowners; burghers threatened by the power of national capital and wanting to keep political control by municipal governments; and workers' organisations which wanted to democratise the state and increase democratic control over private property and strengthen the capacity of the state to intervene in the exploitative, unstable, inequitable and anti-democratic social relations of capitalism.

In the case of the Paris Commune (1870–1), the working-class communards found themselves facing a state which had both remnant characteristics of the feudal state and nascent characteristics of the capitalist state. Almost a hundred years after the first French Revolution, some parts of the centralised power of the French state were still organised along feudal lines: the standing army, police, bureaucracy, clergy, judicature and other government departments were still 'clogged by all manner of medieval rubbish, seigniorial rights, local privileges, municipal and guild monopolies, and provincial constitutions'.[39]

'Only under the second Bonaparte does the state seem to have made itself completely independent … vis-à-vis civil society.'[40] When this occurred:

the government, placed under parliamentary control – that is, under the direct control of the propertied classes – became not only a hotbed of huge national debts and crushing taxes; with its irresistible allurements of place, pelf, and patronage, it became not only the bone of contention between the rival factions and adventurers of the ruling classes; but its political character changed simultaneously with the economic changes of society … state power assumed more and more the character of the national power of capital over labour, of a public force organized for social enslavement, of an engine of class despotism.[41]

On the other hand, and unlike the experiences of Europe and Asia, the capitalist state in the United States developed differently. It did not develop through the breakdown of long-standing feudal polities and feudal obligations in Europe, or the overthrow of despotic polities in Asia. Instead, the capitalist state in the United States was formed by property owners including slave owners who established the various state governments and the national government in ways that made the US state, from its beginning, subordinate to the interests of capital.[42] This is why, Marx says 'The most perfect example of the modern State is North America ... the State exists only for the sake of private property.'[43]

Every nation that has developed on the foundations of the capitalist mode of production has developed capitalist states in historically particular ways. However, there are a number of features that are common to all these states. Every capitalist state continues to deliver the three traditional imperatives that apply to all polities: to defend the society, the national territory and the state from attack; to support the mode of production so that the society and its people have the material goods and services needed for their sustenance and the reproduction of the society over time; and to ensure the state has the legitimacy and material resources needed to carry out its first two roles.

More specifically, the capitalist state has a limited role in the operation of the capitalist economy 'Because the bourgeois do not allow the state to interfere in their private interests and give it only as much power as is necessary for their own safety and the maintenance of competition and because the bourgeois in general act as citizens only to the extent that their private interests demand it.'[44] Capitalist states are structured to support the capitalist mode of production (within the limits of the state's dependence on the capitalist economy for resources and for its legitimacy). The state's legislation (including property, industrial relations, and trade laws and regulations), infrastructure (including the provision of ports, roads, railways, electricity and telecommunications) and taxation arrangements are structured in ways to make profit the principal basis of the economy, to allow capitalists (rather than landowners, employees or the state) to appropriate the whole surplus labour and surplus product (wealth) produced by the direct producers on condition that the capitalists provide a small portion of their surplus to landowners (as rent) and the state (as taxes).[45] Third, the capitalist state must carry out its roles within the limits set by its contradictory social relations with the economy, where the state protects and supports the capitalist economy in return for taxing capital and labour so it has resources to carry out its functions and to maintain its own legitimacy.

The fiscal, bureaucratic, regulatory, taxation and other forms of the capitalist state are never static: they change continuously in response to struggles within and between capital, labour, the landed property class, other interest groups and through struggles within the state over the role of the state itself. At first, the capitalist state had a mutual but contradictory dependence on *national* capital for its resources, taxes and legitimacy. In the late twentieth century, with the development of global capitalism, states increasingly restructured national laws (applying to, for example, trade, finance copyright and intellectual property law) to support the *international* production, circulation and realisation of capital. National governments established international forms of the capitalist state (such as the World Bank, International Monetary Fund and Bank for International Settlements) which generally support multinational private property and promote international institutions of market competition, free trade and globalised systems of finance while simultaneously protecting capital (by minimising international tax obligations and maximising the protection of capital against reparations to individuals, communities and the environment for the pollution, ecological destruction, unemployment, inequality, poverty and other societal damage caused by the production and circulation of capital).

In summary, and unlike ancient, Asiatic and feudal polities, the capitalist mode of production divides societies into two mutually dependent but contradictory spheres, one based on private power (extensive 'economic' control by capital over labour and the means of production) and the other based on public power (limited 'political' control by the state over the economy). This situation is not inevitable or permanent. As will be discussed in Chapter 7, one of the most important strategies to take to transform capitalism is to democratise both the private power of property and the public power of the state that supports it.[46]

Communist polity

Marx wrote relatively few comments about the organisation and practice of communist societies. His early writings tended to be broad statements of principle, and his later writings tended to be more specific. Land, and how the social relations of landed property would need to change, are continually mentioned in his discussions of communism. In communism, a democratic polity would play an essential role. It would take collective ownership and control of the means of production (including land). The state, under the direction of citizens, would plan and assist all citizens to provide the labour needed to produce their own necessary goods and services and to support the reproduction of the society as a whole. After providing this necessary and surplus labour, all people would then have the time they need for their own personal, professional and other development as human beings: this is 'the true realm of freedom'.[47]

In a communist society, the communist state would not 'wither away'[48] but be made subordinate to the 'real community'.[49] With the state and the economy organised and governed to resource human freedom and promote the common good (rather than private profit), 'all the springs of co-operative wealth flow more abundantly' and the classic goal associated with communism would be achieved: society and production will be organised on the basis of 'From each according to his ability, to each according to his needs!'[50]

Marx emphasised there was no single path to a communist society. Each country would need to develop its own unique historically contingent revolutionary course of action. While political and economic change at the local or national level could produce partial victories, in the same way capitalism has become global, so too would communism be based on 'the union and agreement of the democratic parties of all countries'.[51]

In his early *Philosophic Manuscripts*, Marx proposed that communist societies would develop through a three-stage process. In the first stage of communism, 'crude' communism would replace the capitalist state (or other polity) with a revolutionary dictatorship of the proletariat. This communist polity would annul private property; that is, own all land and the other means of production.[52] Indeed, the first 'generally applicable' policy of communism is 'Abolition of property in land and application of all rents of land to public purposes'.[53] In addition to the socialisation of land, 'The proletariat will use its political supremacy to wrest, by degree, all capital from the bourgeoisie, to centralise all instruments of production in the hands of the State, *i.e.*, of the proletariat organised as the ruling class; and to increase the total productive forces as rapidly as possible.'[54] There would be an equality of *wages* for all workers which would be paid out by the state's (communal) capital.

These first-stage developments to establish a 'crude' communist society would be, as has always occurred throughout history, resisted by the bourgeoisie who would lose the benefits they had been accruing from their private control over the means of production. Another essential role of the working-class-controlled communist polity, therefore, would be to establish a proletarian army to support the state and the working class from internal or external attack.[55]

The second, more advanced form of communist polity would use the Paris Commune as a model. Here the centralised polity of 'crude' communism, the revolutionary dictatorship of the proletariat, would be replaced with organisations of workers and the community with direct, democratic control over both the state itself and the means of production owned by the state.[56] This would occur in two ways. First, all the means of production would be concentrated in the hands of a vast association of the direct producers of the nation. For example, multiple cooperative societies owning and managing their own land, tools, equipment, machinery and other means of production would work together with other collective, syndicalist and cooperative firms to regulate national production using a national economic and political plan.

In effect, the state's 'crude' economic role of owning, planning, managing and paying for all economic activity would be replaced by large cooperatives or collectives of free and associated labourers who would decide how the means of production (land and capital) would be used to produce the sustenance needed by all and for the common good.[57] The administrators or managers needed in such an associated polity would be 'chosen by universal suffrage ... [and be] revocable at short term'. In addition, those carrying out these planning and managing roles would be paid a wage at the same rate as all other workers.[58] These organisations would ensure democratic participation by the working class in all aspects of the planning, management and operation of the economy.

With the means of production owned and democratically managed by the direct producers (and not by a party leadership that represents and acts on behalf of the working class), the old capitalist divisions of society (such as the division between the polity and the economy) would be overcome. Democratic control over the means of production would supersede the capitalist mode of production (and its associated conditions of exploitation and oppression), ensure every able-bodied individual worked for a living (instead of letting a minority live off their appropriation of rent or profit), provide the sustenance needed for people to live and do so in ways that were consistent with human self-emancipation.

In the third stage of the development of communist societies, with the total replacement of exploitative and alienating private property and its related political and economic institutions, people would have developed a society where people would be free, without unmet needs and one which would bring about 'the genuine resolution of the conflict between man and nature, and between man and man'.[59]

Conclusion

The last four chapters have summarised Marx's writings about landed property, rent and the landed property class with a focus on these phenomena in cities. The historical approach has shown how different modes of production (the indigenous, ancient, Asiatic, feudal, capitalist and communist modes of production) have made land, rent and class take different forms and have established cities with different functions, resources and forms of governance.

Marx's approach, while based on the study of historical communities and societies, is directly relevant to contemporary urban land policy strategies including land taxes, land nationalisation, indigenous land rights and the creation of land trusts (to be discussed in the next chapter).

Notes

1. K. Marx and F. Engels, *The German Ideology*, pt 3.K, Moscow, Progress Publishers, 1968, https://www.marxists.org/archive/marx/works/1845/german-ideology/ch03k.htm
2. In volume I of *Capital*, for example, Marx referred to 'the power of the State, the concentrated and organised force of society', adding 'force is the midwife of every old society pregnant with a new one'. He was not alone in treating the state as having a monopoly of violence. Max Weber, in the generation after Marx and a founder of sociology, said in his 1918 lecture 'The Profession and Vocation of Politics': 'In the past, the most varied

institutions – beginning with the *Sippe* [i.e. clan, kindred, extended family] – have known the use of physical force as quite normal. Today, however, we have to say that a state is a human community that (successfully) claims the monopoly of the legitimate use of physical force within a given territory. Note that 'territory' is one of the characteristics of the state.' M. Weber, *Political Writings*, https://web.archive.org/web/20001207134100/http://bertie.la.utexas.edu/course-materials/government/32570/vocation/vocation.html

3. Marx and Engels, *The German Ideology*, pt 1.C, https://www.marxists.org/archive/marx/works/1845/german-ideology/ch01c.htm

4. K. Marx, *Capital*, vol. I, ch. 1, Moscow, Progress Publishers, 1887, https://www.marxists.org/archive/marx/works/1857/precapitalist/ch01.htm

5. K. Marx, 'Private Property and Communism', *Economic and Philosophic Manuscripts of 1844*, Moscow, Progress Publishers, 1959, https://www.marxists.org/archive/marx/works/1844/epm/3rd.htm

6. K. Marx, 'The Duchess of Sutherland and Slavery', *The People's Paper*, no. 45, 12 Mar. 1853, London, https://www.marxists.org/archive/marx/works/1853/03/12.htm

7. Ibid.

8. Ibid.

9. Marx and Engels, *The German Ideology*, pt 1.A, https://www.marxists.org/archive/marx/works/1845/german-ideology/ch01a.htm

10. K. Marx, 'Forms Which Precede Capitalist Production', *Grundrisse*, ch. 9, London, Penguin Books in association with *New Left Review*, 1973, https://www.marxists.org/archive/marx/works/1857/grundrisse/ch09.htm

11. Ibid.

12. For a similar example where a Central Mexican indigenous community established a polity made up of 'commoners' rather than the nobility, see L. Fargher, R. Blanton and V. Espinoza, 'Egalitarian Ideology and Political Power in Prehispanic Central Mexico: The Case of Tlaxcallan', *Latin American Antiquity*, vol. 21, no. 3, 2010, pp. 227–51.

13. Marx and Engels, *The German Ideology*, pt 1.A, https://www.marxists.org/archive/marx/works/1845/german-ideology/ch01a.htm

14. Moveable property is distinct both from landed property, or real estate, which consists of the rights of owners and non-owners over the use of a fixed real property (namely land and buildings affixed to the land), and from chattels (moveable property for personal use such as furniture, clothing and jewellery).

15. K. Marx, 'The Chapter on Capital (cont.)', *Grundrisse*, ch. 9, London, Penguin Books in association with *New Left Review*, 1973, https://www.marxists.org/archive/marx/works/1857/grundrisse/ch09.htm

16. Marx and Engels, *The German Ideology*, pt 1.A, https://www.marxists.org/archive/marx/works/1845/german-ideology/ch01a.htm

17. Emperors and other monarchs in East Asia were often called 'the Son of Heaven' or 'ruler of the world', a sacred title which helped legitimise their secular rule.

18. K. Marx, *Capital*, vol. III, ch. 47, New York, International Publishers, 1959, https://www.marxists.org/archive/marx/works/1894-c3/ch47.htm

19. K. Marx, 'India', *New-York Daily Tribune*, 5 Aug. 1853, https://www.marxists.org/archive/marx/works/1853/08/05.htm

20. K. Marx, 'Original Accumulation of Capital', *Grundrisse*, ch. 9, London, Penguin Books in association with *New Left Review*, 1973, https://www.marxists.org/archive/marx/works/1857/grundrisse/ch09.htm

21. Marx, *Capital*, vol. I, ch. 16, https://www.marxists.org/archive/marx/works/1867-c1/ch16.htm#7a
22. Marx, 'Original Accumulation of Capital'.
23. Britannica, The Editors of Encyclopaedia, 'Cao', *Encyclopedia Britannica*, Chicago, IL, 2021, https://www.britannica.com/biography/Cao-Cao
24. K. Marx, 'The Chapter on Capital (cont.)', *Grundrisse*, ch. 9, London, Penguin Books in association with *New Left Review*, 1973, https://www.marxists.org/archive/marx/works/1857/grundrisse/ch09.htm
25. Ibid.
26. Marx and Engels, *The German Ideology*, ch. 3, https://www.marxists.org/archive/marx/works/1845/german-ideology/ch03abs.htm
27. K. Marx, *The Eighteenth Brumaire of Louis Bonaparte*, ch. 7, Marx/Engels Internet Archive, 1995, https://www.marxists.org/archive/marx/works/1852/18th-brumaire/ch07.htm
28. H. J. Berman, *Law and Revolution: The Formation of the Western Legal Tradition*, Cambridge, MA, Harvard University Press, 1983.
29. K. Marx and F. Engels, *The Manifesto of the Communist Party*, pt I, in *Marx/Engels Selected Works*, vol. I, Moscow, Progress Publishers, 1969, https://www.marxists.org/archive/marx/works/1848/communist-manifesto/ch01.htm
30. Marx and Engels, *The German Ideology*, pt 1.D, https://www.marxists.org/archive/marx/works/1845/german-ideology/ch01d.htm
31. Berman, *Law and Revolution*.
32. Marx and Engels, *The German Ideology*, pt 1.C, https://www.marxists.org/archive/marx/works/1845/german-ideology/ch01c.htm
33. Marx and Engels, *The Manifesto of the Communist Party*, pt I, https://www.marxists.org/archive/marx/works/1848/communist-manifesto/ch01.htm
34. Marx's view of 'civil society' as the economic sphere of capitalism differs from the late twentieth-century view that civil society refers to 'social capital' or the 'third sector' of society distinct from government and the economy which includes non-government organisations, religious groups and other interest groups. For a critique of this interpretation of civil society, see B. Fine, *Social Capital Versus Social Theory*, London, Routledge, 2001.
35. K. Marx, *Critique of Hegel's Philosophy of Right*, pt 5, ed. J. O'Malley, Cambridge, Cambridge University Press, 1970, https://www.marxists.org/archive/marx/works/1843/critique-hpr/ch05.htm#087
36. Quoted by K. Marx, 'Wages of Labour', *Economic and Philosophic Manuscripts of 1844*, Moscow, Progress Publishers, 1959, https://www.marxists.org/archive/marx/works/1844/epm/1st.htm
37. Ibid.
38. Marx and Engels, *The German Ideology*, pt 1.C, https://www.marxists.org/archive/marx/works/1845/german-ideology/ch01c.htm
39. K. Marx, 'The Paris Commune', *The Civil War in France*, ch. 5, London, General Council of the International Workingmen's Association, 1871, https://www.marxists.org/archive/marx/works/1871/civil-war-france/ch05.htm
40. Marx, *The Eighteenth Brumaire of Louis Bonaparte*, ch. 7, https://www.marxists.org/archive/marx/works/1852/18th-brumaire/ch07.htm
41. Marx, 'The Paris Commune'.

42. K. Marx, 'Bastiat and Carey', *Grundrisse*, ch. 17, London, Penguin Books in association with *New Left Review*, 1973, https://www.marxists.org/archive/marx/works/1857/grundrisse/ch17.htm

43. Marx and Engels, *The German Ideology*, pt 1.C, https://www.marxists.org/archive/marx/works/1845/german-ideology/ch01c.htm

44. Ibid., pt 3.B, https://www.marxists.org/archive/marx/works/1845/german-ideology/ch03k.htm

45. K. Marx, *Theories of Surplus Value*, ch. 24, Moscow, Progress Publishers, 1969, https://www.marxists.org/archive/marx/works/1863/theories-surplus-value/ch24.htm

46. Marx and Engels, *The Manifesto of the Communist Party*, pt IV, https://www.marxists.org/archive/marx/works/1848/communist-manifesto/ch04.htm

47. Marx, *Capital*, vol. III, ch. 48, https://www.marxists.org/archive/marx/works/1894-c3/ch48.htm

48. For a discussion of whether the state 'withers away' or is 'superseded', see S. Avineri, 'The Hegelian Origins of Marx's Political Thought', *The Review of Metaphysics* 21:1 (1967), 33–56.

49. K. Marx, 'Critique of the Gotha Program', pt IV, *Marx/Engels Selected Works*, vol. III, Moscow, Progress Publishers, 1970, https://www.marxists.org/archive/marx/works/1875/gotha/ch04.htm

50. Ibid., ch. 1, https://www.marxists.org/archive/marx/works/1875/gotha/ch01.htm

51. Marx and Engels, *The Manifesto of the Communist Party*, pt IV, https://www.marxists.org/archive/marx/works/1848/communist-manifesto/ch04.htm

52. K. Marx, 'The Nationalisation of the Land', *The International Herald*, no. 11, 15 June 1872, https://www.marxists.org/archive/marx/works/1872/04/nationalisation-land.htm

53. K. Marx and F. Engels, *The Manifesto of the Communist Party*, part II, in *Marx/Engels Selected Works*, vol. I, Moscow, Progress Publishers, 1969, https://www.marxists.org/archive/marx/works/1848/communist-manifesto/ch02.htm

54. Ibid.

55. K. Marx, 'Speech on the Seventh Anniversary of the International', *The First International and After*, Harmondsworth, Penguin, 1974, https://www.marxists.org/archive/marx/bio/media/marx/71_10_15.htm

56. K. Marx and J. Guesde, 'The Programme of the Parti Ouvrier', in J. Guesde, *Textes choisis 1867–1882*, Paris, Éditions sociales, 1959, trans. B. Moss for Marx/Engels Internet Archive, https://www.marxists.org/archive/marx/works/1880/05/parti-ouvrier.htm

57. K. Marx, 'The Paris Commune', *The Civil War in France*, London, General Council of the International Workingmen's Association, 1871, https://www.marxists.org/archive/marx/works/1871/civil-war-france/ch05.htm

58. Ibid.

59. Marx and Engels, *The Manifesto of the Communist Party*, pt II, https://www.marxists.org/archive/marx/works/1848/communist-manifesto/ch02.htm

CHAPTER 7

Implications for Urban Land Strategies

> The distinguishing feature of Communism is not the abolition of property generally, but the abolition of bourgeois property.[1]

Introduction

The urban problems occurring around the world are serious, affect millions of people, and without intervention, will worsen. They include unaffordable house prices, homelessness, the distribution of employment and unemployment in cities, failing urban infrastructure, the financialisation of land assets, and the capacity of governments to provide city planning, urban transport and other infrastructure and social services. In the Global South, cities also face pressures arising from the colonialisation of land, the privatisation of customary land ('land grabbing'), inadequate housing, urban congestion and pollution, and corruption.

Critically informed urban policies can play a key role in addressing these problems. Successful policies need to tackle the underlying, structural causes of urban development rather than providing temporary solutions, or, worse, providing free-market-based 'solutions' that exacerbate exploitation, increase inequalities and reduce democratic control over our lives. Marx's urban political economy, with its critique of urban development processes, provides a theoretical framework that can be used to develop urban policies with the goals of economic development, social justice, environmental sustainability and political integrity.

Typically, urban policies are complex documents that consider multiple topics (such as the planning, designing, and financing of cities) and multiple stakeholders who affect urban development. In general, these policies focus on decentralisation, entrepreneurialism, and democratisation. Urban governance itself involves a wide range of actors, from the provincial to the global, public, private, and civil society. The 'New Urban Agenda'[2] developed by the United Nations Human Settlements Programme (UN-HABITAT), for example, provides general principles about the content of urban development (such as urban population, immigration and refugees; sustainable urban development; urban planning and infrastructure provision for water, electricity, roads and so on; affordable housing; urban safety and security, especially for women; and the impact of cities on climate change) and the process of urban development (such as the need for consultation, transparency and sound financial systems).

This chapter, however, focuses on one element of urban policies: urban land, including landownership, land use management and land taxation. This focus on land is deliberately singular because so many other urban strategies – such as urban investment, employment, affordable housing, infrastructure and service delivery – are directly enabled or limited by the form of landownership and the issues of rent that exists in cities, as shown in the previous chapters.

Specifically, this chapter proposes four urban land strategies: leave land in private ownership but tax land value (a land value tax); nationalise land and put land use under the control of the state (land nationalisation); strengthen and expand customary land title; and establish community ownership and control of land (community land trusts). These four proposals are discussed in the next four sections.

Land value tax

One urban land strategy is to introduce a tax on the value of land. A tax on the value of land has been promoted since the earliest days of political economic thought. Adam Smith and David Ricardo advocated such a tax, but it is most commonly associated with Henry George.[3] George proposed that exclusive private ownership of land created unwarranted special privileges and, rather than removing these private privileges by nationalising land, another option was for the state to capture any increases in land value by 'taking, in the form of a tax, as nearly as may be, the equivalent of that value which attaches to land by reason of the growth and advance of society.'[4]

Marx and Engels, on the other hand, had called for the overthrow of private property in land and the privatisation of rent in *The Communist Manifesto*: specifically, the 'Abolition of property in land and application of all rents of land to public purposes'. Marx was critical of George's view, which he summarised as: 'everything would be all right if ground rent were paid to the state' because it did not call for the replacement of private property and also left 'wage labour and therefore capitalist production in existence'.[5]

More recently, scholars such as Stiglitz have put similar arguments that inequalities in capitalism can be compensated for by increasing taxes: for example, he suggests that 'A tax on the return to land, and even more so, on the capital gains from land, would reduce inequality and, by encouraging more investment into real capital, actually enhance growth.'[6] The practicalities of a land tax have been analysed in more detail since George's time. In Singapore, for example, where all land is state-owned but buildings on land can be privately owned, Haila researched Singapore's 'Georgian land rent tax, aimed at capturing unearned increment' arising from increases in land value that result from planning, zoning or development changes.[7] Ho subsequently clarified that Singapore differs from the Georgist model in that land is not privately owned but the property of the state.[8] Nevertheless, the Singapore 'development charge' is a flexible policy instrument that can be adapted to real estate cycles: for example, in the 1985 recession, the development charge was lowered from 70 per cent (of the appreciation in land value) to 50 per cent, but then returned to 70 per cent in 2007 when there was a buoyant real estate market.

Types of land value tax

A land value tax is one that taxes increases in land values. Land value taxes have been used throughout history and on all continents of the world.[9] Taxes on solely the value of land are rare, as most governments typically tax the value of land and buildings or, rarely, increases in the value of buildings (but not land). Currently, around thirty countries use some sort of land value tax.[10] In the Global North, for example in Europe, revenue raised exclusively from land taxes is highest in Denmark, Slovenia and Estonia with around 1 per cent of GDP and 2.5 per cent of total tax revenues. Some subnational jurisdictions in Australia, New Zealand and the UK also have land tax regimes.[11] Land taxes also operate in Singapore (as discussed above).

In the Global South, land value taxes have proliferated in nations where a system of registration of title or deeds was already in place (such as Fiji, Kenya and South Africa), and where there are no major issues arising from tenure insecurity and boundary disputes. Land and property taxes are often important sources of local revenue, and thus have historically been locally governed (with a few exceptions like Ethiopia, Jamaica and Chile, where national governments regulate and administer the tax). Recently, in Africa, Lagos combined three different rates on land and property into one land value tax, while countries such as Rwanda, Malawi, Zambia and Botswana have instituted separate taxes on the value of land and the value of the buildings on the land.[12] Recent quantitative simulations of land value tax reforms for Rwanda, Peru, Nicaragua and Indonesia found land taxes provide a substantial untapped potential for tax revenues at minimal deadweight losses; that tax schemes can be designed which avoid adverse effects on the poor; and that, with technological advances, administrative costs of land taxes have reduced substantially and are outweighed by the tax revenues that can be collected.[13]

Implementation

The implementation of a successful land value tax regime relies on the existence of several important administrative systems. These are often specified in the relevant land tax legislation and the legislation and policies of associated public administration bodies (such as anti-corruption bodies). There are four systems that are particularly important.

The first is a land value registration system. An urban land valuation and registration system is a basis for a land value tax regime.[14] Professional bodies (such as the

International Federation of Surveyors (FIG), a United Nations and World Bank–recognised non-governmental organisation of national associations of surveyors and associated professionals) are able to provide advice on a best-design-for-use system. This system will include legislation, regulations, the development of trained professionals to register land, and the establishment of administrative arrangements such as record keeping, use of technology and financial arrangements.

Second is a land value tax system. A land value tax system consists of legislation, regulations, the development of trained professionals to establish and record land values and establish and operate administrative arrangements such as recordkeeping, use of technology and financial arrangements. If there are exceptions for some landowners (such as urban homeowners or tenants), then these criteria need to be specified in the legislation. An appropriate rate of tax will also need to be set. There will also need to be communication strategies for potential taxpayers (so they are aware of their tax payment obligations) and for the public (so they are aware of how they will benefit from the new tax system).

Third is a transparent use of land taxes. The lack of government accountability is one of the key issues undermining the Lagos State Land Use Charge Law 2018.[15] The government (national, provincial or local, as appropriate) must use the new tax revenue in a transparent, accountable and productive manner to deliver economic and social infrastructure and other public interest benefits to the people. This will both increase acceptance of the tax by the public and support taxpayer compliance.

Fourth is a powerful, independent anti-corruption authority. Given the significance of this institution for all land regimes, it is discussed separately below.

Assessment of land value taxation

Land value taxes are simpler and fairer than many other forms of taxation. Land value taxes are a progressive tax in the sense that the tax is imposed only on land title holders and in proportion to the value of the land. The tax falls mostly on those who own large amounts of expensive urban land; that is, people who are highly correlated with having high levels of wealth and income. If land values increase due to demand for land arising from population growth, the addition of urban infrastructure or other reasons, then the increase in the land value is captured by the state rather than the private landowner.

Land taxes are economically efficient because they capture the externalities that arise from government investment in urban infrastructure. John Pullen, for example, has noted that urban development, funded by governments, often delivers benefits to developers and landowners in the form of increased land values.[16] Direct attempts by governments to recoup some of these benefits have rarely been successful, whereas a practical alternative would be to introduce a land value tax. In addition, land value taxes could help reduce land speculation (where speculators withhold land from productive activity in the expectation of an increase in land value) by creating incentives for landowners to use their land for productive investement and job creation.

Land value tax is an administratively efficient tax. Land or property taxes require a system of land registration, or cadastre, which includes fiscal, social, economic, legal and environmental information on land and its owner. The fact that a large number of low-income countries have some form of property taxes suggests that the costs for establishing basic cadastral requirements for land taxation are not prohibitive. Once this system is in place, it is difficult for landowners to hide, avoid or shift their land tax liabilities. Administrative savings are also made if multiple land taxes, property taxes and real estate transfer taxes (such as stamp duty) are combined into a single land tax. In addition, such a tax system is more likely to be supported by taxpayers because it is simple, transparent and predictable.

Land value taxes are also politically feasible. Often, the introduction of land taxes is challenged by a well-organised, vocal but small number of large landowners and property developers in the landed property class. However, by making the benefits clear to the rest of the population, the majority of the population will support the reforms. For example, the International Growth Centre, associated with the London School of Economics and University of Oxford, found that Lagos successfully introduced land tax reforms by directly linking the tax to new expenditures in visible, costly and popular infrastructure projects (such as hospitals and road improvements). As a result of the introduction of a land tax, annual capital spending in Lagos grew from $600 million in 2006 to $1.7 billion in 2011 (in inflation-adjusted 2012 figures).[17] A similar situation has occurred in Singapore where much of the infrastructure central to Singapore's economic and political success has been funded through land value capture.[18]

For all these reasons, land value taxes can be a useful reform if it is decided to leave urban land in private ownership. However, as shown in the case of the global financial crisis (Chapter 4), the price of urban land for housing in capitalist economies can be strongly distorted by the finance sector, insurance companies and the real estate industry to suit their financial interests. Legislative and other changes would also be needed to ensure the finance, insurance and real estate industries did not undermine the effectiveness and simplicity of the tax. Finally, as Marx noted, this is always a transitional policy because it will not fundamentally change the prevailing mode of production that heavily influences how urban land is used, where and to whose benefit.

Nationalisation of urban land

A second urban land strategy open to governments to ensure economically efficient, socially just and environmentally sustainable use of a nation's land is to nationalise urban land.

Nationalisation occurs when economic assets, previously held in private or municipal ownership, are transferred into public ownership by the national or provincial state. There are two common arguments for the nationalisation of economic assets: the nation (or province) as a whole becomes the owner of certain instruments of production (such as land); and the profit motive is replaced with other motives such as 'public service', the 'national interest' or 'social responsibility'.[19] Nationalisation compares with privatisation (when assets are transferred into private control) and municipalisation (when assets are transferred into municipal control).[20]

There are two main forms of nationalisation. First, there is the nationalisation of *production* to deliver social, economic or environmental priorities (to compensate for market failure, to democratise companies, and to stop the exploitation of workers, and in times of war when government control of the economy is essential for national survival). Second, there can be the nationalisation of *consumption* (where governments own and operate companies or industries to provide cheaper services or to provide services that are not profitable for companies to provide). In some cases, such as the nationalisation of Northern Rail (after years of late-running rail services, high ticket prices and poor labour relations overseen by the company running the rail service) by the United Kingdom's Conservative government,[21] nationalisation achieves both goals by improving freight and other production-related objectives as well as providing better-quality services than can be provided by private sector companies.

During the four decades when neoclassical economics and ideology dominated public policy around the world,[22] nationalisation was typically discounted as a policy option in favour of the 'privatisation of the public sphere, deregulation of the corporate sector, and the lowering of income and corporate taxes, paid for with cuts to public spending'.[23] However, nationalisation is being used as a policy option to address the failures caused by neoliberal policies (such as the global financial crisis beginning in 2007–8, the global recession in the late 2000s, and the increasing disparities between rich and poor in capitalist countries)[24] and to address new challenges facing nations (such as climate change caused by industrial-scale burning of fossil fuels and the destruction of the environment, the 'great lockdown' of the world in 2020–1 resulting from the COVID-19 pandemic, and the emergence of economic and superpower rivalry between the United States and China).

Types of land nationalisation

As with all economic policies, such as nationalisation, how it is carried out and who benefits depends on the societal context. Nationalisation of land, industries or organisations in a society with a capitalist mode of production will have significantly different effects compared with nationalisations that occur in other modes of production.

Marx noted, for example, that in societies with a capitalist mode of production, there would be many benefits for capital if land was nationalised. The abolition of landed property (in the sense that privately owned land in a capitalist society is converted into state-owned land) would result in capitalists paying rent to the state (instead of the private landlord) for the use of that land. This would be highly beneficial to capital as a whole because the rental income to the state would reduce the overall tax payment.[25] The nationalisation of land would change the recipient of rent (from the private landlord to the state) but make no systemic change to the circuit of capital: 'Abolition of interest and of interest-bearing capital, on the other hand, means the abolition of capital and of capitalist production itself.'[26]

Nationalisation of land, however, has different effects within communist modes of production. The classic model of land nationalisation was established by Russia's Bolshevik government in 1917. This abolished private ownership of land and put the ownership and use of land in the control of the state, while maintaining the existence of private ownership of buildings (such as houses) on the land. The renting or exchange of land was legally forbidden (but, in practice, it was rife immediately after the revolution).[27] However, even though all land was nationalised and most of the dwellings in cities were built and owned by the local city government, after World War II there was a greater emphasis on small houseowners building and living in their privately owned homes in the suburbs.[28] This experiment in the nationalisation of urban land ceased with the collapse of the Soviet Union in 1991 when all land was privatised.

In China, urban land was nationalised as part of the 1949 revolution (along with the collectivisation of rural land into the hands of rural peasants). All urban land is owned by the state. For more than thirty years, urban land was allocated to various uses (such as housing, industry and so on) through administrative decisions. As there was no concept of a 'land value' or rent, land users paid a 'resettlement fee' to the state in return for 'land use rights' over particular blocks of land, a fee which became regarded as the effective 'price' for land.

In the mid-1980s, two major urban land reforms were instituted. While the public ownership of land continued, the government created the capacity for owners of 'land use rights' to legally transfer (trade, sell, sublease or mortgage) their land use rights to other owners, essentially establishing a land market. Within a decade or so, a three-level land market was operating made up of the primary land market (where the state sells land use rights over portions of land to property developers), the secondary land market (where developers sell land use rights to final land users such as residential householders), and the tertiary land market (where final land users transfer land among themselves).[29]

These new markets were reinforced by the second major urban land reform: the capacity for local governments to levy land taxes. The revenue from land use rights sales is important for local governments' budgets. This new source of revenue was particularly important for local governments which were under increasing demand for new urban infrastructure. This mutually beneficial, self-reinforcing relationship of dependency between property developers making high urban land use rights profits and local government revenues (and the delivery of urban infrastructure which, in turn, promotes more urban development) is a special feature of China's real estate market.

At first, this capacity to trade land use rights only applied to new urban land being opened up for development. However, by 1990, trials were undertaken to introduce land use rights markets to replace the previous practice of administratively allocating land to particular land uses, with payment for the ownership of land use rights paid to the state. With the creation of a land market for land use rights, the landscape of Chinese cities began to change; for example, the warehouses and factories in central business districts (which were characteristic of the period of the administrative allocation of land use rights) have been replaced with high-rise residential and commercial buildings and urban transport and other infrastructure.[30] Despite the exuberance of the land (land use rights) market, by 2002, the administrative allocation of land remained the dominant form of land use supply in most urban areas.

Real estate investment grew rapidly from about 4 per cent of GDP in 1997 to 15 per cent of GDP in 2014.[31] Residential investment, in particular, was high compared with that in other countries, and it accounted for about 15 per cent of fixed asset investment and 15 per cent of total urban employment. Bank lending to the sector accounted for 20 per cent of total loans.

Local government in China was often caught up in the web of real estate–finance interdependencies. The sale of real estate user rights continues to be a key source of local public finance. In addition, land owned by local governments is a principal source of investment, extrabudgetary revenue and collateral for debt borrowings. When the value of land use rights is increasing, the budgetary dependence on land is relatively secure: however, when the value of land falls, local governments will be forced to sell land use rights in a falling market. As well as undermining the revenue streams for local governments as they are forced to sell land use rights at reduced prices, there would also be a domino effect that would undermine the profitability of the construction and real estate sectors attempting to sell property in a falling market.[32]

These changes have established an ambiguous property rights system that creates complex and uncertain property relations between the state and private land developers.[33] One result is that, at the time of writing, after a period of massive growth,[34] China's second largest property developer, Evergrande, was struggling to repay more than $300 billion in liabilities, including nearly $20 billion of offshore bonds deemed in cross-default by ratings agencies.[35] In addition, this approach to land nationalisation by China appears to have established numerous opportunities for speculation and corruption. Data on more than one million land transactions during 2004–16, where local governments were the sole seller of land use rights, showed firms linked to some members of China's supreme political elites obtained a price discount ranging from 55.4 to 59.9 per cent compared with those without the same connections; and, in return, the provincial party secretaries who provided the discount to these 'princeling' firms were 23.4 per cent more likely to be promoted to positions of national leadership.[36]

Implementation

The successful implementation of urban land nationalisation would have, at a minimum, four high-level components.

First, there must be an efficient, transparent and accessible landownership and land registration system. Such as system would be based on a clear legal framework (with a clear definition, recognition and enforcement of the different types of land users' rights, including individual, usufruct and customary land rights);[37] professional land surveying; land titles registration system; and a cadastre which registers details of the ownership, boundaries and the value of real property in a region and which can be used for, at a minimum, tax assessment.

Second, there must be a transparent, democratic land use planning and management system. Typically, such a system is administered by local government or other local or regional authority with land planning, allocating and taxing powers. The land management system would be explicit about its multiple objectives (such as economic development, commercial viability, operating within budget settings, delivering public good objectives, workplace safety and inclusion, customer satisfaction and environmental sustainability, accountability to the government and transparency to the public).

Most importantly, the legislation and regulations establishing the land authority and the land use management system would specify the weighting to be given to these multiple objectives. In addition, membership of the land use planning and allocation authority would be based on a broad representation of key stakeholder groups elected by local city inhabitants and national governments. Any individuals or groups with actual or perceived conflict of interest with the role of the land use authority – and, in particular, property developers, real estate operators and financial institutions – would be barred from funding or in any other way participating in the management of the land authority.

Third, there must be an economic planning and monitoring authority accountable to government. All urban land use affects not just the direct users of land but has significant flow on effects to the whole economy including economic development, investment, employment, housing, transport and other infrastructure, and the credit and finance system. In many countries, urban land use also has particular foreign investment and national security implications. For all these reasons, the landownership and land registration system, the land use planning and management system, and the anti-corruption authority would need to be guided by longer-term, strategic economy-wide plans and oversight, led by a powerful economic planning and monitoring authority. Such an authority, with its high-level objectives set by government, would act to ensure the land strategy, institutions, policies and practices integrated with, and supported, the high-level, societal objectives of economic productivity, employment and financial stability, social equality, political freedom and environmental sustainability. The authority would also be responsible for measuring the productivity and performance of the land sector and disseminating these data to the public. Lastly, it would have the power to recommend to government any corrective actions needed to ensure stability in the links between the land administration and planning authorities, the real estate and land development industries, the finance sector and the nation's tax system.

Fourth, there must be a powerful, independent anti-corruption authority. Given the significance of this institution for all land regimes, it is discussed separately below.

Assessment of land nationalisation

Any assessment of the nationalisation of urban land needs to consider both the effectiveness of the state's administrative arrangements for holding and using land, and the degree to which the nationalisation of urban land has contributed to the public good.

As shown in the case of China, discussed above, and in Singapore (where almost all land is owned by the state),[38] the effective administrative of nationalised urban land can occur if there is a well-managed system of landownership and land registration which includes: a sound legal framework; long-term integrated land use planning; professional land surveying; a land titles registration system; and a cadastre which registers details of the ownership, boundaries and the value of real property in a region and which can be used for, at a minimum, tax assessment purposes.[39] Many of the necessary elements of a legal and institutional framework for land are well known and have been promoted over the past decade by bodies such as the World Bank.[40]

Effective land nationalisation also requires a well-funded corruption prevention, investigation and prosecution strategy and authority. Given land administration is one of the top three most bribed institutions in capitalist and non-capitalist countries around the world (after the police and the judiciary),[41] a crucial institutional element of any system of land nationalisation is a strong, independent anti-corruption oversight and prosecutorial body.

As indicated in the China case study above, the administration of nationalised land also needs a supporting institutional framework to integrate sound land

management practices with policies on municipal finance, bank and credit policies, and real estate development policies. The use of real estate for speculation
rather than meeting the needs of urban inhabitants, in particular, needs to be
guarded against. Another area of contention to be addressed in any comprehensive land nationalisation framework is the rural–urban interface where policies
on the use of rural land can conflict with those applying to urban land, especially
because the process of rezoning rural land into land for urban uses is often one
rife with mismanagement and corruption.[42]

The second element in the assessment of urban land nationalisation is to evaluate the degree to which the nationalisation of urban land has contributed to the
public good. For example, a study of nationalisation of industries and companies
in the United Kingdom in around 1951 noted industries qualified for nationalisation should be subject to five tests:

> (a) Will it increase the people's power over their own destinies? (b) Does it lead to
> a higher standard of life by enabling industry to perform a better and more eco-
> nomical service to the nation? (c) Does it lead to a more equal standard of life? (d)
> Does it lead to a more stable standard, by promoting full employment? (e) Does it
> extend industrial democracy? These are nothing else but the well-known 'welfare
> criteria': maximization, stability, equality, and freedom.[43]

These are useful criteria which can be used, or modified, to evaluate the nationalisation of urban land. They could be supplemented with additional questions of
crucial significance at the beginning of the twenty-first century. Does the nationalisation of urban land: reduce the impact of urban land on climate change;
improve ecological sustainability and diversity; and promote the equitable access
to urban land by women and other marginalised groups?

It is not possible to provide any definitive answer to these questions at the
moment given macro-assessments of the societal benefits of land nationalisation
is a major gap in the urban land literature. The most appropriate economic disci-
pline to undertake such assessments is welfare economics. Unfortunately, for the
last half of the twentieth century, welfare economics was dominated by neoclassical microeconomic modellers investigating the conditions under which a competitive market would come up with a *pareto optimal* allocation of resources such
that no individual consumer in society could be made better off without making
at least one other individual consumer worse off.[44]

The welfare criteria noted above, of maximisation, stability, equality, freedom
and environmental sustainability are not considered by neoclassical models wanting to maximise individual consumption. This narrow view of welfare economics
(and the associated field of public economics) was challenged in the 1980s by
scholars such as Nobel Prize–winning Amartya Sen and philosopher Martha
Nussbaum who argued that 'social welfare' is much broader than individual utility (happiness or satisfaction); is affected by the actual capabilities, resources and

freedoms of people wishing to improve their quality of life; and is affected by societal factors such as human rights, political freedom and other non-utility factors. However, much more work is needed, theoretically, methodologically and empirically, before the nationalisation of urban land can be properly assessed in terms of its impact on a society's economic productivity, employment and financial stability, social equality, political freedom and environmental sustainability.

Customary landownership

A third urban land strategy open to societies is to strengthen and extend the customary rights of ownership over land. There are more than 476.6 million indigenous people living in more than 90 countries around the world. Asia and the Pacific have the highest proportion of indigenous peoples (70.5 per cent), followed by Africa (16.3 per cent), Latin America and the Caribbean (11.5 per cent), Northern America (1.6 per cent), and Europe and Central Asia (0.1 per cent). Overall, indigenous people represent 6.2 per cent of the world's population, which far exceeds the population of the United States and Canada combined.[45] Indigenous peoples and their communities customarily manage over 50 per cent of the global land mass, but legally own just 10 per cent.[46]

Urban policymakers often assume customary land is predominantly non-urban land and not relevant for urban land planning. In fact, more than one-quarter of the world's indigenous people live in urban areas; but 70 per cent of Pacific Islands' indigenous people,[47] 52.2 per cent of Latin America's and the Caribbean's indigenous people, and 69.0 per cent of the Northern America's indigenous people are urban dwellers.[48]

Types of customary landownership

Customary tenure systems are unique to each community that has title over its land. However, these tenures tend to have some or all of four characteristics.[49] These are: collective ownership or possession and control over land and its associated natural resources; community-based jurisdiction over the land, most often on the basis of customary norms and obligations; acknowledgement within the customary sector that each community owns and controls discrete areas and may access other's land by customary rights of access; and the size of customary territories is periodically adjusted to remain at a scale over which community-based control can be effective.

In addition, customary tenure systems often have one or more of seven additional characteristics.[50] First, customary tenure systems gain their legitimacy from the trust a community places in the people and institutions that govern the system. The repository of land tenure norms and rules are often respected elders, who also have responsibility for enforcing the customs. Second, customary tenure mirrors the cultural and social values of the community and is not merely an economic asset. Third, while customary tenure often favours the rights of first occupants and those who initially invested labour to clear the land, they may also have mechanisms for latecomers to enter the system. Typically, newcomers gain progressively stronger rights through intermarriage with the founding families or by being a responsible neighbour and investing in the local community.

Fourth, customary tenure may differentiate rights between community members and those considered to be outsiders. Fifth, customary tenure frequently disaggregates rights to resources found in a particular locale, allowing multiple uses and users of resources found in the territory. The complex, differentiated tenure rules found in customary systems often protect the interests of disadvantaged, vulnerable and minority populations. Sixth, customary tenure often makes provision for collective (as opposed to individual) ownership or management of the locale. For example, the entire territory is the collective property of the community which then allocates specific rights to designated resources within the territory. Finally, and very importantly, customary tenure is a 'living institution'. Customary tenure systems evolve over time in response to changes in the institutional, economic and physical environment.

Assessment of customary landownership

Most customary land tenure around the world is under threat from local and international interests that seize land for agricultural, mining, speculation, development and other projects. These actions have been reinforced by neoclassical economic-based policies lauding land privatisation, land markets, the commodification of land, and the use of land for profit rather than community life. Bodies such as the World Bank and the International Monetary Fund argue that customary land tenure is a barrier to national and international profit-making via the capitalist exploitation of agriculture, mining, forestry and other land uses. They and their supporters ignore or downplay the economic, social, cultural and spiritual use of the land by local indigenous people that has occurred successfully for thousands of years.

One major issue undermining customary land rights is the security of land tenure. Tenure security refers to the legal and practical ability of communities to defend their ownership, occupation, use of and access to customary land from interference by others. In sub-Saharan Africa, for example, there is evidence that 'new' forms of 'customary tenure', based on neoclassical economic theory is undermining traditional customary rights and obligations including the security of the communities' tenure over land and the traditional institutions of governance over the land.[51]

Another issue undermining customary land tenure is the pressure to change customary governance institutions where elders, traditional councils and other forms of customary governance are accountable to the community members. Traditional communal governance is often manipulated, undermined or replaced with the objective to change customary title land into private or state title land for the financial benefit of property developers, real estate speculators, land grabbers, mining companies and the state.

For example, South Africa's Communal Land Rights Act (2004) and other similar legislation were attempts made over twenty years to bolster customary land rights. However, 'it seems evident that the powerful rural elites (including traditional leaders, land speculators and international and local corporations) have been disproportionately advantaged by the legislative and policy framework put forward by government, while the rights and interests of individuals and families living on communal land have been systematically undermined or ignored.[52]

A related issue is that, even when community-owned land is recognised in legislation, political action is often needed to overcome stakeholder and bureaucratic opposition to the implementation of the legislation. The Kenyan Community Land Act 2016, for example, permitted the conversion of community land into private land (if ratified by the community assembly), the conversion of public land into community land, and the conversion of private land to community land. However, little progress was made until 2019 when collective action by paralegal professionals forced applications for community land title to be processed by the state.[53]

Implementation of customary landownership
There are four key strategies to strengthen customary ownership of land around the globe. First, new laws need to be developed, or existing customary land laws need to be strengthened, to recognise customary land title, including customary institutions of decision making over the use of the land. The recent emphasis on the need for state legislation to build on local tenure systems (rather than attempting to 'replace' them with systems 'imported' from elsewhere) is a major step forward.[54]

Second, accessible, transparent and well-resourced land title administration arrangements need to be developed. These would include professional land surveying; a land titles registration system; and a cadastre which registers details of the ownership, boundaries and the value of real property in a region and which can be used for, at a minimum, tax assessment purposes. In some instances, customary organisations can develop a local land registry that will complement or, if necessary, challenge the land registry of the state. Such an alternative land registry allows indigenous and local communities to document recognition of the borders of their land and the customary land rights over that land.[55] This non-governmental alternative to state-run land title and registration systems can also prevent, or help remedy, land grabbing.

Third, there is also the need for a powerful, independent anti-corruption authority (for reasons discussed at the end of this chapter).

Fourth, communities with customary land title often feel isolated, especially when under threat from national and international companies wishing to take control of their land. This can be addressed by assisting customary bodies to build social solidarity within and between similar communities on land rights and related matters.

There is much evidence to show that customary land rights will always have to be fought for. There will often be the need for direct action, where urban residents occupy and control land and their associated buildings through organised or informal squatting, land settlement or some other forms of adverse possession (also known as 'squatters' rights'). For example, one-quarter of the world's urban population lives in informal settlements they have established through adverse possession. In sub-Saharan Africa there are more than 200 million people (62 per cent of Africa's urban population) living in informal settlements.[56]

Direct action is necessary, but outcomes always depend on local factors and the extent to which customary groups receive financial, political, media and other support. In Zimbabwe, for example, there was a massive rural to urban migration in the 1980s which led to the rapid growth of slums across the nation's major towns and cities. Prime Minister Mugabe's government in 2005 implemented a nationwide slum clearance campaign (Operation Murambatsvina, or 'Move the Rubbish'). It was officially promoted as eliminating crime, cleaning up the streets and regularising the informal sector, but despite international condemnation, the operation destroyed 92,460 homes.[57]

However, there have been examples of successful direct action to defend customary land rights in cities. In the face of pressure to rezone large tracts of urban land into 'Special Employment Zones', direct action has hindered the private sector from displacing urban inhabitants from their urban settlements, and, in some cases, secured compensation for those who were displaced.[58]

Community land trusts

The fourth strategy to modernise urban land use with a comprehensive urban policy is to replace private landownership and state-owned land with community ownership of land, especially as trusts. Community land trusts are a classic example of the *Gesellschaft* societies discussed in Chapter 4.

Types of community land trusts

In many countries, community landownership is undertaken by community land trusts. The distinguishing feature between a trust and other corporate structures is that the purpose of a trust is to *protect* assets, while other legal structures are established to *utilise* assets.[59] Trusts must also benefit a defined community, members of a trust control it either directly or through a board elected by members, and the surpluses produced by trusts through their business operations must be used to benefit that community. While most urban land trusts operate locally, the trust model has great flexibility. For example, the World Land Trust, a charity registered in England and Wales, operates internationally, working with partner organisations in Kenya, Zambia and many countries in Latin America and Asia to purchase, protect and manage trust land.

Trusts are established to provide continuous, community control and stewardship of land. The trust is often managed by a committee of elected *resident members* comprising adults who live in or use the leased land (leaseholders); *community members* comprising adults who live in the targeted area; and *public interest members* made up of local representatives from government, funding agencies and other stakeholder groups.[60] Typically, the common and shared ownership of the urban land does not extend to the buildings on the land, which may be owned (or leased long-term) by individual residents, businesses and/or other organisations. Revenues (such as rent) generated from the urban land are used by the legal body to maintain, protect and expand the asset, and are not used for the personal benefit of individual members. There is a strict prohibition on the misapplication of the land. One of the most common social objectives of community land trusts is to establish affordable housing in urban areas.[61]Cooperatives (including producer cooperatives and consumer cooperatives) are similar organisations or businesses that are owned and democratically governed by its members, in accordance with the social or economic purposes for which it was established.[62]

Community land trusts also exist in the Global South. In Brazil, for example, approximately 1,000 favelas, ranging in size from tens to 200,000 people, have a form of collective ownership where urban land is held by the government with the purpose of providing a 'social benefit'.[63] People who originally had little choice but to set up informal settlements (favelas) after their escape from war, social conflict or other dire circumstances, have slowly established more secure housing in their townships. Similarly, in the case of the Martín Peña Canal in Puerto Rico, collective ownership of the once-polluted and unsanitary canal land lies with a government-facilitated community land trust that owns the land but grants residents with surface rights (including the right to inherit and maintain ownership of their home). In 2004, residents established a non-profit organisation to promote the economic, social and community development of the region, support the community land trust, and ensure compliance with the region's Comprehensive Development Plan. The separation of landownership from house ownership insulates residents from rising real estate values that typically arise from the gentrification that occurs after urban redevelopment; as a result, residents can capitalise on the rising values of their home but not the land underneath.

Note that community landownership is not to be confused with 'commons' land (or 'common property' land). 'Commons' land is land that has no ownership or management structure, and where an unlimited number of individual land users can utilise the land for their own interests with no duty of care for future owners.[64] This results in the 'tragedy of the commons' where individuals using an unregulated common good (land), acting in their own self-interest and with no regard for community obligations, will overexploit and in other ways destroy that common good.[65]

Similarly, phrases such as 'the commons' and 'community landownership' have been co-opted to perpetuate privatised ownership of real estate, property development and environmental resources. The United Nations, for example, published reports on the need to protect the 'global commons', which discussed how to better manage and exploit resources in the world outside the control of national jurisdictions (such as the high seas, the atmosphere, Antarctica and outer space) and 'Resources of interest or value to the welfare of the community of nations – such as tropical rain forests and biodiversity'.[66] Similarly World Bank–funded bodies such as the Global Environment Facility, which funds local municipalities to carry out 'integrated urban planning' that will produce 'better demand-management measures and improved assets utilisation',[67] have set out private sector profit-based proposals with titles such as 'Our Global Commons: Sustainable Cities' which have little to do with protecting community-owned assets and keeping them under the democratic control of members.[68]

Implementation of community land trusts
There are four key elements in strategies to strengthen community ownership of urban land.

The first element of this urban land strategy is to acquire land. Every city has land, including pockets of underutilised land or underdeveloped urban areas, that can be converted into community-owned property. Gaining access to this land can occur through one or a combination of four types of action: state provision of land, private purchase or provision of land, non-government access to land (such as by churches and trade unions) and direct action (such as squatting). For example, councils can require property developers to donate land or money to community land organisations as a condition for urban development approval.[69] Provincial, national and international government bodies can assist through their taxing, funding, regulatory, urban infrastructure and other programmes. For example, the then mayor of Burlington, Vermont, Bernie Sanders, supported by the Progressive Coalition and under attack from property developers and others, working in partnership with the local community, established the Burlington Community Land Trust in 1984.[70] A rationale for this type of action is that, in the same way conservation trusts take land out of the market to protect the natural environment, so, too, 'Community land trusts take land out of market to protect the urban environment including the people who live there.'[71]

In Europe, municipal, provincial, national and international state bodies have created or supported the purchase or appropriation of urban land for collective ownership through initiatives such as the Sustainable Housing for Inclusive and Cohesive Cities programme.[72] Land can also be acquired with the assistance of the private sector, including philanthropists. In some nations, these groups have purchased or donated urban land to community land groups for community purposes. For example, the Charities Aid Foundation, which is both a charity and a bank, has supported community land trusts since 2008.[73] The Charities Aid Foundation also works with partner bodies to promote private donations of money and land in Bulgaria, Brazil, India, Russia and Southern Africa as well as Global North countries.

Non-government organisations are also important supporters of community-owned land. Trade unions have established both the cooperative ownership of community land and the cooperative management of munici-pally owned land. In the case of the Federación Uruguaya de Cooperativas de Vivienda por Ayuda Mutua (FUCVAM), the Uruguayan Federation of Mutual-Aid Housing Cooperatives was established by the Uruguayan trade union movement to provide urban housing for working-class people and create neighbourhoods that would provide a dignified and decent life for inhabitants.[74] FUCVAM understands land and housing as common property and manages community land and the building process in ways that foster community solidar-ity, social empowerment and democratic action: houses built by the cooperative can be mortgaged against but never be sold.[75] This approach promotes local eco-nomic development and jobs (e.g. through employment in housing construction); raises the standard of living of working-class families and promotes social inclu-sion through, for example, support for libraries, childcare centres, health centres, schools, shopping centres and other services; and promotes democratic worker self-management. Trade unions have also played a role in protecting urban land from exploitation as occurred with the 'green bans'[76] in Sydney as well as in supporting other forms of mutual aid, civil disobedience or militancy such as blockades and rent strikes.

As shown throughout this book, the urban landless (and their allies) often need to take direct action to secure access to, use of and management of land. Land non-owners can take economic, political and other direct action against those who own land, and often need to do so in concert with direct action against the governments that establish, perpetuate and enforce the rights of landowners over the rights of those who need urban land for employment, housing and other social and environmental purposes. When they do appropriate land for social uses, they often have to take direct action to defend their land ownership.

The second element of this urban land strategy is to ensure there is demo-cratic governance of the land. Community urban land is democratically con-trolled by the members of the community who own the land. This is a defining feature of community land trusts and other community organisations such as cooperatives.[77] At least 12 per cent of the world's population are members of three million cooperatives. Successful cooperatives operate in the Global North (such as Canada, most countries in Europe, Japan, Korea and the United States)[78] and, in fewer numbers, in the Global South (in countries such as Argentina, Brazil, Colombia, Costa Rica, India, Kenya and Uruguay.) In 2018, the 300 largest cooperatives in the world generated US$2,146 billion per annum in turnover while also providing services and infrastructure their members and societies needed to thrive.[79] Cooperatives have a proven record of creating and sustaining employment and provide at least 279 million jobs, promoting decent work while also advancing socially equitable and environmentally sustainable goals.[80]

Although there are many different types of cooperatives around the world,[81] most are organised on the basis of the Rochdale Principles (including voluntary and open membership, democratic member control and member economic participation). Neoliberal economic modelling has shown that cooperatives play a crucial role in an economy by addressing market failures, counteracting the concentration of market power, internalising social costs, reducing information asymmetries, and putting pressure on competitors to provide better services to their customers and employees.[82]

The third element of this urban land strategy is for individual land trusts to build alliances and collaborations with other like-minded bodies. Even the best-run communally owned and run organisation, with the most dedicated people, can fail if it is isolated. Practical solidarity relations, including trade and the exchange of personnel, will be mutually beneficial for all trusts and cooperatives.

For example, the largest coalition of worker cooperatives in the world is the Mondragon Corporation, a federation of numerous worker cooperatives based in the Basque region of Spain.[83] It has been operating for more than sixty years, employs more than 81,000 people, has sales in more than 150 countries and is one of the largest businesses in Spain. Worker management occurs through the governing council and the cooperative congress which sets strategic directions for the corporation. One of the worker management challenges facing Mondragon is how to perpetuate its democratic and participative model of worker management to subsidiaries outside Spain, such as in Mondragon's Chinese subsidiaries.[84]

A second model of trust and cooperative self-support is in the Emilia Romagna region of Italy. This cooperative movement is more a networked ecosystem than a single, overarching corporation like Mondragon. The Emilia Romagna region of Italy has one of the densest cooperative economies in the world where there are numerous horizontal, vertical and complementary networks between cooperatives that support each other financially.[85] About two out of every three inhabitants of the region are cooperative members, and they produce around 30 per cent of the region's GDP. The growth of Italian cooperatives has been fuelled by deep connections to broader sets of political commitments and values. The largest two federations, Legacoop (Lega Nazionale delle

Cooperative e Mutue) and Confcooperative (Confederazione delle Cooperative Italiane), are organized with strong historic ties to the Catholic Church and the Italian Communist Party, respectively. Both emphasise strong communitarian philosophies that have helped people set up businesses grounded in solidarity rather than pure profit. The Italian state supports cooperatives in many ways: the Italian constitution explicitly recognises the social contribution of cooperatives and directs that legislation should promote and favour cooperatives; tax legislation treats worker cooperatives as non-profit entities, requires the surplus to be invested for further job creation and requires 3 per cent of each cooperative's surplus to go into a fund to develop new cooperatives; and the government assists cooperatives through direct financial contributions that facilitate capital investment their growth.[86]

Another model of self-supporting trusts and cooperatives is in Venezuela. Cecosesola, the Central Cooperativa de Servicios Sociales des Estado Lara, is a network of about sixty cooperatives and grassroots organisations which have in total around 20,000 members. Cecosesola was established in Barquisimeto, capital of Lara State, as a cooperative integration organisation in 1967. It facilitates networking and coordination between its member cooperatives in agricultural production, small-scale agro-industrial production, funeral services, health services, savings and loans, mutual aid funds and food distribution.[87] It is the largest community organisation for the distribution of goods and services in Venezuela.[88] Cecosesola operates without directors, managers or supervisors, and through its coordination efforts its members assist more than 200,000 families each year and generate more than US$180 million in annual revenue.

The fourth crucial element of this urban land strategy is to always promote transparency, accountability and integrity. Public confidence in community ownership of urban land requires transparency, accountability and integrity *within* the organisation and *between* the organisation and other bodies (such as government, the media and the public). Such an approach also will prevent the common problems in many societies of corruption and the misuse of funds and resources.[89]

There is also the need for a powerful, independent anti-corruption authority (for reasons discussed at the end of this chapter).

Assessment of community land trusts
There are two types of community landownership: 'transformational' and 'non-transformational'.[90] Transformational ownership explicitly works to build alternatives to capitalist forms of property (such as community ownership of land), modes of production (such as worker cooperatives) and state control (such as participatory democracy). Transformational community land organisations recognise the danger of class-based counterattacks that aim to privatise community land and use it in production for profit. Transformational organisations often

build a united front, collaborating with labour unions, women's organisations, homelessness and other groups disenfranchised by capitalism to address both immediate issues and longer-term societal structural change.

On the other hand, non-transformational landownership occurs when people build collective forms of organisations (such as companies) to exploit land assets. Non-transformational community organisations, while promoting some level of cooperative behaviour, are vulnerable to co-option by the state or the private sector.

An anti-corruption authority

All the land initiatives discussed in this chapter recommend they be accompanied by a strong, anti-corruption authority. Urban development is full of opportunities for finance lenders, property owners, property developers, politicians and others to profit from bribery, corruption and other illegal activities in the Global North and South.[91] Transparency International has estimated that, across the globe, one in every five people has paid a bribe to access land services.[92] In part, this is because 'there are some cultural features of real estate development which make it susceptible to corruption'.[93] Corruption can occur at every stage of the land development process. For example, urban planning processes create opportunities and large financial incentives for urban plans to be formulated, revised and approved on the basis of investors' commercial interests (rather than for the public good). Furthermore, planning processes create opportunities for investors to bribe state officials and other decision makers with a share of the absolute rent created by the rezoning of land with a low-value zoning to a high-value zoning.[94]

A well-funded, independent land anti-corruption body is essential to monitor compliance with the land ownership, development, governance and stewardship framework and practices, including the regulation, operations, management and outcomes of land registration, titles, planning, and taxation systems, and to investigate and prosecute tax evaders, corrupt officials and other threats to the integrity of the land system.

In addition to government anti-corruption initiatives, an independent media is another key stakeholder for corruption prevention.[95] Other non-government bodies can also play an important part in identifying the conditions that make corruption and bribery possible, and in reporting corruption.[96]

Conclusion

This chapter has discussed four options for governments (and communities) to develop urban land policies for inclusive and socially equitable urban development. Each of the proposals – a land value tax, land nationalisation, customary land title and community land trusts – can be applied in different cities depending on their current mode of production, and their level of political and community support for economically efficient, socially just, democratic and environmentally sustainable forms of urban development.

Importantly, these strategies have been applied in cities and nations throughout the Global South and North. These experiences have shown that the options can be successful, as well as the political, legal and administrative conditions needed for them to be successful. Despite their differences, what they have in common is that they will be strongly resisted by the status quo, especially those who are currently profiting from privatised land, lightly regulated real estate markets, and the speculation and development of land for profit rather than for the benefit of urban residents.

Finally, it is important to emphasise that cities are structured primarily by the mode of production, of which land is a part. Changing the social relations of land is a necessary but not sufficient strategy to bring about structural change in societies. What is needed in addition are strategies to address the essential source of all urban economic growth: the production by labour of a surplus which, in capitalism, is produced by labour but appropriated by capitalists as unpaid surplus labour.

Notes

1. K. Marx and F. Engels, *The Manifesto of the Communist Party*, pt II, in *Marx/Engels Selected Works*, vol. I, Moscow, Progress Publishers, 1969, https://www.marxists.org/archive/marx/works/1848/communist-manifesto/ch02.htm
2. United Nations Habitat, *New Urban Agenda*, Nairobi, Kenya, United Nations Habitat (Human Settlements Programme), https://habitat3.org/the-new-urban-agenda/
3. Although best known for his land value tax, George also had a theory of labour: H. George, *The Condition of Labor: An Open Letter to Pope Leo XIII*, 1891, http://www.wealthandwant.com/HG/the_condition_of_labor.htm; and F. Obeng-Odoom, 'Rethinking Development Economics: Problems and Prospects of Georgist Political Economy', *Review of Political Economy*, 2021, DOI: 10.1080/09538259.2021.1928334
4. H. George, 'The Inwardness of a Boom', *The Standard*, vol. 2, 6 Aug. 1887, http://henrygeorgethestandard.org/volume-2-august-6-1887/
5. K. Marx, 'Letter to Friedrich Adolph Sorge, 20 June 1881', *Karl Marx and Frederick Engels, Selected Correspondence*, Moscow, Progress Publishers, 1975, https://www.marxists.org/archive/marx/works/1881/letters/81_06_20.htm
6. J. Stiglitz, 'The Origins of Inequality, and Policies to Contain It', *National Tax Journal*, vol. 68, no. 2 (2), 2015, pp. 425–48.
7. A. Haila, *Urban Land Rent: Singapore as a Property State*, Hoboken, NJ, Wiley-Blackwell, 2015.
8. K. C. Ho, 'Land and Housing in Singapore: Three Conversations with Anne Haila', *American Journal of Economics and Sociology*, vol. 80, no. 2, pp. 325–51.
9. R. Andelson, 'Land-Value Taxation around the World', *The American Journal of Economics and Sociology*, vol. 59, no. 5, 2000.

10. M. Kalkuhl, B. F. Milan, G. Schwerhoff, M. Jakob, M. Hahnen and F. Creutzig, 'Can Land Taxes Foster Sustainable Development? An Assessment of Fiscal, Distributional and Implementation Issues', *Land Use Policy*, vol. 78, 2018, pp. 338–52.

11. London Assembly Planning Committee, *Tax Trial: A Land Value Tax for London?*, London, Greater London Authority, 2016, https://www.london.gov.uk/sites/default/files/final-draft-lvt-report_2.pdf

12. P. Collier, E. Glaeser, T. Venables, P. Manwaring and M. Blake, *Land and Property Taxes: Exploiting Untapped Municipal Revenues*, London, International Growth Centre, 2018, https://www.theigc.org/wp-content/uploads/2017/08/Land-and-property-taxes-policy-brief_updated.pdf

13. Kalkuhl et al., 'Can Land Taxes Foster Sustainable Development?'

14. For example, Singapore's Property Tax Act 1960 and the Land Tax Management Act 1956 of New South Wales, Australia.

15. C. Ezomike and O. Isiadinso, 'Property Taxation in Lagos State: A Review of the Lagos State Land Use Charge Law 2018', *Andersen Tax Digest*, 10 Apr. 2018, https://drive.google.com/file/d/1a-noYABg0_7Omjs9NTr5fInW95sl8n3q/view

16. J. Pullen, 'Government Infrastructure Investment Dividends and Urban Development', *American Journal of Economics and Sociology*, vol. 80, no. 2, 2021, pp. 721–45.

17. P. Collier, E. Glaeser, T. Venables, P. Manwaring and M. Blake, *Land and Property Taxes: Exploiting Untapped Municipal Revenues*, London, International Growth Centre, 2018, https://www.theigc.org/wp-content/uploads/2017/08/Land-and-property-taxes-policy-brief_updated.pdf

18. E. Loo, *Lessons from Singapore about Land Value Capture*, London, Royal Town Planning Institute, 2017, https://www.rtpi.org.uk/blog/2017/april/lessons-from-singapore-about-land-value-capture/

19. A. De Neuman, 'Some Economic Aspects of Nationalization', *Law and Contemporary Problems*, vol. 16, nos. 4/9, 1951, pp. 702–51, https://scholarship.law.duke.edu/cgi/viewcontent.cgi?article=2509&context=lcp

20. For an early example of municipalisation, see the speech made by Thomas Spence entitled 'Property in Land Every One's Right', in A. Bonnett and K. Armstrong (eds), *Thomas Spence: The Poor Man's Revolutionary*, London, Breviary Stuff Publications, 2014, https://www.marxists.org/history/england/britdem/people/spence/property/property.htm

21. W. Gritten, 'Why the Northern Rail Franchise is being Nationalised', *The Week*, London, Dennis Publishing, 30 January 2020, https://www.theweek.co.uk/105444/why-the-northern-rail-franchise-is-being-nationalised

22. A. Kliman, 'The Great Recession and Marx's Crisis Theory', *American Journal of Economics and Sociology*, vol. 74, no. 2, 2015, pp. 236–77.

23. N. Klein, *This Changes Everything: Capitalism vs the Climate*, London, Penguin Books, 2015.

24. T. Piketty, *Capital in the Twenty-First Century*, Cambridge, MA, Harvard University Press, 2017.

25. K. Marx, *Theories of Surplus Value*, https://www.marxists.org/archive/marx/works/1863/theories-surplus-value/add3.htm#_ftn8

26. Ibid.

27. J. Channon, 'The Bolsheviks and the Peasantry: The Land Question during the First Eight Months of Soviet Rule', *The Slavonic and East European Review*, vol. 66, no. 4, 1988, pp. 593–624.

28. J. N. Hazard, 'Soviet Property Law', *Cornell Law Review*, vol. 30, no. 4, 1945, pp. 466–87.

29. Q. Xie, A. Parsa and B. Redding, 'The Emergence of the Urban Land Market in China: Evolution, Structure, Constraints and Perspectives', *Urban Studies*, vol. 39, no. 8, 2002, pp. 1375–98.

30. Ibid.

31. M. Chivakul, W. Lam, R. Waikei, X. Liu, W. Maliszewski and A. Schipke, *Understanding Residential Real Estate in China*, International Monetary Fund Working Paper 15/84, Washington, DC, International Monetary Fund, 2015, https://www.imf.org/en/Publications/WP/Issues/2016/12/31/Understanding-Residential-Real-Estate-in-China-42873

32. Y. Lu and T. Sun, *Local Government Financing Platforms in China: A Fortune of Misfortune?*, International Monetary Fund Working Paper 13/243, Washington, DC, International Monetary Fund, 2013, https://www.imf.org/external/pubs/ft/wp/2013/wp13243.pdf

33. Y. Wang and J. Chen, 'Privatizing the Urban Commons under Ambiguous Property Rights in China: Is Marketization a Remedy to the Tragedy of the Commons?', *American Journal of Economics and Sociology*, vol. 80, no. 2, 2021, pp. 503–47.

34. L. Zhang and Q. Gou, 'Demystifying China's Economic Growth: Retrospect and Prospect', in United Nations Conference on Trade and Development, *Rethinking Development Strategies after the Financial Crisis – Volume II: Country Studies and International Comparisons*, Geneva, United Nations Conference on Trade and Development, 2016, https://unctad.org/webflyer/rethinking-development-strategies-after-financial-crisis-volume-ii-country-studies-and

35. The Economic Times, 'With Evergrande Debt Relief Deal, China Signals Stability Trumps Austerity', *The Economic Times*, 14 Jan. 2022, https://economictimes.indiatimes.com/news/international/business/with-evergrande-debt-relief-deal-china-signals-stability-trumps-austerity/articleshow/88895109.cms

36. T. Chen and J. Kung, 'Busting the "Princelings": The Campaign against Corruption in China's Primary Land Market', *The Quarterly Journal of Economics*, vol. 134, no. 1, Feb. 2019, pp. 185–226. Also H. Cai, J. Henderson and Q. Zhang, *National Bureau of Economic Research Working Paper 15067: China's Land Market Auctions: Evidence of Corruption?*, Cambridge, MA, National Bureau of Economic Research, 2013, https://www.nber.org/system/files/working_papers/w15067/w15067.pdf

37. N. Zuniga, *Land Corruption*, Berlin, Transparency International, 2018, https://knowledgehub.transparency.org/product/topic-guide-on-land-corruption

38. A. Haila, *Urban Land Rent: Singapore as a Property State*, Hoboken, NJ, Wiley-Blackwell, 2015.

39. M. Ng and C. C. Pong, *Land Framework of Singapore: Building a Sound Land Administration and Management System*, Singapore, Centre for Liveable Cities, 2018, https://www.clc.gov.sg/docs/default-source/urban-systems-studies/uss-land-framework-of-singapore.pdf

40. K. Deininger, H. Selod and T. Burns, *Land Governance Assessment Framework*, Washington, DC, World Bank, 2011, https://openknowledge.worldbank.org/bitstream/handle/10986/2376/657430PUB0EPI1065724B09780821387580.pdf?sequence=1

41. Transparency International, *Global Corruption Barometer (2003–2017)*, Berlin, Transparency International, 2017, https://www.transparency.org/en/gcb

42. H. L. Nguyen, J. Duan and G. C. Zhang, 'Land Politics under Market Socialism: The State, Land Policies, and Rural–Urban Land Conversion in China and Vietnam', *Land*, vol. 7, no. 2, 2018, https://www.mdpi.com/2073-445X/7/2/51

43. A. M. De Neuman, 'Some Economic Aspects of Nationalization', *Law and Contemporary Problems*, vol. 16, nos. 4/9, 1951, pp. 702–51.

44. R. Backhouse, A. Baujard and T. Nishizawa (eds), *Welfare Theory, Public Action, and Ethical Values: Revisiting the History of Welfare Economics*, Cambridge, Cambridge University Press, 2021.

45. International Labour Organization, 'Implementing the ILO Indigenous and Tribal Peoples Convention No. 169: Towards an inclusive, sustainable and just future', Geneva, International Labour Organization, 2019, https://www.ilo.org/wcmsp5/groups/public /—dgreports/—dcomm/—publ/documents/publication/wcms_735607.pdf

46. International Work Group for Indigenous Affairs, *Global Report on the Situation of Lands, Territories and Resources of Indigenous Peoples*, Indigenous Peoples Major Group for Sustainable Development, 2019, https://www.iwgia.org/images/documents/briefings/ IPMGpercent20Globalpercent20Reportpercent20FINAL.pdf

47. Ibid.

48. Ibid.

49. L. A. Wily, 'Customary Land Tenure in the Modern World, Rights and Resources Initiative', Washington, DC, Rights and Resources Group, 2011, https://dlc.dlib. indiana.edu/dlc/bitstream/handle/10535/7713/customary%20land%20tenure%20 in%20the%20modern%20world.pdf?sequence=1

50. M. Freudenberger, 'The Future of Customary Tenure: Options for Policymakers', *Land Links*, Washington, DC, Land and Resource Governance Division, United States Agency for International Development (USAID), 2013, https://www.land-links.org/issue-brief/ the-future-of-customary-tenure/

51. A. Chimhowu, 'The "New" African Customary Land Tenure. Characteristic, Features and Policy Implications of a New Paradigm', *Land Use Policy*, vol. 81, 2019, pp. 897–903.

52. M. Clark and N. Luwaya, 'Communal Land Tenure 1994–2017: Commissioned Report for High Level Panel on the Assessment of Key Legislation and the Acceleration of Fundamental Change, an initiative of the Parliament of South Africa', Cape Town, Parliament of South Africa, 2017, https://www.parliament.gov.za/storage/app/media/ Pages/2017/october/High_Level_Panel/Commissioned_Report_land/Commisioned_ Report_on_Tenure_Reform_LARC.pdf

53. J. Vogelsang, 'A Historic Step towards Securing Community Land Rights in Kenya', London, Thomson Reuters Foundation, 2019, https://news.trust.org/item/201907301 51357-yl708

54. L. Cotula (ed.), *Changes in 'Customary' Land Tenure Systems in* Africa, International Institute for Environment and Development, London, 2007, https://pubs.iied.org/sites/default/ files/pdfs/migrate/12537IIED.pdf

55. International Land Coalition, 'Effective Actions against Land Grabbing', Rome, International Land Coalition, https://d3o3cb4w253x5q.cloudfront.net/media/docu ments/toolkit_9_landgrabbing_en.pdf

56. J. Mutero and M. Chege, 'Bridging the Affordability Gap: Towards a Financing Mechanism for Slum Upgrading at Scale in Nairobi', Nairobi, Urban Economy and Finance Branch, United Nations Human Settlements Programme (UN-Habitat), 2019, https://unhabitat.org/sites/default/files/2020/05/financing_mechanism_for_slum_ upgrading_at_scale_in_nairobi.pdf

57. Amnesty International, 'Zimbabwe: Housing Policy Built on Foundation of Failures and Lies', London, Amnesty International, 2006, https://web.archive.org/web/2006101019 0256/http://news.amnesty.org/index/ENGAFR460152006

58. R. S. Wall, J. Maseland, K. Rochell and M. Spaliviero, 'The State of African Cities 2018: The Geography of African Investment', United Nations Human Settlements Programme

(UN-Habitat) and IHS-Erasmus University Rotterdam, 2018, https://unhabitat.org/sites/default/files/download-manager-files/Thepercent20Statepercent20ofpercent20Africanpercent20Cities.pdf

59. L. Crabtree, P. Phibbs, V. Milligan and H. Blunden, 'Principles and Practices of an Affordable Housing Land Trust Model', Melbourne, Australian Housing and Urban Research Institute, 2012, https://www.ahuri.edu.au/sites/default/files/migration/documents/AHURI_Research_Paper_Principles-and-practices-of-an-affordable-housing-community-land-trust-model.pdf

60. Ibid.

61. For example, Champlain Housing Trust, 'Board of Directors', Vermont, Champlain Housing Trust, https://www.getahome.org/board-of-directors/

62. International Cooperative Alliance, 'Cooperative Identity, Values and Principles', Brussels, International Cooperative Alliance, https://www.ica.coop/en/whats-co-op/co-operative-identity-values-principles?_ga=2.156019067.1180638431.1633314535-350852483.1633314535

63. T. Williamson, 'Community Land Trusts in Rio's Favelas', *Land Lines*, vol. 30, no. 3, July 2018, Cambridge, MA, The Lincoln Institute of Land Policy, https://www.lincolninst.edu/sites/default/files/pubfiles/land-lines-july-2018-full_2.pdf

64. E. Ostrom, 'Beyond Markets and States: Polycentric governance of complex economic systems', Nobel Prize Lecture, Stockholm, The Nobel Foundation, 2009, https://www.nobelprize.org/uploads/2018/06/ostrom_lecture.pdf

65. F. Obeng-Odoom, *The Commons in an Age of Uncertainty: Decolonizing Nature, Economy, and Society*, Toronto, University of Toronto Press, 2021.

66. UN System Task Team on the Post-2015 UN Development Agenda, 'Global Governance and Governance of the Global Commons in the Global Partnership for Development beyond 2015', New York, Department of Economic and Social Affairs, https://www.un.org/en/development/desa/policy/untaskteam_undf/thinkpieces/24_thinkpiece_global_governance.pdf

67. Global Environment Facility, 'Sustainable Cities Program', Washington, DC, Global Environment Facility, https://www.thegef.org/sites/default/files/publications/GEF_SDG_Sustainable_Cities2017_CRA_112817-3.pdf

68. Global Environment Facility, 'Our Global Commons: Sustainable Cities', Washington, DC, Global Environment Facility, 2018, https://www.youtube.com/watch?v=DtdcWkdSLZQ

69. The World Bank, 'Inclusionary Zoning', Washington, DC, The World Bank, https://urban-regeneration.worldbank.org/node/46

70. Champlain Housing Trust, 'History and Awards', Burlington, VT, Champlain Housing Trust, https://www.getahome.org/history-awards/

71. D. Fireside, 'Burlington Busts the Affordable Housing Debate', *Dollars & Sense*, no. 258, Mar./Apr. 2005, http://dollarsandsense.org/archives/2005/0305fireside.html

72. C. Boulanger and D. Pialucha, *Community Land Trusts Finance: Understanding the diversity of models in Europe*, Montreuil, Global Fund for Cities' Development, 2019, https://fmdv.net/admin/Images/Publications/124/0_190904_FinancialCS_VF2-light.pdf

73. S. Halilovic, 'Community Land Trust Fund I: What We've Learned by Supporting Communities to Build Their Forever Affordable Homes', London, Charities Aid Foundation, 2016, https://www.cafonline.org/docs/default-source/charity-finance-and-fundraising/clt-i-fund-closing-paper_final.pdf?sfvrsn=0

74. National Assembly of FUCVAM (1999), Declaration of Principles, Montevideo, Federación Uruguaya de Cooperativas de vivienda por Ayuda Mutua, https://www.fucvam.org.uy/wp-content/uploads/2017/08/DeclaracipercentC3percentB3n-de-Principios.pdf

75. Federación Uruguaya de Cooperativas de vivienda por Ayuda Mutua, 'New Groups', Montevideo, Federación Uruguaya de Cooperativas de vivienda por Ayuda Mutua, https://www.fucvam.org.uy/nuevos-grupos/

76. Action taken by a trade union or other organised labour association for environmental or conservation purposes including to defend open urban spaces, preserve older-style buildings and protect existing housing stock from commercial development: M. Bergmann and V. Burgmann, 'Green Bans Movement', *Dictionary of Sydney*, 2011, Sydney, State Library of New South Wales, https://dictionaryofsydney.org/entry/green_bans_movement

77. International Labour Organization, 'Cooperatives', Geneva, International Labour Organization, https://www.ilo.org/global/topics/cooperatives/lang--en/index.htm

78. In the United States in 2009, for example, there were nearly 30,000 cooperatives operating at 73,000 places of business throughout the country earning nearly US$654 billion in revenue, employing more than 2 million workers and paying US$75 billion in wages and benefits per annum. For details, see S. Deller, A. Hoyt, B. Hueth and R. Sundaram-Stukel, 'Research on the Economic Impact of Cooperatives', Madison, WI, University of Wisconsin Center for Cooperatives, 2009, http://reic.uwcc.wisc.edu/sites/all/REIC_FINAL.pdf

79. EURICSE, 'Exploring the Cooperative Economy', World Cooperative Monitor, 2020, https://monitor.coop/sites/default/files/publication-files/wcm2020web-final-1083463041.pdf

80. International Labour Organization, 'Cooperatives', Geneva, International Labour Organization, https://www.ilo.org/global/topics/cooperatives/lang--en/index.htm

81. J. Orizet, 'The Co-operative Movement since the First World War', *International Labour Review*, vol. 100, no. 1, 1969, pp. 23–50.

82. J. Royer, 'The Neoclassical Theory of Cooperatives', *Journal of Cooperatives*, vol. 28 (special edn), 2014, pp. 2014.

83. Mondragon Corporation, 'Press Dossier', Mondragón, Mondragon Corporation, https://www.mondragon-corporation.com/wp-content/uploads/docs/MONDRAGONnotadeprensa_EN.pdf

84. A. Errasti, 'Mondragon's Chinese Subsidiaries: Coopitalist Multinationals in Practice', *Economic and Industrial Democracy*, vol. 36, no. 3, 2015, pp. 479–99, https://doi.org/10.1177/0143831X13511503

85. J. Duda, 'The Italian Region Where Co-ops Produce a Third of Its GDP', *Yes!*, 5 July 2016, https://www.yesmagazine.org/economy/2016/07/05/the-italian-place-where-co-ops-drive-the-economy-and-most-people-are-members

86. M. J. Adeler, 'Enabling Policy Environments for Co-operative Development: A Comparative Experience Centre for the Study of Co-operatives', Winnipeg, University of Saskatchewan Institute of Urban Studies, University of Winnipeg, 2009, https://institute.coop/sites/default/files/resources/225 per cent202009_Juarez per cent20Adeler_Enabling per cent20policy per cent20environments per cent20for per cent20cooperative per cent20development.pdf

87. Cecosesola, 'About Us', Cecosesola, https://cecosesola.org/acerca-de/

88. Cooperativa Gestión Participativa, 'Cecosesola', Caracas, Cooperativa Gestión Participativa https://www.gestionparticipativa.coop/portal/index.php?option=com_content&view=article&id=215&Itemid=435

89. Transparency International, 'How Corrupt Are Different Institutions and Groups in Society – Global Average?' Berlin, Transparency International, 2017, https://www.transparency.org/en/gcb/global/global-corruption-barometer-2017. See also W. Chibamba, E. B. Koroma, F. Mutondori, M. M. Nkutawala, M. H. Okai, K. Rafitoson and L. Z. Senteza, 'Combating Land Corruption in Africa', Berlin, Transparency International, 2019, https://images.transparencycdn.org/images/2019_Guide_CombattingLandCorruptionAfrica_English.pdf; and D. Kaufmann and P. C. Vicente, 'Legal Corruption', Second Draft, Washington, DC, World Bank, 2005, http://web.worldbank.org/archive/website00818/WEB/LEGALCOR.HTM

90. R. Hollender, 'A Politics of the Commons or Commoning the Political? Distinct Possibilities for Post-Capitalist Transformation', *Spectra*, vol. 5, no. 1, 2016.

91. J. Dodson, E. Coiacetto and C. Ellway, 'Corruption in the Australian Land Development Process: Identifying a Research Agenda', *Refereed Proceedings of the 2nd Bi-Annual National Conference on the State of Australian Cities*, Griffith, Griffith University, 2006; J. Zhu, 'The Shadow of the Skyscrapers: Real Estate Corruption in China', *Journal of Contemporary China*, vol. 21, 2012, pp. 243–60.

92. Transparency International, *Land Corruption* [online resources], Berlin, Transparency International, n.d., https://www.transparency.org/en/our-priorities/land-corruption

93. M. H. Krieger, 'Corruption and the Culture of Real Estate Development', *Business and Professional Ethics Journal*, vol. 13, no. 3, 1994, pp. 19–32.

94. A. Garrido, M. Delfina, J. Anderson, S. Davidsen, D. H. Vo, D. N. Dinh and H. T. L. Tran, *Recognizing and Reducing Corruption Risks in Land Management in Vietnam*, Washington, DC, World Bank Group, 2011, http://documents.worldbank.org/curated/en/918551468322441320/Recognizing-and-reducing-corruption-risks-in-land-management-in-Vietnam

95. Reporters Without Borders, 'Global Communication and Information Space: A Common Good of Gumankind', Paris, Reporters Without Borders, https://rsf.org/en/global-communication-and-information-space-common-good-humankind

96. Independent Commission Against Corruption, 'Conditions That May Allow Corruption to Occur', Sydney, Independent Commission Against Corruption, https://www.icac.nsw.gov.au/about-corruption/conditions-that-may-allow-corruption-to-occur-

CHAPTER 8

Conclusion

> From the standpoint of a higher economic form of society, private ownership of the globe by single individuals will appear quite as absurd as private ownership of one man by another.[1]

This book has argued that one of Marx's crucial, but under-recognised, insights is that land (by which he meant nature) is the most basic economic resource upon which all communities and societies rely. Capitalism (and all other modes of production) require labour to be applied to land, to transform the raw materials or 'natural resources' (the soils, minerals, plants and animals, waters and atmosphere of the environment) into the goods and services needed by people individually and collectively to live.

Except for the indigenous and communist modes of production, all other modes of production establish a societal division between those who own land (landowners) and those who are excluded from owning the land but need the land to live (the tenants, serfs, peasants and so on). This division of society is only possible when a relatively small number of individuals capture, steal or in other ways appropriate parts of the earth's surface as 'their property'. This establishes a social (property) relation of dependency and obligation between two classes of people; a social relation of property that is reinforced politically, legally and through the powers of the state.

With the creation of property rights, landowners (or the state) were able to control the lives of the majority by determining who can use the land, for how long and in return for the payment of compensation (rent). Marx also showed that the creation of property rights over land was integrally linked with the formation of the world's greatest cities. In other words, land is not a commodity, a form of capital or 'space'; Marx always stressed any reference to land is a reference to the social relations of power embedded in landed property.

Landed property rights have continually been the hidden political economic force that has structured the functions and morphology of cities, the location and nature of urban housing, the placement and mix of urban infrastructure, and other factors of urban life including wars over territory, land taxes, suburban poverty and wealth, and urban environmental sustainability. Marx showed how landed property affected the location, functions, design and operation of urban economies and urban polities.

Unfortunately, the theoretical lacuna of political economy to land in general, and urban land in particular, has been reinforced politically by those who have assumed that the 'land question' refers to agricultural land, agrarian land reforms and the potential of landless peasants as revolutionaries. This was historically relevant in the past; but today and for the foreseeable future, when more than half the world's people live in cities, the land question is now both an urban question and a question about the destruction of the environment upon which we all depend.

Furthermore, Marx's critique of the social relations of landed property has one other implication for radical practice. One of the greatest powers of those who own landed property, like the owners of capital, is their capacity to exploit those who need access to land (or capital) to live, but who are the non-owners of land and capital. Specifically, workers have no choice but to provide an amount of unpaid, surplus labour (as rent) to landowners (and as profit to the owners of capital). The solution to this exploitation of labour by the owners of private property is democracy: the replacement of privatised ownership of property with democratic, social control of land. Chapter 7 considered four practical urban policy strategies that can be used, to various degrees, to ensure land is used for the benefit of people and not primarily to create income for landowners.

The urban land question asks how landownership, rent and the landed property class shapes our cities and the lives of urban dwellers, and what can be done to ensure cities are built to meet the needs of urban residents. The urban land question includes: what is the mode of production of the community or society and what function does land play in perpetuating that mode of production; who owns which land (and who is a land non-owner) and what rights do they have over the use and disposal of that land; how does the ownership of urban land affect the built environment of cities, the location of urban economic development and employment, and the quality of life of urban residents; how does land contribute to the creation of wealth and poverty (including unemployment and homelessness); is the urban land use environmentally sustainability; and finally, to what extent does the landed property sector influence or control the governance of the city, province and nation?

The need for action to resolve the issues of urban land is becoming more important every year. Urgent action is needed to prepare for a world where two-thirds of the world's people live in cities by 2050.[2] New policies are needed that do not repeat the mistakes of the past; policies that will promote prosperous cities where the inhabitants have access to high-quality and affordable transport and communications, a quality built environment, a sustainable natural environment, inclusive and safe communities, effective health, housing and education services, a vibrant cultural life, and good governance with community participation in decision making.

When pursuing answers to the urban question, this book has shown that no cities are the same. Cities in the Global North differ significantly from those in the Global South – not least in terms of their forms of land tenure, the complexity of land use and land markets, and the interests and capacities of local and national governments to ensure urban landownership benefits all city residents – and cities within each of these two spheres also differ considerably. Today, as in the past, different cities play each city plays its own unique combination of roles within its community and nation, including but not limited to defence, production, trade, finance, residential housing and other quality-of-life services, consumption and state administration; and these roles often change over time.

However, all cities are major contributors to the economic production and consumption of their nations, and today, the reproduction of national and global political economic systems also relies on the economic strength and political stability of cities.

The role of cities, and the economic and social opportunities they can hold for people, are not static or automatic: they are not mechanically derived from the operation of the economy, the development of technology or other factors. They are always the outcomes of struggles between urban groups (worker trade unions, student associations, local community organisations and social movements) – the majority of people living in cities who want a better quality of life for themselves, their families and their grandchildren – and the powerful and resourced beneficiaries of the current urban arrangements who wish to consolidate and extend their economic and political power.

Many powerful institutions (such as the World Bank, the International Monetary Fund and the Organisation for Economic Co-operation and Development) continue to promote and fund economic development policies that assume cities and nations will only develop by privatising indigenous and common land; establishing free markets for land (not fair markets); treating land as an asset for speculation or development for profit; pursuing ever-increasing growth; and overlooking the social and environmental consequences. After decades of failure by those promoting neoliberal economic policies, it is time for new approaches to urban land.

Transforming cities to be inclusive, equitable and sustainable requires structural change to the ownership of urban land. New land policies such as designing creative land value taxation, establishing effective forms of land nationalisation, strengthening customary land rights and/or establishing community-owned landed property are germane for such goals, with great potential to be strengthened and extended. They are tangible, measurable and understandable; they make it possible to deliver concrete services (such as affordable housing) to members and the broader urban community; they provide demonstrable alternatives to the 'laws' of the capitalist market and profit; and they help build the skills people need for a fairer, more democratic and environmentally sustainable economy and society. These strategies also provide opportunities to transform the state by promoting the 'practices of direct democracy, the horizontal distribution of power, and collective decision-making'.[3]

Time for change

Finally, social change has almost always occurred slowly over centuries, and only very rarely through the rapid revolutionary change that is most commonly associated with the idea of Marxism. A better world is practical and achievable: a world based on common ownership of urban land (not private or state ownership), economic and social collaboration (not competition), fair trade (not free trade), production for people's needs (not profit), direct democratic participation in the polity and the economy (not oligarchies), and a world that is environmentally sustainable (not wasteful and environmentally destructive).

These changes are already under way around the world and are being implemented through the efforts of many people taking small, day-by-day, often mundane-seeming actions, with the occasional major structural change. Change is being made, despite the resistance of the members of the status quo, including those who will lose their privileges from their private ownership of land. Landed property, one of the most important underpinnings of our societies and our cities, has been changed many times in the past, and by working together, we can make it change again for the better.

Notes

1. K. Marx, *Capital*, vol. III, ch. 46, New York, International Publishers, 1959, https://www.marxists.org/archive/marx/works/1894-c3/ch46.htm
2. United Nations, Department of Economic and Social Affairs, '68% of the World Population Projected to Live in Urban Areas by 2050, Says UN', New York, United Nations Department of Economic and Social Affairs, 2018, https://www.un.org/development/desa/en/news/population/2018-revision-of-world-urbanization-prospects.html
3. S. R. Cayuela, 'The Commons', *Uneven Earth*, 12 Apr. 2021, http://unevenearth.org/2021/04/the-commons/

Bibliography

Aalbers, M., *Subprime Cities: The Political Economy of Mortgage Markets*, Hoboken, NJ, Wiley-Blackwell, 2012.

Aalbers, M., *The Financialisation of Housing*, London, Routledge, 2016.

Adeler, M. C., 'Enabling Policy Environments for Co-operative Development: A Comparative Experience', *Canadian Public Policy / Analyse de Politiques*, vol. 40, 2014, S50–S59.

Alhadeff-Jones, M., 'Beyond Space and Time: Conceiving the Rhythmic Configurations of Adult Education through Lefebvre's Rhythmanalysis', *Journal for Research on Adult Education*, vol. 42, 2019, pp. 165–81.

Amirtahmasebi, R., Orloff, M., Wahba, S. and Altman, A., *Regenerating Urban Land: A Practitioner's Guide to Leveraging Private Investment*, Washington, DC, World Bank, 2016, https://www.worldbank.org/en/topic/urbandevelopment/publication/regenerating-urban-land-a-practitioners-guide-to-leveraging-private-investment

Amnesty International, 'Zimbabwe: Housing Policy Built on Foundation of Failures and Lies', *News Amnesty*, London, Amnesty International, 2006, https://web.archive.org/web/20061010190256/http://news.amnesty.org/index/ENGAFR460152006

Andelson, R., 'Land-Value Taxation around the World', *The American Journal of Economics and Sociology*, vol. 59, no. 5, 2000, pp. I–490.

Andersen, I., 'First Person: COVID-19 is Not a Silver Lining for the Climate, Says UN Environment Chief', *UN News*, 5 Apr. 2020, https://news.un.org/en/story/2020/04/1061082

Anderson, K. B., *Marx at the Margins: On Nationalism, Ethnicity, and Non-Western Societies*, Chicago, IL, University of Chicago Press, 2016.

Anderson, P., *Passages from Antiquity to Feudalism*, London, Verso, 1975.

Appelbaum, E. and Katz, E., 'Seeking Rents by Setting Rents: The Political Economy of Rent Seeking', *The Economic Journal*, vol. 97, no. 3, 1987, pp. 685–99.

Australian Council of Social Service, *An Affordable Housing Reform Agenda: Goals and Recommendations for Reform*, Canberra, ACOSS, 2015, p. 12, https://www.acoss.org.au/images/uploads/Housing_paper_March_2015_final.pdf

Avineri, S., 'The Hegelian Origins of Marx's Political Thought', *The Review of Metaphysics*, vol. 21, no. 1, 1967, pp. 33–56.

Backhouse, R., Baujard, A. and Nishizawa, T. (eds), *Welfare Theory, Public Action, and Ethical Values: Revisiting the History of Welfare Economics*, Cambridge, Cambridge University Press, 2021.

Badcock, B., 'An Australian View of the Rent Gap Hypothesis', *Annals of the Association of American Geographers*, vol. 79, no. 1, 1989, pp. 125–45.

Barber, W. J., *A History of Economic Thought*, London, Penguin Books, 1991.

Barendse, R. J., 'The Feudal Mutation: Military and Economic Transformations of the Ethnosphere in the Tenth to Thirteenth Centuries', *Journal of World History*, vol. 14, no. 4, 2003, pp. 503–29.

Barnes, T, *Informal Labour in Urban India: Three Cities, Three Journeys*, London, Routledge, 2015.

Barnes, T., *Making Cars in the New India: Industry, Precarity and Informality*, Cambridge, Cambridge University Press, 2018.

Beamish, R., 'Base and Superstructure', in G. Ritzer (ed.), *Blackwell Encyclopedia of Sociology*, Hoboken, NJ, John Wiley & Sons, 2017, pp. 244–6.

Beitel, K., 'The Affordable Housing Crisis: Its Capitalist Roots and the Socialist Alternative', *Socialist Register*, vol. 56, 2020.

Beitel, K., 'Circuits of Capital, Ground Rent and the Production of the Built Environment: A (New) Framework for Analysis', *Human Geography*, vol. 9, no. 3, 2016, pp. 27–42.

Bellamy Foster, J., Clark, B. and York, R., *The Ecological Rift: Capitalism's War on the Earth*, New York, New York University Press, 2010.

Belussi, F. and Caldari, K., 'At the Origin of the Industrial District: Alfred Marshall and the Cambridge School', *Cambridge Journal of Economics*, vol. 33, no. 2, Mar. 2009, pp. 335–55.

Bems, R., Johnson, R. C. and Yi, K. M., *Demand Spillovers and the Collapse of Trade in the Global Recession*, Washington, DC, International Monetary Fund, 2010, https://www.imf.org/en/Publications/WP/Issues/2016/12/31/Demand-Spillovers-and-the-Collapse-of-Trade-in-the-Global-Recession-23946

Benton, T., 'What Karl Marx Has to Say about Today's Environmental Problems', *The Conversation*, (Australian edn), 5 June 2018, https://theconversation.com/what-karl-marx-has-to-say-about-todays-environmental-problems-97479

Bergmann, M. and Burgmann, V., 'Green Bans Movement', *Dictionary of Sydney*, Sydney, State Library of New South Wales, 2011, https://dictionaryofsydney.org/entry/green_bans_movement

Berman, H.J., *Law and Revolution: The Formation of the Western Legal Tradition*, Cambridge, MA, Harvard University Press, 1983.

Bloch, M., *Feudal Society*, London, Routledge, 2014.

Bond, N., 'Ferdinand Tönnies' Appraisal of Karl Marx: Debts and Distance', *Journal of Classical Sociology*, vol. 13, no. 1, 2013, pp. 136–62.

Boulanger, C. and Pialucha, D., *Community Land Trusts Finance: Understanding the Diversity of Models in Europe*, Global Fund for Cities' Development, Montreuil, France, 2019, https://fmdv.net/admin/Images/Publications/124/0_190904_FinancialCS_VF2-light.pdf

Bourdeau-Lepage, L. and Huriot, J. M., 'Megacities without Global Functions, *Belgian Journal of Geography*, no. 1, 2007, pp. 95–114.

British Broadcasting Corporation, 'Episode 25 – Gold Coins of Croesus (transcript)', *A History of the World*, London, British Broadcasting Corporation and British Museum, 2010, https://web.archive.org/web/20100227235939/http://www.bbc.co.uk/ahistoryoftheworld/about/transcripts/episode25/

Bromley, D., 'Formalising Property Relations in the Developing World: The Wrong Prescription for the Wrong Malady', *Land Use Policy*, vol. 26, 2008, pp. 20–7.

Burkett, P., *Marx and Nature: A Red and Green Perspective*, Chicago, IL, Haymarket Books, 2014.

Byres, T. and Mukhia, H., *Feudalism and Non-European Societies*, Bristol, Stonebridge Press, 1985.

Cahill, K., *Who Owns the World: The Hidden Facts behind Landownership*, New York, Grand Central Publishing, 2010.

Cai, H., Henderson, J. and Zhang, Q., *National Bureau of Economic Research Working Paper 15067: China's Land Market Auctions: Evidence of Corruption?*, Cambridge, MA, National Bureau of Economic Research, 2013, https://www.nber.org/system/files/working_papers/w15067/w15067.pdf

Cambridge Dictionary, Cambridge, Cambridge University Press, https://dictionary.cambridge. org/dictionary/english/land

Carchedi, G. and Roberts, M., 'The Long Roots of the Present Crisis: Keynesians, Austerians and Marx's Law', *World Review of Political Economy*, vol. 4, no. 1, 2013, pp. 86–115.

Cartledge, P. and Konstan, D., 'Marxism and Classical Antiquity', in S. Hornblower, A. Spawforth and E. Eidinow (eds), *Oxford Classical Dictionary*, 4th edn, Oxford, Oxford University Press, 2016.

Castells, M., *The Urban Question: A Marxist Approach*, trans. A. Sheridan, London, Edward Arnold, 1977.

Cayuela, S. R., 'The Commons', *Uneven Earth*, 12 Apr. 2021, http://unevenearth. org/2021/04/the-commons/

Cecosesola, 'About Us', Cecosesola, https://cecosesola.org/acerca-de/

Centre for Public Integrity, *Industry Political Donations and Disclosable Payments: Case Study: The Property and Construction Industry*, Sydney, Australia, The Centre for Public Integrity, 2021, https://publicintegrity.org.au/wp-content/uploads/2021/01/Donations-case-study-property-and-construction-industry-1.pdf

Centers for Disease Control and Prevention, *2009 H1N1 Pandemic (H1N1pdm09 virus)*, Washington, DC, Centers for Disease Control, 2019, https://www.cdc.gov/flu/pandemi c-resources/2009-h1n1-pandemic.html

Champlain Housing Trust, *History and Awards*, Burlington, VT, Champlain Housing Trust, https://www.getahome.org/history-awards/

Channon, J., 'The Bolsheviks and the Peasantry: The Land Question during the First Eight Months of Soviet Rule', *The Slavonic and East European Review*, vol. 66, no. 4, 1988, pp. 593–624.

Chen, T. and Kung, J., 'Busting the "Princelings": The Campaign against Corruption in China's Primary Land Market', *Quarterly Journal of Economics*, vol. 134, no. 1, Feb. 2019, pp. 185–226.

Chibamba, W., Koroma, E. B., Mutondori, F., Nkutawala, M. M., Okai, M. H., Rafitoson, K. and Senteza, L. Z., *Combating Land Corruption in Africa*, Berlin, Transparency International, 2019, https://images.transparencycdn.org/images/2019_Guide_CombattingLandCorru ptionAfrica_English.pdf

Chibber, V., *Postcolonial Theory and the Spectre of Capital*, London, Verso, 2012.

Chivakul, M., Lam, W. R., Liu, X., Maliszewski, W. and Schipke, A., *International Monetary Fund Working Paper 15/84: Understanding Residential Real Estate in China*, Washington, DC, International Monetary Fund, 2015, https://www.imf.org/en/Publications/WP/Issues/ 2016/12/31/Understanding-Residential-Real-Estate-in-China-42873

Christophers, B., *Rentier Capitalism: Who Owns the Economy, and Who Pays for It?*, London, Verso, 2020.

Clapp, J., 'Land and Financialization: Role of International Financial Actors in Land Deals in Africa' [online video], *Exploring Economics*, Heidelberg, Germany, 2013, https://www. exploring-economics.org/en/discover/land-and-financialization-role-of-international/

Clark, C., 'Von Thunen's Isolated State', *Oxford Economic Papers*, vol. 19, no. 3, 1967, pp. 370–7.

Clark, G. and Dear, M., 'The State in Capitalism and the Capitalist State', in M. Dear and A. J. Scott, eds, *Urbanisation and Urban Planning in Capitalist Society*, London, Routledge, 1981.

Clarkson, C. et al., 'Human Occupation of Northern Australia by 65,000 years ago', *Nature*, no. 547, 2017, pp. 306–10.

Clift, J., 'Hearing the Dogs Bark', *Finance and Development Magazine*, Washington, DC, International Monetary Fund, Washington, DC, Dec. 2003, pp. 8–11, https://www.imf.org/external/pubs/ft/fandd/2003/12/pdf/people.pdf

Coase, R. H., 'The Problem of Social Cost', *Journal of Law and Economics*, vol. 3, 1960, pp. 1–44.

Cockburn, C., *Local State: Management of Cities and People*, London, Pluto Press, 1977.

Collier, P., Glaeser, E., Venables, T., Manwaring, P. and Blake, M., *Land and Property Taxes: Exploiting Untapped Municipal Revenues*, London, International Growth Centre, 2018, https://www.theigc.org/wp-content/uploads/2017/08/Land-and-property-taxes-policy-brief_updated.pdf

Columbia Encyclopedia, 6th edn, New York, Columbia University Press, 2008, www.encycloped ia.com

Cooperativa Gestión Participativa, 'Cecosesola', Caracas, Cooperativa Gestión Participativa https://www.gestionparticipativa.coop/portal/index.php? option=com_content&view=a rticle&id=215&Itemid=435

Cotula, L. (ed.), *Changes in 'Customary' Land Tenure Systems in Africa*, International Institute for Environment and Development, London, 2007, https://pubs.iied.org/sites/default/files/pdfs/migrate/12537IIED.pdf

Cotula, L., Toulmin, C. and Hesse, C., *Land Tenure and Administration in Africa: Lessons of Experience and Emerging Issues*, London, International Institute for Environment and Development, 2004, http://www.hubrural.org/IMG/pdf/iied_lt_cotula.pdf

Crabtree, L., Phibbs, P., Milligan, V. and Blunden, H., 'Principles and Practices of an Affordable Housing Land Trust Model', Australian Housing and Urban Research Institute, 2012, https://www.ahuri.edu.au/sites/default/files/migration/documents/AHURI_Research_Paper_Principles-and-practices-of-an-affordable-housing-community-land-trust-model.pdf

Crosby, N., Gibson, V. and Murdock, S., 'UK Commercial Property Lease Structures: Landlord and Tenant Mismatch', *Urban Studies*, vol. 40, no. 8, 2003, pp. 1487–516.

Das, R., 'David Harvey's Theory of Accumulation by Dispossession: A Marxist Critique', *World Review of Political Economy*, vol. 8, no. 4 (Winter 2017), pp. 590–616.

Dear, M. and Scott, A. J., 'Towards a Framework for Analysis' in M. Dear and A.J. Scott, eds, *Urbanisation and Urban Planning in Capitalist Society*, London, Routledge, 1981.

Deininger, K., Selod, H. and Burns, T., *Land Governance Assessment Framework*, World Bank, Washington, DC, 2011, https://openknowledge.worldbank.org/bitstream/handle/10986/2376/657430PUB0EPI1065724B09780821387580.pdf?sequence=1

Deller, S., Hoyt, A., Hueth, B. and Sundaram-Stukel, R., *Research on the Economic Impact of Cooperatives*, 2009, Madison, WI, University of Wisconsin Centre for Cooperatives, http://reic.uwcc.wisc.edu/sites/all/REIC_FINAL.pdf

de Neuman, A. M., 'Some Economic Aspects of Nationalization', *Law and Contemporary Problems*, vol. 16, nos. 4/9, 1951, pp. 702–51.

de Ste. Croix, G. E. M., *The Class Struggle in the Ancient Greek World from the Archaic Age to the Arab Conquests*, Ithaca, New York, Cornell University Press, 1981.

de Vivo, G., 'Malthus's Theory of the Constant Value of Labour', *Contributions to Political Economy*, vol. 31, no. 1, 2012, pp. 103–20.

Dodson, J., Coiacetto, E. and Ellway, C., 'Corruption in the Australian Land Development Process: Identifying a Research Agenda', *Refereed Proceedings of the 2nd Bi-Annual National Conference on the State of Australian Cities*, Griffith, Griffith University, 2006, https://research-repository.griffith.edu.au/handle/10072/11501

Duda, J., 'The Italian Region Where Co-ops Produce a Third of Its GDP', *Yes Magazine*, 2016, https://www.yesmagazine.org/economy/2016/07/05/the-italian-place-where-co-ops-drive-the-economy-and-most-people-are-members

Dunn, B., *Keynes and Marx*, Manchester, Manchester University Press, 2021.

Durand, C., *Fictitious Capital: How Finance Is Appropriating Our Future*, Verso, London, 2017.

Duranton, G. and Puga, D., *The Growth of Cities*, Paris, Organisation for Economic Co-operation and Development, 2013, https://www.oecd.org/economy/growth/Growth_of_cities_Duranton.pdf

Economic Times, 'With Evergrande Debt Relief Deal, China Signals Stability Trumps Austerity', Mumbai, India, *The Economic Times*, 14 Jan. 2022, https://economictimes.indiatimes.com/news/international/business/with-evergrande-debt-relief-deal-china-signals-stability-trumps-austerity/articleshow/88895109.cms

The Economist Intelligence Unit, *The Global Livability Index 2019*, London, The Economist Group, 2019, https://www.eiu.com/public/topical_report.aspx?campaignid=liveability2019

Edel, M., 'Capitalism, Accumulation and the Explanation of Urban Phenomena', in M. Dear and A. J. Scott (eds), *Urbanisation and Urban Planning in Capitalist Society*, London, Routledge, 1981.

Edel, M., *Development or Dispersal? Approaches to Ghetto Poverty*, Cambridge, MA, Center for Community Economic Development, 1970.

Edel, M., 'Rent Theory and Labor Strategy: Marx, George and the Urban Crisis', *Review of Radical Political Economics*, no. 4, 1977, pp. 1–15.

Edel, M., *Urban and Regional Economics: Marxist Perspectives*, London, Routledge, 1991.

Edel, M., 'Urban Renewal and Land Use Conflicts', *Review of Radical Political Economics*, vol. 3, no. 3, 1971, pp. 76–89.

Edwards, M. and Lovatt, D., 'Review: Capital and Land', *Capital and Class*, vol. 3, no. 3, 1979, pp. 144–6.

Embassy of the Socialist Republic of Vietnam in the United States of America, *Land Regulations*, Washington, DC, Embassy of the Socialist Republic of Vietnam in the United States of America, n.d., http://vietnamembassy-usa.org/basic-page/land-regulations

Engels, F. *The Condition of the Working Class in England* [1845], London, Panther Books, 1969, https://www.marxists.org/archive/marx/works/1845/condition-working-class/index.htm

Engels, F., *The Housing Question*, Marx/Engels Internet Archive, https://www.marxists.org/archive/marx/works/1872/housing-question/

Engels, F., *Ludwig Feuerbach and the End of Classical German Philosophy*, Moscow, Progress Publishers, 1946, https://www.marxists.org/archive/marx/works/subject/hist-mat/ecgp-marx.htm

Engels, F., *The Peasant War in Germany*, New York, International Publishers, n.d., https://www.marxists.org/archive/marx/works/1850/peasant-war-germany/

Errasti, A., 'Mondragon's Chinese Subsidiaries: Coopitalist Multinationals in Practice', *Economic and Industrial Democracy*, vol. 36, no. 3, 2015, pp. 479–99.

European Research Institute on Cooperative and Social Enterprise, 'Exploring the Cooperative Economy', *World Cooperative Monitor, 2020*, Trento, 2020, https://monitor.coop/sites/default/files/publication-files/wcm2020web-final-1083463041.pdf

Ezomike, C. and Isiadinso, O., 'Property Taxation in Lagos State: A Review of the Lagos State Land Use Charge Law 2018', *Andersen Tax Digest*, 10 Apr. 2018.

Fargher, L., Blanton, R. and Espinoza, V., 'Egalitarian Ideology and Political Power in Prehispanic Central Mexico: The Case of Tlaxcallan', *Latin American Antiquity*, vol. 21, no. 3, 2010, pp. 227–51.

Federación Uruguaya de Cooperativas de vivienda por Ayuda Mutua, 'New Groups', Montevideo, Federación Uruguaya de Cooperativas de vivienda por Ayuda Mutua, https://www.fucvam.org.uy/nuevos-grupos/

Ferrando, T., 'The Financialization of Land and Agriculture: Mechanisms, Implications and Responses', Social Science Research Network (now SSRN), 2017, http://dx.doi.org/10.2139/ssrn.2916112

Financial Crisis Inquiry Commission, *The Financial Crisis Inquiry Report: Final Report of the National Commission on the Causes of the Financial and Economic Crisis in the United States*, Washington, DC, Financial Crisis Inquiry Commission, 2011, https://www.govinfo.gov/content/pkg/GPO-FCIC/pdf/GPO-FCIC.pdf

Fine, B., 'Marx's Rent Theory Revisited? Landed Property, Nature and Value', *Economy and Society*, vol. 48, no. 3, 2019, pp. 450–61.

Fine, B., 'On Marx's Theory of Agricultural Rent', *Economy and Society*, vol. 8, no. 3, 1979, pp. 241–78.

Fine, B., *Social Capital versus Social Theory*, London, Routledge, 2001.

Fine, B. and Saad-Filho, A., *Marx's Capital*, 6th edn, London, Pluto Press, 2016.

Fireside, D., 'Burlington Busts the Affordable Housing Debate', *Dollars and Sense*, Economic Affairs Bureau, Union for Radical Political Economics, Portsmouth, NH, 2005, http://dollarsandsense.org/archives/2005/0305fireside.html

Food and Agriculture Organization, *Voluntary Guidelines on the Responsible Governance of Tenure of Land, Fisheries and Forests in the Context of National Food Security*, Rome, Food and Agriculture Organization, 2012, http://www.fao.org/3/i2801e/i2801e.pdf

Freudenberger, M., 'The Future of Customary Tenure: Options for Policymakers', *Land Links*, Washington, DC, Land and Resource Governance Division, United States Agency for International Development (USAID), 2013, https://www.land-links.org/issue-brief/the-future-of-customary-tenure/

Fukuyama, F., 'The End of History?' *The National Interest*, vol. 16, 1989, pp. 3–18.

Furniss, N., 'The Political Implications of the Public Choice-Property Rights School', *The American Political Science Review*, vol. 72, no. 2, 1978, pp. 399–410.

Gailey, C., 'Community, State and Questions of Social Evolution in Marx's Ethnological Notebooks', *Anthropologica*, vol. 45, no. 1, 2003, pp. 45–57.

Garrido, A., Delfina, M., Anderson, J., Davidsen, S., Vo, D. H., Dinh, D. N. and Tran, H. T. L., *Recognizing and Reducing Corruption Risks in Land Management in Vietnam*, Washington, DC, World Bank Group, 2011, http://documents.worldbank.org/curated/en/918551468322441320/Recognizing-and-reducing-corruption-risks-in-land-management-in-Vietnam

George, H., *The Condition of Labor: An Open Letter to Pope Leo XIII*, 1891, http://www.wealthandwant.com/HG/the_condition_of_labor.htm

George, H., 'The Inwardness of a Boom', *The Standard*, vol. 2, 6 Aug. 1887, p. 4, http://henrygeorgethestandard.org/volume-2-august-6-1887/

George, H., *Progress and Poverty: An Inquiry into the Cause of Industrial Depressions and of Increase of want with Increase of Wealth; the Remedy*, New York, Doubleday, Page & Company, 1916, https://archive.org/details/progresspovertyi01geor/page/n15/mode/2up.

Giampaoli, P. and Aggarwal, S., *USAID Issue Brief: Land Tenure and Property Rights in Pakistan*, Washington, DC, United States Agency for International Development, 2010, https://www.land-links.org/wp-content/uploads/2016/09/USAID_Land_Tenure_Pakistan_Issue_Brief-2.pdf

Gibson-Graham, J. K., *A Postcapitalist Politics*, Minneapolis, MN, University of Minnesota Press, 2006.

Gilbert, A., 'On the *Mystery of Capital* and the Myths of Hernando de Soto: What Difference Does Legal Title Make?', *International Development Planning Review* (formerly *Third World Planning Review*), vol. 24, no. 1, 2002, pp. 1–19.

Glasow, R. von, Jickells, T. D., Baklanov, A., Carmichael, G. R., Church, T. M., Gallardo, L., Hughes, C., Kanakidou, M., Liss, P. S., Mee, L., Raine, R., Ramachandran, P., Ramesh, R., Sundseth, K., Tsunogai, U., Uematsu, M. and Zhu, T., 'Megacities and Large Urban Agglomerations in the Coastal Zone: Interactions between Atmosphere, Land, and Marine Ecosystems', *Ambio*, vol. 42, no. 1, 2013, pp. 13–28.

Global Change Data Lab, 'Urbanization over the Past 500 Years, 1500 to 2016', *Our World in Data*, Oxford, Global Change Data Lab, n.d., https://ourworldindata.org/grapher/urbanization-last-500-years

Graeber, D., *Debt: The First 5,000 Years*, New York, Melville House Publishing, 2011.

Grafton, R. Q. and Williams, J., 'Rent-seeking Behaviour and Regulatory Capture in the Murray–Darling Basin, Australia', *International Journal of Water Resources Development*, vol. 36, no. 2, 2020, pp. 484–504.

Gray, N., 'Whose Rebel City?', *Mute*, 18 Dec. 2012, https://www.metamute.org/editorial/articles/whose-rebel-city

Gritten, W., 'Why the Northern Rail Franchise is Being Nationalised', *The Week*, London, Dennis Publishing, 30 Jan. 2020, https://www.theweek.co.uk/105444/why-the-northern-rail-franchise-is-being-nationalised

Haila, A., *Urban Land Rent: Singapore as a Property State*, Hoboken, NJ, Wiley-Blackwell, 2015.

Halilovic, S., *Community Land Trust Fund I: What We've Learned by Supporting Communities to Build Their Forever Affordable Homes*, London, Charities Aid Foundation, 2016, https://www.cafonline.org/docs/default-source/charity-finance-and-fundraising/clt-i-fund-closing-paper_final.pdf?sfvrsn=0

Halvitigala, D., Murphy, L. and Levy, D., 'The Impacts of Commercial Lease Structures on Landlord and Tenant Leasing Behaviours and Experiences', *Pacific Rim Property Research Journal*, vol. 17, 2015, pp. 560–83.

Hankin, A., 'Megaprojects' Exclusionary Benefits: The Case of Local Government Policy Benefiting the Privileged Few', *Harvard Real Estate Review*, 17 May 2017, https://medium.com/harvard-real-estate-review/megaprojects-exclusionary-benefits-the-case-of-local-government-policy-benefiting-the-privileged-db4d1a8228bc

Harvey, D., 'A Commentary on the Falling Rate of Profit in Marx's Crisis Theory' [online video], *The Great Meltdown of 2008: Systemic, Conjunctural or Policy-created*, conference at Izmir University of Economics, Izmir, Turkey, Oct. 2014, https://www.youtube.com/watch?v=-ZJrNgb-iiY

Harvey, D., 'David Harvey on Class Struggle', video, LABOURNET TV, 2011, https://en.labournet.tv/video/6260/david-harvey-class-struggle

Harvey, D., *The Limits to Capital*, Oxford, Basil Blackwell, 1982.

Harvey, D., *Megacities Lecture 4*, Amersfoort, Twynstra Gudde Management Consultants, 2000, https://www.kas.de/c/document_library/get_file?uuid=1463ff93-1eab-8877-edfc-ccef8540c262&groupId=252038

Harvey, D., 'Reflections on an Academic Life', *Human Geography*, vol. 15, no. 1, 2021, pp. 14–24.

Harvey, D., 'The Social Construction of Space and Time: A Relational Theory', *Geographical Review of Japan*, vol. 67 (Ser. B), no. 2, 1994, pp. 126–35.

Harvey, D., *Social Justice and the City*, Athens, GA, University of Georgia Press, 2009.

Harvey, D., 'Space as a Key Word', *Marx and Philosophy Conference*, London, Institute of Education, 29 May 2004, http://frontdeskapparatus.com/files/harvey2004.pdf

Harvey, D., 'The Urbanisation of Capitalism', *Actuel Marx*, vol. 35, no. 1, 2004, pp. 41–70.

Harvey, D., 'The Urban Process under Capitalism: A Framework for Analysis', in M. Dear and A. J. Scott, eds, *Urbanisation and Urban Planning in Capitalist Society*, London, Routledge, 1981.

Hatfield, R. and Davies, J., *Global Review of the Economics of Pastoralism*, Nairobi, International Union for the Conservation of Nature, 2006, https://www.iucn.org/sites/dev/files/import/downloads/global_review_ofthe_economicsof_pastoralism_en_1.pdf

Havel M. B., 'The Effect of Formal Property Rights Regime on Urban Development and Planning Methods in the Context of Post-Socialist Transformation: An Institutional Approach', in R. Levine-Schnur (ed.), *Measuring the Effectiveness of Real Estate Regulation*. SpringerLink, 2020.

Hazard, J. N., 'Soviet Property Law', *Cornell Law Review*, vol. 30., no. 4, 1945, pp. 466–87.

He, J., Qian, J. and Strahan, P. E., 'Credit Ratings and the Evolution of the Mortgage-Backed Securities Market', *American Economic Review*, vol. 101, no. 3, 2011, pp. 131–5.

Heller, H., *The Birth of Capitalism: A 21st-Century Perspective*, London, Pluto Press, 2011, pp. 215–42.

Henry George Foundation, *Economic Rent*, London, Henry George Foundation, n.d., https://www.henrygeorgefoundation.org/the-science-of-economics/economic-rent.html

Hindess, B. and Hirst, P. Q., *Pre-Capitalist Modes of Production*, Abingdon, Routledge, 2018.

Ho, K. C., 'Land and Housing in Singapore: Three Conversations with Anne Haila', *American Journal of Economics and Sociology*, vol. 80, no. 2, 2021, pp. 325–51.

Hobsbawm, E. J., *Pre-Capitalist Economic Formations*, New York, International Publishers, 1965.

Hodgson, G. M., *How Economics Forgot History: The Problem of Historical Specificity in Social Science*, London, Routledge, 2001.

Hollender, R., 'A Politics of the Commons or Commoning the Political? Distinct Possibilities for Post-Capitalist Transformation', *Spectra*, vol. 5, no. 1, 2016, n.p.

Hudson, M., 'From Marx to Goldman Sachs: The Fictions of Fictitious Capital, and the Financialization of Industry', *Critique*, vol. 38, 2010, pp. 419–44.

Independent Commission Against Corruption, *Conditions That May Allow Corruption to Occur*, Sydney, Independent Commission Against Corruption, 2018, https://www.icac.nsw.gov.au/about-corruption/conditions-that-may-allow-corruption-to-occur-

Indigenous Peoples Major Group for Sustainable Development, *Global Report on the Situation of Lands, Territories and Resources of Indigenous Peoples*, Indigenous Peoples Major Group for Sustainable Development, 2019, https://www.iwgia.org/images/documents/briefings/IPMG%20Global%20Report%20FINAL.pdf

Institute on Metropolitan Opportunity, *American Neighborhood Change in the 21st Century*, Minneapolis, MN, Institute on Metropolitan Opportunity, University of Minnesota, 2019, https://www.law.umn.edu/sites/law.umn.edu/files/metro-files/american_neighborhood_change_in_the_21st_century_-_full_report_-_4-1-2019.pdf

International Labour Organization, *Cooperatives*, Geneva, International Labour Organisation, https://www.ilo.org/global/topics/cooperatives/lang–en/index.htm

International Labour Organization, *Implementing the ILO Indigenous and Tribal Peoples Convention No. 169: Towards an Inclusive, Sustainable and Just Future'*, Geneva, International Labour Organization, 2019, https://www.ilo.org/wcmsp5/groups/public/—dgreports/—dcomm/–publ/documents/publication/wcms735607.pdf

Intergovernmental Panel on Climate Change, '1.2.1.2. Land Degradation', *Special Report on Climate Change and Land: An IPCC Special Report on Climate Change, Desertification, Land Degradation, Sustainable Land Management, Food Security, and Greenhouse Gas Fluxes in Terrestrial Systems*, Geneva, Intergovernmental Panel on Climate Change, 2019, https://www.ipcc.ch/srccl/chapter/chapter-1/

Jones, A., 'The Rise and Fall of the Manorial System: A Critical Comment', *Journal of Economic History*, vol. 32, no. 4, 1972, pp. 938–44.

Kalkuhl, M., Milan, B. F., Schwerhoff, G., Jakob, M., Hahnen, M. and Creutzig, F., 'Can Land Taxes Foster Sustainable Development? An Assessment of Fiscal, Distributional and Implementation Issues', *Land Use Policy*, vol. 78, 2018, pp. 338–52.

Katz, S., 'Towards a Sociological Definition of Rent: Notes of David Harvey's *The Limits to Capital*', *Antipode*, vol. 18, no. 1, 1986, pp. 64–78.

Kaufmann, D. and Vicente, P. C., *Legal Corruption*, Second Draft, Washington, DC, World Bank, 2005, http://web.worldbank.org/archive/website00818/WEB/LEGALCOR.HTM

Kawate, L., 'China's Largest "Ghost City" Booms Again Thanks to Education Fever', Tokyo, *Nikkei Asia*, 19 Apr. 2021, https://asia.nikkei.com/Spotlight/Society/China-s-largest-ghost-city-booms-again-thanks-to-education-fever

Kay, J. and King, A., *Radical Uncertainty: Decision-Making Beyond the Numbers*, New York, W. W. Norton & Company, 2020.

Kaye, H., 'Totality: Its Application to Historical and Social Analysis by Wallerstein and Genovese', *Historical Reflections*, vol. 6, no. 2, 1979.

Kearney, *2020 Global Cities Index*, Chicago, IL, Kearney, 2020, https://www.kearney.com/global-cities/2020

Kennedy, M. and Leonard, P., *Dealing with Neighborhood Change: A Primer on Gentrification and Policy Choices*, Washington, DC, The Brookings Institution, 2011, https://www.brookings.edu/wp-content/uploads/2016/06/gentrification.pdf

Keynes, J. M., *A Treatise on Money*, Cambridge, Cambridge University Press, 1930.

Khanna, P., 'Mega-Cities, Not Relations, Are the World's Dominant Enduring Social Structures', *Quartz* [online news organisation], 21 Apr. 2016, https://qz.com/666153/megacities-not-nations-are-the-worlds-most-dominant-enduring-social-structures-adapted-from-connectography/

King, A. D., 'Colonialism and Urban Development' in F. Miraftab and N. Kudva, *Cities of the Global South Reader*, Abingdon, Routledge, 2015.

Kleer, J. and Nawrot, K. A., *The Rise of Megacities: Challenges, Opportunities and Unique Characteristics*, Singapore, World Scientific Publishing Company, 2018.

Klein, N., *This Changes Everything: Capitalism vs the Climate*, London, Penguin Books, 2015.

Kliman, A., 'The Great Recession and Marx's Crisis Theory', *American Journal of Economics and Sociology*, vol. 74, no. 2, 2015, pp. 236–77.

Konaev, M., 'The Future of Urban Warfare in the Age of Megacities', *Focus stratégique*, no. 88, 2019, Paris, Institut français des relations internationales (Ifri), https://www.ifri.org/sites/default/files/atoms/files/konaev_urban_warfare_megacities_2019.pdf

Kose, M. A., Sugawara, N. and Terrones, M. E., *Global Recessions: Policy Research Working Paper 9172*, Washington, USA, World Bank, 2020, https://documents1.worldbank.org/curated/en/185391583249079464/pdf/Global-Recessions.pdf

Kosminsky, E. A., 'Services and Money Rents in the Thirteenth Century', *Economic History Review*, vol. 5, no. 2, 1935, pp. 24–45.

Krieger, M. H., 'Corruption and the Culture of Real Estate Development', *Business and Professional Ethics Journal*, vol. 13, no. 3, 1994, pp. 19–32.

Kulish, M., Richards, A. and Gillitzer, C., *RDP 2011-03: Urban Structure and Housing Prices: Some Evidence from Australian Cities*, Sydney, Reserve Bank of Australia, 2011, https://www.rba.gov.au/publications/rdp/2011/2011-03/introduction.html

Kulp, S. A. and Strauss, B. H., 'New Elevation Data Triple Estimates of Global Vulnerability to Sea-level Rise and Coastal Flooding', *Nature Communications*, vol. 10, article no. 4844, 2019.

Lall, S. V., Henderson J. V. and Venables, A. J., *Africa's Cities: Opening Doors to the World*, Washington, DC, World Bank, 2017, https://openknowledge.worldbank.org/handle/10986/25896

Land Portal, *Collective Property in South America, Challenges and Perspectives*, Groningen, The Netherlands, Land Portal, 2017, https://landportal.org/debates/2017/collective-property-south-america-challenges-and-prospects

Lapavitsas, C., and Aguila, N., 'Monetary Policy Is Ultimately Based on a Theory of Money: A Marxist Critique of MMT', *Developing Economics*, 17 Mar. 2021, https://developingeconomics.org/2021/03/17/monetary-policy-is-ultimately-based-on-a-theory-of-money-a-marxist-critique-of-mmt/

Lazarus, M., 'Marx's Concept of Class and the Athenian Polis', *Eras Journal*, vol. 18, no. 1, pp. 21–37.

Lefebvre, H., *The Production of Space*, Hoboken, NJ, Wiley-Blackwell, 1991.

Lefebvre, H., *The Right to the City* in H. Lefebvre, *Writings on Cities*, ed. and trans. E. Kofman and E. Lebas, Hoboken, NJ, Wiley-Blackwell, 1995.

Lefebvre, H., *The Urban Revolution*, Minneapolis, MN, University of Minnesota Press, 2003.

Le Page, M., 'Destruction of Nature Is as Big a Threat to Humanity as Climate Change', *New Scientist*, no. 3229, 11 May 2019, https://www.newscientist.com/article/2201697-destruction-of-nature-is-as-big-a-threat-to-humanity-as-climate-change/

Li, J., *Chinese Civilization in the Making, 1766–221 BC*, London, Palgrave Macmillan, 1996.

Li, W., *Ethnoburb: The New Ethnic Community in Urban America*, Manoa, HI, University of Hawaii Press, 2012.

Liu, Z. and Liang, M. 'Study on Dual-Track System of Chinese Land Ownership', *Cross-Cultural Communication*, vol. 11, no. 9, 2015, pp. 24–8.

Locke, J., *Second Treatise of Government* [1690], Cambridge, MA, Hackett Publishing Company, 1980.

London Assembly Planning Committee, *Tax Trial: A Land Value Tax for London?*, London, Greater London Authority, 2016, https://www.london.gov.uk/sites/default/files/final-draft-lvt-report_2.pdf

Loo, E., *Lessons from Singapore about Land Value Capture*, London, Royal Town Planning Institute, 2017, https://www.rtpi.org.uk/blog/2017/april/lessons-from-singapore-about-land-value-capture/

Löscher, A. 'Financialisation and Development: A Case Study of Ethiopia', *Qualitative Research in Financial Markets*, vol. 11, no. 2, 2019, pp. 138–96.

Lu, Y. and Sun, T, *International Monetary Fund Working Paper 13/243: Local Government Financing Platforms in China: A Fortune of Misfortune?*, Washington, DC, International Monetary Fund, 2013, https://www.imf.org/external/pubs/ft/wp/2013/wp13243.pdf

Lukacs, G., 'The Marxism of Rosa Luxemburg', *History and Class Consciousness*, London, Merlin Press, 1967, https://www.marxists.org/archive/lukacs/works/history/ch02.htm

McChesney, F., 'Rent Extraction and Rent Creation in the Economic Theory of Regulation', *Journal of Legal Studies*, vol. 16, no. 1, 1987, pp. 101–18.

Mahowald, M., 'Marx's "Gemeinschaft": Another Interpretation', *Philosophy and Phenomenological Research*, vol. 33, no. 4, 1973, pp. 472–88.

Major, J. R., ' 'Bastard Feudalism' and the Kiss: Changing Social Mores in Late Medieval and Early Modern France', *Journal of Interdisciplinary History*, vol. 17, no. 3, 1987, pp. 509–35.

Marx, K., *A Contribution to the Critique of Hegel's Philosophy of Right*, Marx/Engels Internet Archive, n.d., https://www.marxists.org/archive/marx/works/1843/critique-hpr/intro.htm

Marx, K., *A Contribution to the Critique of Political Economy*, Moscow, Russia, Progress Publishers, 1977, https://www.marxists.org/archive/marx/works/1859/critique-pol-economy/index.htm

Marx, K., 'Address of the Central Committee to the Communist League', *Marx/Engels Selected Works*, Moscow, Progress Publishers, 1970, https://www.marxists.org/archive/marx/works/subject/hist-mat/com-leag.htm

Marx, K., 'The British Rule in India', *New-York Daily Tribune*, 25 June 1853 https://www.marxists.org/archive/marx/works/1853/06/25.htm

Marx, K., *Capital*, vol. I, Moscow, Progress Publishers, 1887, https://www.marxists.org/archive/marx/works/1867-c1/index.htm

Marx, K., *Capital*, vol. II, Moscow, Progress Publishers, 1956, https://www.marxists.org/archive/marx/works/1885-c2/index.htm

Marx, K., *Capital*, vol. III, New York, International Publishers, 1959, https://www.marxists.org/archive/marx/works/1894-c3/

Marx, K., *The Civil War in France*, London, General Council of the International Workingmen's Association, 1871, https://www.marxists.org/archive/marx/works/1871/civil-war-france/index.htm

Marx, K., *Communism and the Augsburg* Allgemeine Zeitung, Marx/Engels Internet Archive, n.d., https://www.marxists.org/archive/marx/works/1842/10/16.htm

Marx, K., 'Critique of the Gotha Programme', *Marx/Engels Selected Works, Vol. Three*, Moscow, Progress Publishers, 1970, pp. 13–30, https://www.marxists.org/archive/marx/works/1875/gotha/index.htm

Marx, K., *Critique of Hegel's Philosophy of Right*, ed. J. O'Malley, Cambridge, Cambridge University Press, 1970, https://www.marxists.org/archive/marx/works/1843/critique-hpr/index.htm

Marx, K., 'The Duchess of Sutherland and Slavery', *The People's Paper*, London, no. 45, 12 Mar. 1853, https://www.marxists.org/archive/marx/works/1853/03/12.htm

Marx, K., *Economic and Philosophic Manuscripts of 1844*, Moscow, Progress Publishers, 1959, https://www.marxists.org/archive/marx/works/1844/manuscripts/preface.htm

Marx, K., *The Eighteenth Brumaire of Louis Bonaparte*, Marx/Engels Internet Archive, 1995, https://www.marxists.org/archive/marx/works/1852/18th-brumaire/ch01.htm

Marx, K., *The Ethnological Notebooks of Karl Marx*, Assen, van Gorcum and Company, 1974, https://www.marxists.org/archive/marx/works/1881/ethnographical-notebooks/notebooks.pdf

Marx, K., 'The First Draft' (of Marx's reply to a letter from Vera Zasulich), in T. Shanin (ed.), *Late Marx and the Russian Road: Marx and the 'Peripheries of Capitalism'*, New York, Monthly Review Press, 1983, https://www.marxists.org/archive/marx/works/1881/zasulich/draft-1.htm

Marx, K., *Grundrisse*, London, Penguin Books in association with *New Left Review*, 1973, https://www.marxists.org/archive/marx/works/1857/grundrisse/index.htm

Marx, K., 'India', *New-York Daily Tribune*, 5 Aug. 1853, https://www.marxists.org/archive/marx/works/1853/08/05.htm

Marx, K., 'Instructions for the Delegates of the Provisional General Council of the International Workingmen's Association', *The International Courier*, nos. 6/7, 20 Feb. 1867 and nos. 8/10, 13 Mar. 1867, https://www.marxists.org/archive/marx/works/1866/08/instructions.htm

Marx, K., 'Letter to Friedrich Adolph Sorge, 20 June 1881', *Karl Marx and Frederick Engels, Selected Correspondence*, Moscow, Progress Publishers, 1975, https://www.marxists.org/archive/marx/works/1881/letters/81_06_20.htm

Marx, K., 'Letter to Arnold Ruge, May 1843', *Marx/Engels Internet Archive*, n.d., https://www.marxists.org/archive/marx/works/1843/letters/43_05.htm

Marx, K., 'Letter to Nikolai Danielson in St Petersburg, 19 February 1881', *Marx and Engels Correspondence*, Moscow, International Publishers, 1968.

Marx, K., 'Marx-Zasulich Correspondence', in T. Shanin (ed.), *Late Marx and the Russian Road: Marx and the 'peripheries of capitalism'*, New York, Monthly Review Press, 1983, https://www.marxists.org/archive/marx/works/1881/zasulich/index.htm.

Marx, K., 'The Nationalisation of the Land', *The International Herald*, no. 11, 15 June 1872, https://www.marxists.org/archive/marx/works/1872/04/nationalisation-land.htm

Marx, K., 'Nature and Growth of Capital', *Wage Labour and Capital*, Marxists Internet Archive, 1993, https://www.marxists.org/archive/marx/works/1847/wage-labour/ch05.htm

Marx, K., *On the Jewish Question*, Marx/Engels Internet Archive, 2020, https://www.marxists.org/archive/marx/works/1844/jewish-question/

Marx, K., 'The Paris Commune', *The Civil War in France*, London, General Council of the International Workingmen's Association, 1871, https://www.marxists.org/archive/marx/works/1871/civil-war-france/ch05.htm

Marx, K., *The Poverty of Philosophy*, Moscow, Progress Publishers, 1955, https://www.marxists.org/archive/marx/works/1847/poverty-philosophy/index.htm

Marx, K., *Pre-Capitalist Economic Formations*, New York, International Publishers, 1964, https://www.marxists.org/archive/marx/works/1857/precapitalist/index.htm

Marx, K., 'Reply to Vasulich', in T. Shanin (ed.), *Late Marx and the Russian Road: Marx and the 'Peripheries of Capitalism'*, New York, Monthly Review Press, 1983, https://www.marxists.org/archive/marx/works/1881/zasulich/reply.htm

Marx, K., 'Revolutionary Spain', *New-York Daily Tribune*, New York, 20 Nov. 1854, https://www.marxists.org/archive/marx/works/1854/revolutionary-spain/ch06.htm

Marx, K., 'The Second Draft' (of reply to a letter from Vera Zasulich), in T. Shanin (ed.), *Late Marx and the Russian Road: Marx and the 'peripheries of capitalism'*, New York, Monthly Review Press, 1983, https://www.marxists.org/archive/marx/works/1881/zasulich/draft-2.htm

Marx, K., 'Speech on the Seventh Anniversary of the International', *The First International and After*, Harmondsworth, Penguin, 1974, https://www.marxists.org/archive/marx/bio/media/marx/71_10_15.htm

Marx, K., *Theories of Surplus Value*, Moscow, Progress Publishers, 1969, https://www.marxists.org/archive/marx/works/1863/theories-surplus-value/

Marx, K., *Theses on Feuerbach*, Moscow, Progress Publishers, 1969, https://www.marxists.org/archive/marx/works/1845/theses/theses.htm

Marx, K., *Wage Labour and Capital*, Marx/Engels Internet Archive, 1993, https://www.marxists.org/archive/marx/works/1847/wage-labour/index.htm

Marx, K. and Engels, F., *The German Ideology*, Moscow, Progress Publishers, 1968, https://www.marxists.org/archive/marx/works/1845/german-ideology/index.htm

Marx, K. and Engels, F., *The Manifesto of the Communist Party*, in *Marx/Engels Selected Works*, vol. I, Moscow, Progress Publishers, 1969, pp. 98–137, https://www.marxists.org/archive/marx/works/1848/communist-manifesto/index.htm

Marx, K. and Guesde, J., 'The Programme of the Parti Ouvrier', in J. Guesde, *Textes choisis 1867–1882*, Paris, Éditions Sociales, 1959, pp. 117–19, trans. B. Moss for Marx/Engels Internet Archive, https://www.marxists.org/archive/marx/works/1880/05/parti-ouvrier.htm

Mason, J. W., 'In Defence of David Graeber's Debt', *Jacobin*, vol. 3, Sept. 2012, n.p., https://jacobinmag.com/2012/09/in-defense-of-david-graebers-debt

Massey, D., *Spatial Divisions of Labour: Social Structures and the Geography of Production*, 2nd edn, New York, Routledge, 1995.

Massey, D. and Catalano, A., *Capital and Land: Land Ownership by Capital in Great Britain*, London, E. Arnold, 1978.

Maybee, J. E., 'Hegel's Dialectics', in E. N. Zalta (ed.), *Stanford Encyclopedia of Philosophy*, Winter 2020, https://plato.stanford.edu/archives/win2020/entries/hegel-dialectics/

Merrifield, A., *The New Urban Question*, London, Pluto Press, 2014.

Mondragon Corporation, *Press Dossier*, Mondragón, Mondragon Corporation, https://www.mondragon-corporation.com/wp-content/uploads/docs/MONDRAGONnotadeprensa_EN.pdf

Monzon, R., 'Introducing Private-Property Rights to Cuba: How Cuba's New Constitution Paves the Way for Economic Growth', *Case Western Reserve Journal of International Law*, vol. 52, no. 1, 2020, pp. 629–68.

Morange, M. and Spire, A., 'The Right to the City in the Global South. Perspectives from Africa', *Cybergeo: European Journal of Geography* (online), 20 May 2019, n.p., https://journals.openedition.org/cybergeo/32217#quotation

Mutero, J. and Chege, M., *Bridging the Affordability Gap: Towards a Financing Mechanism for Slum Upgrading at Scale in Nairobi*, Nairobi, United Nations Habitat (Human Settlements Programme), 2019, https://unhabitat.org/sites/default/files/2020/05/financing_mechanism_for_slum_upgrading_at_scale_in_nairobi.pdf

National Assembly of FUCVAM, Declaration of Principles, Federación Uruguaya de Cooperativas de vivienda por Ayuda Mutua, Montevideo, 1999, https://www.fucvam.org.uy/wp-content/uploads/2017/08/Declaraci per centC3 per centB3n-de-Principios.pdf

Ng, M. and Pong, C.C., *Land Framework of Singapore: Building a Sound Land Administration and Management System*, Singapore, Centre for Liveable Cities, 2018, https://www.clc.gov.sg/docs/default-source/urban-systems-studies/uss-land-framework-of-singapore.pdf

Nguyen, H. L., Duan J. and Zhang G. Q., 'Land Politics under Market Socialism: The State, Land Policies, and Rural–Urban Land Conversion in China and Vietnam', *Land*, vol. 7, no. 2, 2018, https://www.mdpi.com/2073-445X/7/2/51

Obeng-Odoom, F., '"Abnormal" Urbanization in Africa: A Dissenting View', *African Geographical Review*, vol. 29, 2010, pp. 13–40.

Obeng-Odoom, F., *The Commons in an Age of Uncertainty: Decolonizing Nature, Economy, and Society*, Toronto, University of Toronto Press, 2020.

Obeng-Odoom, F., 'Oil Cities in Africa: Beyond Just Transition', *American Journal of Economics and Sociology*, vol. 80, no. 2, 2021, pp. 777–821.

Obeng-Odoom, F., *Oiling the Urban Economy: Land, Labour, Capital, and the State in Sekondi-Takoradi, Ghana*, London, Routledge, 2014.

Obeng-Odoom, F., 'Private Urban Land Tenure: Revisiting Anne Haila's Work on Its Nature, Critique, and Alternatives', *American Journal of Economics and Sociology*, vol. 80, no. 2, 2021, pp. 291–324.

Obeng-Odoom, F., *Property, Institutions, and Social Stratification in Africa*, Cambridge, Cambridge University Press, 2020.

Obeng-Odoom, F., *Reconstructing Urban Economics: Towards a Political Economy of the Built Environment*, London, Zed Books, 2016.

Obeng-Odoom, F., 'Rethinking Development Economics: Problems and Prospects of Georgist Political Economy', *Review of Political Economy*, 2021, DOI: 10.1080/09538259. 2021.1928334.

Obeng-Odoom, F., 'Transnational Corporations and Urban Development', *American Journal of Economics and Sociology*, vol. 77, no. 2, 2018, pp. 447–510.

Obeng-Odoom, F., 'Valuing Unregistered Urban Land in Indonesia', *Evolutionary and Institutional Economics Review*, vol. 15, 2018, pp. 315–340.

Obeng-Odoom, F. and Stilwell, F., 'Security of Tenure in International Development Discourse', *International Development Planning Review*, vol. 35, no. 4, 2013, pp. 315–33.

O'Connor, J., 'Marxism and the Three Movements of Neoliberalism', *Critical Sociology*, vol. 36, no. 5, 2010, pp. 691–715.

O'Connor, J., *Natural Causes: Essays in Ecological Marxism*, New York, Guilford Press, 1998.

Orizet, J., 'The Co-operative Movement since the First World War', *International Labour Review*, vol. 2, no. 100, 1969, pp. 23–50.

Oust, A. and Hrafnkelsson, K., 'What Is a Housing Bubble?', *Economics Bulletin*, vol. 37, no. 2, 2017, pp. 806–36.

Pacific Data Hub, *National Minimum Development Indicators for Population*, Noumea, New Caledonia, The Pacific Community, 2020, https://stats.pacificdata.org/vis?data query=A..._T._T._T..&period=2020percent2C2020&frequency=A&locale=en& facet=2GnE9Xll4JueXZO6PCaYVMITvuuMAH&constraints[0]=2GnE9X ll4JueXZO6PCaYVMITvuuMAHpercent2C0percent7CNationalpercent20Min imumpercent20Developmentpercent20Indicatorspercent23NMDIpercent23& dataflow[datasourceId]=SPC2&dataflow[dataflowId]=DF_NMDI_POP&data flow[agencyId]=SPC&dataflow[version]=1.0&filter=PANEL_PERIOD

Pejovich, S. (ed.), *The Economics of Property Rights*, Cheltenham, Edward Elgar Publishing, 2001.

Picard, P. M. and Selod, H., *Customary Land Conversion and the Formation of the African City*, Washington, DC, World Bank, 2020, https://openknowledge.worldbank.org/bitstream/ handle/10986/33484/Customary-Land-Conversion-and-the-Formation-of-the-African-City.pdf?sequence=1&isAllowed=y

Piketty, T., *Capital in the Twenty-First Century*, Cambridge, MA, Harvard University Press, 2017.

Pisarev, A., 'Soviet Sinology and Two Approaches to an Understanding of Chinese History', *China Review*, vol. 14, no. 2, pp. 113–30.

Polanyi, K., *The Great Transformation: The Political and Economic Origins of our Time*, Boston, MA, Beacon Press, 2018.

Prum, D.A., 'Commercial-Property Leases as a Means for Private Environmental Governance', *Georgia State University Law Review*, vol. 35, no. 3, 2019, pp. 727–75.

Pullen, D., 'Government Infrastructure Investment Dividends and Urban Development', *American Journal of Economics and Sociology*, vol. 80, no. 2, 2021, pp. 721–45.

Pumain, D. (ed.), *Theories and Models of Urbanisation: Geography, Economics and Computing Sciences*, Berlin, Springer, 2020.

Purcell, M., 'Excavating Lefebvre: The Right to the City and Its Urban Politics of the Inhabitant', *GeoJournal*, no. 58, 2002, pp. 99–108.

Rasmus, J., 'The Deepening Global Financial Crisis: From Minsky to Marx and Beyond', *Critique*, vol. 36, no. 1, 2008, pp. 5–29.

Red-Green Study Group, *What on Earth Is to Be Done?*, Manchester, 1995, http://redgreen studygroup.org.uk/what-on-earth-is-to-be-done/

Reporters Without Borders, *Global Communication and Information Space: A Common good of Humankind*, Paris, Reporters Without Borders, https://rsf.org/en/global-communication-and-information-space-common-good-humankind.

Resonance Consultancy, *The World's Best Cities 2021*, Vancouver, Resonance Consultancy, 2021, https://www.bestcities.org/

Restrepo Cadavid, P., Cineas, G., Quintero, L. E. and Zhukova, S., *Cities in Europe and Central Asia: A Shifting Story of Urban Growth and Decline*, Washington, DC, World Bank Group, 2017, https://openknowledge.worldbank.org/handle/10986/28972?locale-attribute=en

Reydon, B. P. and Fernandes, V. B., 'Financialization, Land Prices and Land Grab: A Study Based on the Brazilian Reality', *Economia e Sociedade*, vol. 26, 2017, pp. 1149–79.

Reynolds, S., *Fiefs and Vassals: The Medieval Evidence Reinterpreted*, Oxford, Oxford University Press, 1996.

Ricardo, D., *On the Principles of Political Economy, and Taxation*, London, John Murray, 1817, p. 49.

Rights and Resources Initiative, *Who Owns the World's Land? A Global Baseline of Formally Recognised Indigenous and Community Land Rights*, Washington, DC, Rights and Resources Initiative, 2015, https://rightsandresources.org/wp-content/uploads/GlobalBaseline_web.pdf

Roberts, M., 'Modern Monetary Theory: A Marxist Critique', *Class, Race and Corporate Power*, vol. 7, no. 1, n.p.

Rodriguez, L., *A Global Perspective on the Total Economic Value of Pastoralism: Global Synthesis Report based on six Country Valuations*, Nairobi, World Initiative for Sustainable Pastoralism, 2008, https://www.iucn.org/sites/dev/files/import/downloads/tev_report.pdf

Rolston, H., 'Values in Nature', *Environmental Ethics*, vol. 3, Summer 1981, pp. 113–28.

Rosenthal, S. S. and Strange, W. C., 'How Close Is Close? The Spatial Reach of Agglomeration Economies', *Journal of Economic Perspectives*, vol. 34, no. 3, 2020, pp. 27–49.

Royer, J., 'The Neoclassical Theory of Cooperatives', *Journal of Cooperatives*, vol. 28, 2014, pp. 1–35.

Ryan, A. E. and Koch, A. B., 'COVID-19 and Lease Negotiations: Early Termination Provisions', *Law Journal Newsletters*, Jan. 2022, https://www.lawjournalnewsletters.com/2022/01/01/covid-19-and-lease-negotiations-early-termination-provisions/

Ryan-Collins, J., Lloyd, T. and Macfarlane, L., *Rethinking the Economics of Land and Housing*, London, Zed Books, 2017.

Sandercock, L., *The Land Racket: The Real Costs of Property Speculation*, Canberra, Silverfish, 1979.

Satterthwaite, D., 'Will Africa Have Most of the World's Largest Cities in 2100?', *Environment and Urbanisation*, vol. 29, no. 1, 2017, pp. 217–20.

Scott, A. J. and Storper, M., 'The Nature of Cities: The Scope and Limits of Urban Theory', *International Journal of Urban and Regional Research*, 2014, pp. 1–15.

Shaikh, A., *Capitalism: Competition, Conflict, Crises*, New York, Oxford University Press, 2016.

Shaikh, A. M. and Tonak, A., *Measuring the Wealth of Nations: The Political Economy of National Accounts*, Cambridge, Cambridge University Press, 1996.

Shang, L., 'Migration and Privatisation of Space and Power in Late Socialist China', in F. Miraftab and N. Kudva, *Cities of the Global South Reader*, Abingdon, Routledge, 2015.

Sharma, R. S., *Indian Feudalism*, 3rd edn, Delhi, Macmillan Publishers, 2005.

Sheppard, E., 'David Harvey and Dialectical Space-Time', in N. Castree and D. Gregory (eds), *David Harvey: A Critical Reader*, Hoboken, NJ, Wiley-Blackwell, 2006, pp. 121–41.

Smet, K., 'Housing Prices in Urban Areas', *Progress in Human Geography*, vol. 40, no. 4, 2016, pp. 495–510.

Smit, W., 'Urbanisation in the Global South', *Global Public Health*, 26 Apr. 2021, https://oxfordre.com/publichealth/view/10.1093/acrefore/9780190632366.001.0001/acrefore-9780190632366-e-251

Smith, N., 'Gentrification and the Rent Gap', *Annals of the Association of American Geographers*, vol. 77, no. 3, 1987, pp. 462–5.

Spence, T., 'Property in Land Every One's Right', in A. Bonnett and K. Armstrong (eds), *Thomas Spence: The Poor Man's Revolutionary*, London, Breviary Stuff Publications, 2014, https://www.marxists.org/history/england/britdem/people/spence/property/property.htm

Stiglitz, J., 'The Origins of Inequality, and Policies to Contain It', *National Tax Journal*, vol. 68, no. 2 (2), 2015, pp. 425–48.

Stilwell, F., *Economic Crisis, Cities and Regions: Analysis of Urban and Regional Problems in Australia*, Oxford, Pergamon Press, 1980.

Stilwell, F., *Political Economy: The Contest of Economic Ideas*, 3rd edn, Oxford, Oxford University Press, 2011.

Stilwell, F., *Understanding Cities and Regions: Spatial Political Economy*, Leichhardt, Pluto Press Australia, 1995.

Stilwell, F. and Jordan, K., 'Land Tax in Australia: Principles, Problems and Policies', in J. Laurent (ed), *Henry George's Legacy in Economic Thought*, Cheltenham, Edward Elgar, 2005, pp. 216–42.

Strauss, K., 'Beyond Crisis? Using Rent Theory to Understand the Restructuring of Publicly-Funded Seniors' Care in British Columbia, Canada', *Environment and Planning A: Economy and Space*, 25 Jan. 2021, https://journals.sagepub.com/doi/abs/10.1177/0308518X20983152

Survival International, *Fifty Fascinating Facts about Indigenous and Tribal Peoples from around the World*, London, Survival International, 2019, https://www.survivalinternational.org/articles/50facts

Taques, F. H., De Souza, H. P. B. and Alencar, D. A., 'The 2007–08 Financial Crisis from a Marxist View', *Modern Economy*, vol. 8, 2017, pp. 1069–81.

Thompson, E. P., *The Making of the English Working Class*, Harmondsworth, Penguin Books, 1968.

Thompson, E. P., *The Poverty of Theory & other Essays*, London, Merlin Press, 1978.

Ticktin, H. (ed.), *Marxism and the Global Financial Crisis*, London, Routledge, 2013.

Tong, D., Wang, X., Wu, L. and Zhao, N., 'Land Ownership and the Likelihood of Land Development at the Urban Fringe: The case of Shenzhen, China', *Habitat International*, vol. 73, Mar 2018, pp. 43–52.

Transparency International, *Global Corruption Barometer (2003–2017)*, Berlin, Transparency International, 2017, https://www.transparency.org/en/gcb

Transparency International, *How Corrupt Are Different Institutions and Groups in Society – Global Average?*, Transparency International, Berlin, 2017, https://www.transparency.org/en/gcb/global/global-corruption-barometer-2017

Transparency International, *Land Corruption* [online resources], Berlin, Transparency International, n.d., https://www.transparency.org/en/our-priorities/land-corruption

United Nations, 'Cities and Pollution', *Climate Solutions*, New York, United Nations, n.d., https://www.un.org/en/climatechange/climate-solutions/cities-pollution

United Nations, *Declaration on the Rights of Indigenous Peoples*, New York, United Nations, 2007, https://www.un.org/development/desa/indigenouspeoples/wp-content/uploads/sites/19/2018/11/UNDRIP_E_web.pdf

United Nations Department of Economic and Social Affairs, '68% of the World Population Projected to Live in Urban Areas by 2050, Says UN', New York, United Nations Department of Economic and Social Affairs, 2018, https://www.un.org/development/desa/en/news/population/2018-revision-of-world-urbanization-prospects.html

United Nations Department of Economic and Social Affairs, *Transforming Our World: The 2030 Agenda for Sustainable Development*, New York, United Nations Department of Economic and Social Development, 2015, https://sdgs.un.org/2030agenda

United Nations Department of Economic and Social Affairs, *The World's Cities in 2018 – Data Booklet*, New York, United Nations Department of Economic and Social Affairs, 2018, https://www.un.org/en/events/citiesday/assets/pdf/the_worlds_cities_in_2018_data_booklet.pdf

United Nations Department of Economic and Social Affairs, *World Urbanization Prospects: The 2018 Revision*, New York, United Nations Department of Economic and Social Affairs, 2019, https://population.un.org/wup/Publications/Files/WUP2018-Report.pdf

United Nations Educational, Scientific and Cultural Organisation, 'Neolithic Site of Çatalhöyük', *World Heritage List*, Paris, United Nations Educational, Scientific and Cultural Organization, n.d., https://whc.unesco.org/en/list/1405/

United Nations Habitat, *The Challenge of Slums Global Report on Human Settlements*, Nairobi, Kenya, United Nations Habitat (Human Settlements Programme), 2003, https://unhabitat.org/sites/default/files/download-manager-files/The%20Challenge%20of%20Slums%20-%20Global%20Report%20on%20Human%20Settlements%202003.pdf

United Nations Habitat, *National Urban Policy*, United Nations Habitat (Human Settlements Programme), Nairobi, Kenya, n.d., https://unhabitat.org/programme/national-urban-policy

United Nations Habitat, *World Cities Report 2020 – The Value of Sustainable Urbanization*, Nairobi, Kenya, United Nations Habitat (Human Settlements Programme), 2020, https://unhabitat.org/sites/default/files/2020/10/wcr_2020_report.pdf

United Nations Office of the High Commission for Human Rights, *Briefing Note: Indigenous Peoples' Rights and the 2030 Agenda*, Geneva, Office of the High Commission for Human Rights, 2017, https://www.un.org/development/desa/indigenouspeoples/wp-content/uploads/sites/19/2016/10/Briefing-Paper-on-Indigenous-Peoples-Rights-and-the-2030-Agenda.pdf

United States Agency for International Development, 'What Is Land Tenure?', *Land Links*, Washington, DC, United States Agency for International Development, n.d., https://www.land-links.org/what-is-land-tenure/

Walker, A. M. and Frimpong Boamah, E., 'Making the Invisible Hyper-visible: Knowledge Production and the Gendered Power Nexus in Critical Urban Studies', *Human Geography*, vol. 12, no. 2, 2019, pp. 36–50.

Walker, A. M. and Frimpong Boamah, E., 'Map the Gap: Alternative Visualizations of Geographic Knowledge Production', *Geo: Geography and Environment*, vol. 4, no. 2, pp. 1–16.

Wall, R. S., Maseland, J., Rochell, K. and Spaliviero, M., *The State of African Cities 2018: The Geography of African Investment*, United Nations Habitat and IHS-Erasmus University Rotterdam, 2018, https://unhabitat.org/sites/default/files/download-manager-files/The per cent20State per cent20of per cent20African per cent20Cities.pdf

Wang, Y. and Chen, J., 'Privatizing the Urban Commons under Ambiguous Property Rights in China: Is Marketization a Remedy to the Tragedy of the Commons?', *American Journal of Economics and Sociology*, vol. 80, no. 2, 2021, pp. 503–47.

Ward, C. and Aalbers, M. B., 'The Shitty Rent Business: What's the Point of Land Rent Theory?', *Urban Studies*, vol. 53, no. 9, 2016, pp. 1760–83.

Warren, R. (ed.), *The Debate on Postcolonial Theory and the Spectre of Capital*, London, Verso, 2017.

Webster, P. and Burke, J., 'How the Rise of the Megacity Is Changing the Way We Live', *The Guardian*, 22 Jan. 2016, https://www.theguardian.com/society/2012/jan/21/rise-megacity-live

Wood, D., Griffiths, K. and Blane, N., 'The Case for a Rent Holiday for Businesses on the Coronavirus Economic Frontline', *The Conversation*, 27 Mar. 2020, AU edn, https://theconversation.com/the-case-for-a-rent-holiday-for-businesses-on-the-coronavirus-economic-frontline-134890

Wood, E. M., *Democracy against Capitalism: Renewing Historical Materialism*, Cambridge, Cambridge University Press, 1995.

Wood, E. M., *Peasant-Citizen and Slave: The Foundations of Athenian Democracy*, London, Verso, 1988.

World Bank, *Urban Development*, Washington, DC, World Bank, 2020, https://www.worldbank.org/en/topic/urbandevelopment/overview

World Health Organization, 'Climate Change and Infectious Diseases', in *Climate Change and Human Health – Risks and Responses*, Geneva, World Health Organization, 2003, https://www.who.int/globalchange/publications/climchange.pdf

World Health Organization, *COP24 Special Report: Health & Climate Change*, Geneva, World Health Organization, 2018, https://apps.who.int/iris/handle/10665/276405

World Health Organization, *WHO Coronavirus (COVID-19) Dashboard*, Geneva, Switzerland, World Health Organization, 2018, https://covid19.who.int/

World Health Organization, *WHO Releases Country Estimates on Air Pollution Exposure and Health Impact*, Geneva, World Health Organization, 2016, https://www.who.int/news/item/27-09-2016-who-releases-country-estimates-on-air-pollution-exposure-and-health-impact

Xie, Q., Parsa, A. and Redding, B., 'The Emergence of the Urban Land Market in China: Evolution, Structure, Constraints and Perspectives', *Urban Studies*, vol. 39, no. 8, 2002, pp. 1375–98.

Zakout, W., 'Stand with Us to Help Make Land Rights a Reality for Millions of Women around the World', *Sustainable Cities Blog*, Washington, DC, World Bank, 9 May 2019, https://blogs.worldbank.org/sustainablecities/make-land-rights-a-reality-millions-women-around-world

Zasulich, V., 'Letter to Karl Marx', in T. Shanin (ed.), *Late Marx and the Russian Road: Marx and the 'Peripheries of Capitalism'*, New York, Monthly Review Press, 1983, https://www.marxists.org/archive/marx/works/1881/zasulich/zasulich.htm

Zendeli, E., 'The Notion and Legal Space of Exercising the Right to Ownership', *Journal of Civil and Legal Sciences*, vol. 2, 2013, p. 104.

Zhang, L. and Gou, Q., 'Demystifying China's Economic Growth: Retrospect and Prospect', in United Nations Conference on Trade and Development, *Rethinking Development Strategies after the Financial Crisis – Volume II: Country Studies and International Comparisons*, Geneva, 2016, United Nations Conference on Trade and Development, https://unctad.org/webflyer/rethinking-development-strategies-after-financial-crisis-volume-ii-country-studies-and

Zhou, Y., *How to Build a World-class Megacity*, World Economic Forum, 2017, https://www.weforum.org/agenda/2017/06/china-urbanisation-beijing-city-cluster/

Zhu, J., 'The Shadow of the Skyscrapers: Real Estate Corruption in China', *Journal of Contemporary China*, vol. 21, 2012, pp. 243–60.

Zuniga, N., *Land Corruption*, Berlin, Transparency International, 2018, https://knowledgehub.transparency.org/product/topic-guide-on-land-corruption

Index